A Public Philosophy Reader

A Public Philosophy Reader

Richard J. Bishirjian

ARLINGTON HOUSE · PUBLISHERS
NEW ROCHELLE, NEW YORK

To my Country
my Father
my Mother

P10 9 8 7 6 5 4 3 2 1

Book design by Pat Slesarchik

Manufactured in the United States of America

Library of Congress Cataloging in Publication Data
Main entry under title:

A Public philosophy reader.

1. Political science—United States—Addresses, essays, lectures. 2. Political science—United States—History—Addresses, essays, lectures. I. Bishirjian, Richard J.
JA84.U5P79 320.9'73 78-23415
ISBN 0-87000-435-2

Contents

Preface

ANY DISCUSSION OF HOW we, the American people, understand our existence as a community in history must come to grips with the problem that our public life rests on certain myths. These myths articulate the beliefs, commonly shared by all Americans, that hold us together as a political community. We are not a political community merely because it is economically useful, or even because it is safer to live within the protection of a political community amidst the predatory intentions of other communities. A higher level of rationality enables us to cohere as a national unit, gives meaning to our public lives, and informs our private lives with public truths. This level of our common existence is best articulated in public myths about the ends of government, the origin of political authority in "the people," the sovereignty of God, of universal moral obligation, and the nature of man.

In the ancient world also, all societies were intellectually and socially organized by myths. By means of these myths, ancient man represented to himself his experience of participation in a sacred reality greater than himself. Myths integrated political and social order with the order of the gods because society was understood to be an extension of the larger sacred cosmos composed and ruled by the gods. Myths were crucial for the maintenance of the order and health of society. These ancient myths were not "tales," however, in the sense of "false stories," or fairy tales. They interpreted reality and its meaning.

In antiquity, as today, myths were explanations of the "why" of reality. They did not function by arbitrarily giving meaning to events, but interpreted archetypal human reality such as birth; death; the question of the origins of existing things; the presence of evil, of good, justice, injustice, mortality, immortality, order, punishment, social disintegration, and the sacredness of community life. Myths were interpretations of experience in the sense that all "experience" is laden with interpretation, not simply passive reception of stimuli.

Indeed, all societies, modern as well as ancient, are shaped by public myths. Because the ancient myths were the vehicles through which ancient communities were maintained in harmony with the gods, because they articulated an experience of the sacredness of community life, however, some deny they are equivalent to the public myths that hold contemporary Western societies together. It is widely believed that the basis of modern society is founded not on a shared experience of the sacredness of social life, but in economics or pragmatic rationalism. It is sufficient to recall here, however, the judgment of the French sociologist Émile Durkheim that "no society could possibly hold together" if separated from a "non-rational, non-utilitarian scheme of sacred values."

This reader is intended to serve as an introduction to the nature of public philosophy, its role in interpreting and delineating the commonly shared "sacred values" or public myths of the American political community, and with its precarious position in the United States today. Public philosophy is embodied in the public myths of the American republic, but it should not be confused with the public myths. The public myths are passive, the public philosophy is active. Its primary function is to shape the public myths, adapt them to changing circumstances, and give them authority by showing how our myths are grounded in being and reason.

The difficulty is that the public myths of our political life are influenced not only by public philosophy, but also by a type of civil religion that sees the United States as performing an immanent eschatological role: a this-worldly, public salvation. The titles of two recent books illustrate how our public myths have been colored by the enduring presence of such secular eschatological religious speculations: Ernest Lee Tuveson's *Redeemer Nation: The Idea of America's Millennial Role* (1968) and Conrad Cherry's *God's New Israel: Religious Interpretations of American Destiny* (1971). In sum, the public myths upon which American public life rests have been shaped by two opposing intellectual currents, public philosophy and civil religion. At stake in this conflict is the intellectual and spiritual condition of the American soul.

Chapter One of my introductory essay (Part One of the book) examines the nature of public philosophy; Chapter Two, the nature of civil religion as political religion. In Chapter Three, I explore the contributions to public philosophy of American public philosophers Gerhart Niemeyer, Michael Novak, and Robert Nisbet. Chapters Four and Five discuss the origins of

America's civil religion in the development of modern Liberalism and its merger with the millennial tradition in America, what Irving Kristol has called the "prophetic-utopian" tradition. My examination of the American civil religion focuses largely upon Herbert Croly and Woodrow Wilson as its chief exemplars. Chapter Six asks what is *the* American political tradition? and examines the tension between what Kristol has called the "constitutional-legal" tradition and our civil religion.

Part Two consists of selected essays written by representative American public philosophers. The first essay (chronologically) was published in 1955 by Walter Lippmann, and the most recent was published in 1977 by Professor Gerhart Niemeyer. Covering a span of 22 years, these essays were selected to introduce the reader to a range of contemporary commentary on the problems of public philosophy, of American life, and the difficulties of community existence during the second half of the 20th century. Thirteen public philosophers are chosen for their incisive observations: Frederick D. Wilhelmsen, Walter Lippmann, Thomas Molnar, Richard Weaver, M. E. Bradford, Gerhart Niemeyer, Willmoore Kendall, Fr. John Courtney Murray, Robert Nisbet, Irving Kristol, Eric Voegelin, Stephen Tonsor, and Michael Novak. Through their contributions to our understanding of the nature of public philosophy, it is hoped that the reader will come to a fuller appreciation of this essential aspect of our commonly shared political existence.

Acknowledgments

THE INTRODUCTORY ESSAY (Part One) was made possible by a Fellowship Research Grant from the Carthage Foundation. Preparation of the manuscript for publication was made possible by a grant from the Secretarial Assistance Fund of the College of New Rochelle. Special thanks is given to Dr. Angelo Codevilla for his patient editorial advice, and to Mr. Thomas Moore, Serial Librarian at the College of New Rochelle, for his assistance in obtaining copies of articles and books not available in the College's permanent collection. Thanks must also be given to my typist, Mrs. Fran Miceli for her uncommon attention to the difficulties of preparing an errorless manuscript.

Part I:

The Nature of Public Philosophy

1/Public Philosophy

ANCIENT POLITICAL COMMUNITIES were held together by myths that explained the origin of the world, the gods, society, man, and community life in terms of the actions of the gods. Such mythic experience is qualitatively different from our own. Our daily existence is not dominated by the presence of intracosmic deities to whom responsibility for all that happens to us and those about us is attributed. In his book *The New Science of Politics* (1952), Eric Voegelin made the observation that while ancient myths expressed the "cosmological" truth that society is an analogue of the order of intracosmic gods, postmythic order is represented in the "anthropological" truth that society is representative of the order of the soul of man.

The public truths of our postmythic era are "anthropological" because society has been understood as an extension of the order or disorder of the human soul, not as the plaything of the gods. Society is no longer seen as a "microcosmos," but as "macroanthropos," to use Voegelin's concepts. Society is understood to be man writ large. Our civilization lives by the realization that men themselves are responsible for their actions and for the order or disorder of society. In our era, political philosophy, the search for the origins of social order in the human *psyche,* has supplanted cosmological myth as the representative inquiry into public truth.

Plato first identified this distinction between the age of Chronos, when the gods ruled the affairs of man, from the age of Zeus, when man took control of human affairs. Despite the disorder that ensued, we cannot return to the rule of the gods, he said. We should instead allow that which is immortal in us, our *nous,* to govern. For if we do not want to continue in a condition of disorder, it will be necessary to discover the truths of public order anew by personal search for the divine in the depth of the human *psyche.*

We still articulate the substance of political order by means of myths that make our noetic understanding socially effective, but these myths express the truth of the soul, not the "falsehoods" of cosmological order. Public life today is not devoid of myths.

Quite the contrary. We live today in a society governed by public myths, commonly shared beliefs about the nature of man, society, international order, life after death, the origin of political authority in "the people," to mention but a few. But our public myths articulate an experience of reality, truth, which we verify by an intellection that is not mere ratiocination, or logical reasoning; it is noetic.

My use of the concept "noetic" is derived from the Classical definition of man as a rational animal, a man having *nous,* mind or reason. Aristotle's analysis of the nature of man illustrates my meaning. *Nous,* he said, is the highest aspect of man's nature because it is either divine itself or the most divine thing in man. It is that aspect of us which experiences the divine, what Aristotle called *theion nous,* and shapes our consciousness of our humanity. Our creaturely experience of the divine makes us aware of our mortality, while suggesting at the same time that an aspect of our humanity is immortal insofar as it can participate in transcendent reality. Man's *nous,* and not man's passions, defines his nature. Therefore, a society that fosters the dominance of reason over the passions fosters humanity.

The Classical political philosophers saw that political community is not only an alliance for the purpose of survival or of exchange. It is not a mere alliance for the resolution of conflicting interests, though that certainly is involved on the pragmatic level. It is possible after all to resolve conflicts of interest in a manner contrary to the common good. Politics is something more than deciding who gets what, when, and where. It includes that, but also the resolution of questions of a higher sort, such as what is *good* for the community as a whole. Thus Aristotle was critical of politicians who gave no attention to the maintenance of civic virtue, for without virtue a community becomes, simply, an alliance. Political community is, above all, a shared commitment to the good life. Therefore, statesmen must have some notion of human goodness and must try, insofar as circumstances permit, to foster its growth in their people.

On this paradigmatic level, the level of the inquiry into the common good, a special type of political man, and a special type of political discourse is required: the public philosopher and public philosophy. The function of public philosophy is to attempt to turn one's fellow citizens, including the statesmen, away from a life that is untrue to the truth embodied in the myths of their common existence. Perhaps this is what Socrates meant when he said that politics is an art carried out with an eye upon the highest good. True statesmanship, he saw, is concerned with the order of the soul and seeks its fulfillment in political life, though he was aware that Athenian politicians practiced not politics in the paradigmatic sense, but a form of flattery. And yet, since a community cannot permanently endure in a condition of untruth, cannot endure the perennial practice of flattery in the guise of statesmanship, the fate of one's country hangs in the balance.

The nature of public philosophy, originating in the noetic consciousness of order in the human *psyche,* however, contributes to the social fragility of public philosophy, and of society itself in the modern era. Whereas ancient myths were obligatory public definitions of a sacred cosmos, the origin of public philosophy in the reflection of the philosopher causes it to have a tenuous influence on public life. If mythic political order were understood to be part of a larger sacred cosmos permeated by intracosmic gods, the myths that explain the origin, powers, and functions of these gods would dominate public understanding of existence. But because public philosophy articulates the more complex personal consciousness of the order of the soul, indeed is based on the personal insights of daimonic[1] men, an element of contest enters the interpretation of social order.

Who are the public philosophers? This question could not have arisen in mythic societies because the consonance of political order with the order of the cosmos of mythic man was performed by the rulers or priests who were the socially accepted guardians of the myths. The consonance of modern social existence, however, depends chiefly upon the development of virtuous citizens, the receptivity of citizens to good counsel, and the maintenance of a public culture in which men of wisdom are respected. Furthermore, whereas one or two myths could express the public truths and give them social effect, in post-mythic societies this public function is neither performed by one class of citizens, nor capable of being stated in any single systematic manner. It is a continuing vital process of articulation of, and education in, the needs of a healthy political community. I emphasize that it is a public, not a private function, though the persons who develop the public philosophy may not necessarily hold public office. The public philosopher's own virtue is

[1] from δαίμων, personal spirit (Gr.)

the necessary example of the type of civic virtue that the good life requires.

A chief problem of contemporary American life is that we lack authoritative myths that identify for the community the commitments and meaning of our national life. Our past has no authoritative interpretation, since a major contest is currently waged between those, on the one hand, who see the American revolution in terms of a utopian commitment to reconstitute the structure of existence, and, on the other, those who see in our revolutionary history lessons on the constitutional limits of state power. Our present existence has no authoritative interpretation because public discourse is divided by those who see presently constituted American society as fundamentally illegitimate and those who assert its legitimacy. That inescapable feature of life in the United States today contributes to the anxiety, tension, and disorder of our public lives.

I must note also, however, that our contemporary lack of authoritative myths in American society is attributable not merely to the fact that whatever myths claim authority are challenged by competing sources of interpretation. It is also due to the attrition of public philosophy in American culture. We do not live in a society whose public institutions have as their principal ends to create virtuous citizens or to foster civic virtue. What constitutes virtue is a private matter, it is widely believed, and there even exist Constitutional impediments (chiefly the Establishment Clause of the First Amendment) to the maintenance of civic virtue. A current assessment of this problem is Walter Berns', *The First Amendment and the Future of American Democracy* (1976). Nor do we live in a society in which men of wisdom are respected, at least if they are wise about matters that cannot be verified by the scientific method. If the stability of our public order depends upon the continual articulation of the needs of a healthy political community, and the authoritative pronouncements of persons who have made this their life's work, then the future stability of the American political order is indeed questionable. Nevertheless, public philosophy must be concerned with this aspect of our political order.

What, then, is the public philosophy? In *Essays in the Public Philosophy* (1955), Walter Lippmann properly observed that Jeremy Bentham's rejection of a view of community as a corporate reality is at the root of the decline of public philosophy.

> Those who are strongly nominalist in their cast of mind, which modern men tend to be, look upon the abstract concept of a corporate people as mere words and rather like conjuring up spooks. Thus, according to that resolute nominalist Jeremy Bentham, "the community is a fictitious *body*, composed of the individual persons who are considered as constituting as it were its *members*. The interest of the community then is, what?—The sum of the interests of the several members who compose it."

The difficulty with Bentham's position (also held by Hobbes, Locke, and Rousseau) is that it mistakes the apprehension of community for the artificial making of community. The Social Contract tradition sees political community as an artifice created by prepolitical, atomic individuals. Man is not a political animal by nature. The basis of society cannot be found in the social aspect of man's soul, his apprehension of the common reason in himself and in the public myths, which he shares with his fellow citizens. Instead, political community is an artificial construction, an acquired habit easily lost, and thus man lives on the knife's edge between the peace provided by a commonly-assented-to political power and the disorder, inconvenience, and, to Hobbes, the "solitary, poor, nasty, brutish, and short" condition of the state of nature.

The first principle of public philosophy is that political community is not an artifice originating in the passionate appetite to survive, but is based upon the commonly shared apprehension of its members that they in common "hold these truths." The community that gives birth to the public myths itself originates in the public myths. There can be no community until community is apprehended. Men have always been social animals, but they were not political animals, inhabitants of a "political community," until they apprehended the truths that bound them together and enabled them to cohere as a political community. In that sense, public philosophy creates the "experience" of community, though its sensible conditions preceded its discovery. Without public philosophy, therefore, political community cannot endure, though it may prevail in the form of an unjust alliance. Even Thomas Hobbes inadvertently admitted this truth, when, in his *Leviathan* (1651), he spoke of the artificial covenant that brought man out of the state of nature, and the need for a common power to "defend them from the invasion of foreigners. . . ."[1] Did not Hobbes say more than he intended? The apprehension that some people are "foreigners" is itself testimony to the existence of a community of common truths that precedes the social contract, a community that even Hobbesian prepolitical men apprehended.

The second principle of public philosophy is that the public good is not necessarily in agreement with public opinion. Fr. John Courtney Murray made this distinction in *We Hold These Truths* (1960) when he spoke of the public philosophy's objectivity of content and its independence of "either majority or minority opinion." "I would maintain, for instance," he writes, "that the public consensus of the West, and of the United States as an historic participant in the Western style of civilization, would remain the public consensus, even if it were held, as perhaps it is held, only by a minority within the West." To be socially effective, the public philosophy will require public agreement, but that same public agreement or opinion is not, by itself, the public philosophy. At the center of the public philosophy is a moral consensus that does not depend on popular opinion at any given moment. Of course, this raises the dilemma central to our concept of representative government. The corporate interests of the community are as much a part of our concept of representative government as the view that the government should represent the will of the people. But the private interests, however many, must take second place to the interests of the community as a whole (see for example, *Federalist* No. 10). The public interest should have a much greater claim upon government attention than the latest polls. A government is both the representative of the citizens who elected it, and the representative of the nation in history. In its former role it is responsible to the electorate, in its latter role to God. I shall return to the subject of the sovereignty of God in Chapter Three.

The third principle is that the elaboration of the public philosophy is the act of the souls or intellects instructed in and committed to the common good. Yet this does not mean it is by, of, and for a naturally restricted caste of leaders. The essence of philosophic inquiry lies in a personal act. But the personal judgment of what the public truth *is,* which constitutes the act

[1] *Leviathan,* pt. II, chap. 17, par. 13

of public philosophy, is also the basis of the philosophy's commonality to all men. Here we must go as far back as Heraclitus' explication of the *zynon,* the common social element in the human *psyche,* to make our case.

Men have in common not only their animal appetites, economic interests, or social, historical, and cultural similarities. As human beings they share a constitutive element. That, Heraclitus said, is *logos* (reason). Aristotle called it *nous.* A common reason informs our consciousness and is an element of the *zynon.* The rational judgment of the public philosopher, therefore, though a personal act of apprehending reality, is nevertheless an action in the public domain. The function of the public philosopher is to mediate his experience of the good that he has in common with his fellow citizens. This mediation, whether it be in books, articles, classrooms, lectures, or simply common speech, is a "political" act. It can be said that it is even more *public* than the most recent opinion polls because a plurality of private interests does not make the public interest. There is nothing common to be found in the plurality of individual preferences, because as such they are incommensurable, whereas all men to some extent can grasp the truths fundamental to the life they lead.

Fr. Murray asks, "Do we hold these truths because they are true, or are these truths true because we hold them?" Is the public philosophy true because we prefer it, or do we prefer it because it is true? The first formulation asserts that truth is grounded on will, the second that we will rightly when it is in accordance with truth. Our knowledge of the public truth is dependent on its articulation by the public philosophers. But, paradoxically, it is true because they say it is, more than it is true because we find it acceptable.

The fourth principle is that the public philosophy is compatible with, indeed articulates, the theological truths of our public myths. When the President of the United States proclaims a Day of Thanksgiving, when Congress decided that all coins should bear the inscription "In God We Trust," or when, on any public occasion, a representative of the government invokes the sovereignty of God, we witness a few of the countless ways that the American people celebrate the theological mystery underlying their communal existence. Like other peoples, Americans share and celebrate the experience that their political order participates in a higher order, but it is public philosophy which informs that experience with understanding. That was demonstrated by Plato in the *Republic* (Book Two) when he coined the term "theology" to express those truths about the gods that would form the public myths of the best political community. The anthropological truth of Classical political philosophy has as its correlate the theological truth that god is transcendent, not intracosmic, and is the origin of the good, not of evil. Public philosophy today, as we shall examine in Chapter Three, must grapple with these Classical theological truths and the important theological truths of Israel and Christianity. Indeed, a principal weakness of the American political order is, as Thomas Luckmann writes in *The Invisible Religion* (1967), that our public institutions "do not maintain the sacred cosmos; they merely regulate the legal and economic frame within which occurs the competition on the 'ultimate' significance market." On the level of the public truths of the American political order, it is public philosophy alone that attempts to "maintain the sacred cosmos."

In this context we must note the conflict between public philosophy and civil religion. Important writers like Michael Novak and Fr. John Courtney Murray have tended to confuse public philosophy with civil religion. Fr. Murray, for example, writing in his *We Hold These Truths* (1960), observed that the Soviet Union has a public philosophy. And Michael Novak, in *Choosing Our King* (1974), offers a definition of civil religion that approximates our above description of America's public philosophy and public myths:

> a public perception of our national experience, in the light of universal and transcendent claims upon human beings, but especially upon Americans; a set of values, symbols, and rituals institutionalized as the cohesive force and center of meaning uniting our many peoples.

Modern American society is ordered by a public philosophy *and* by civil religion. The conflict between them shapes contemporary American life. And the intensity of that conflict can be seen in the observation that the Soviet Union has a civil religion, but it does not have a public philosophy. In order to understand this paradox, it is necessary to understand the nature of civil religion as political religion.

2/Civil Religion as Political Religion

MODERN TOTALITARIAN IDEOLOGIES, most specialists in this field will agree, are secular religions in which concern for life in this world displaces the transcendent God of philosophy and Christianity. Norman Cohn, for example, has shown in his monumental study of late medieval and early modern millenarianism, *The Pursuit of the Millennium* (1957), the similarity of modern ideologies in structure and experiential content to such revolutionary millennial sects of the early modern era as the Anabaptist followers of Thomas Muentzer. These sects are characterized by the expectation that (a) the world can be made over into a heavenly condition; (b) the existing civil and ecclesiastical authorities are evil incarnate and must be rejected out of hand; (c) the New Jerusalem is imminent, near at hand, and awaits only decisive action, by (d) the bearers of the revolutionary cause, paracletic leaders, who have been appointed by God to transfigure this worldly existence. Though stripped of the Biblical orientation of the earlier period, modern political ideologies present much the same message in secular guise.

The chief modern political ideology, Marxism, is very much a civil religion and the "religious" judgments to be found in it are representative of the species. They are:

a) Reality is defective. The present condition of mankind under capitalism is evil. It degrades man by taking from him the means by which he gives meaning to his own life. Just as man creates himself by his own labor, he saves himself by his own labor. But the capitalist mode of production ennobles only the capitalist. Man's condition, therefore, is one of alienation. His future condition under Communism will be one of wholeness.

b) Paradise is to be *in* this world. The future leads inevitably to revolution and to Communism. Marx claimed he discovered this "economic fact" that has been perpetuated by his followers and present representatives, the world's Communist parties.

c) Revolution is redemptive. The revolution that overturns bourgeois society, the proletarian revolution, will emancipate all mankind, not merely the proletariat, from a fundamentally evil condition.

Perhaps the fullest analysis of this religious nature of Marxism was made by Henri de Lubac, S.J., in his work *The Drama of Atheist Humanism* (1945). In that work, Fr. Lubac explored the furious impulse in Feuerbach, Marx, Nietzsche, and Comte to reject God and restructure man as an autonomous being, free from any obligation to God, because, they believed, man is himself a self-creating being, that is his own Creator. Lubac noted the ersatz god was being worshiped with religious fervor and that his "priests" were claiming a kind of knowledge that surpassed that of orthodox religion.

Later, Eric Voegelin argued in his *The New Science of Politics* (1952) that these modern ideologists had perverted the nature of faith, in the meaning of Hebrews 11:1, as "the substance of things hoped for and the proof of things unseen." Marx's claim, for example, that Communism is the "riddle of history, solved" is a claim to a type of certainty needed by the ideologist who must fill the vacuum of his spiritual life with a more certain faith than Christianity. "Ontologically," Voegelin wrote in 1952,

> the substance of things hoped for [in Christianity] is nowhere to be found but in faith itself; and, epistemologically, there is no proof for things unseen but again this very faith. The bond is tenuous, indeed, and it may snap easily. The life of the soul in openness toward God, the waiting, the periods of aridity and dullness, guilt and despondency, contrition and repentance, forsakenness and hope against hope, the silent stirrings of love and grace, trembling on the verge of a certainty which if gained is loss—the very lightness of this fabric may prove too heavy a burden for men who lust for massively possessive experience.

Marxism is a civil religion, both in theory and in the actual role that it plays in those countries unfortunate enough to be governed by Communist parties. But the analysis of the nature of civil religion cannot be concluded by reference to Marxism alone. Marxism is but the fulfillment of deep civilizational currents in the West, movements that sought the renewal of individuals and of the world *within* history. Movements representative of this type are Renaissance Hermeticism, alchemy, sorcery, millenarianism, and Gnosticism.

In Gnosticism and Renaissance Hermeticism, the latter more commonly known as Neo-Platonism, for example, the Christian faith was eclipsed by the desire to realize the "truth" that man himself was God. The ancient Gnostics had lived by the belief that a divine spark is imprisoned in the human body, construed as evil. That spark, they believed, will be released from matter, by a saving knowledge, *gnosis.* The pneumatic substance to be released is an emanation of the godhead, and its release alters the nature of god.

This ecstatic claim to be God did not die out with the cultural changes of the modern era. Indeed, the greatest currency was given to such claims by the recovery of ancient Hermeticism in the Renaissance. Marsilio Ficino, Giovanni Pico della Mirandola, Giordano Bruno, Tommaso Campanella, and many others, for example, found new inspiration in the Gnostic and pantheistic aspects of the thought of Hermes Trismegistus. Though this area of scholarship is still advancing, some preliminary conclusions can be made. Man was endowed, the Renaissance Hermeticists believed, with divine nature. To fulfill human nature, man was to become God, not to actualize his humanity in the experience of the divine. Paul O. Kristeller, in *The Philosophy of Marsilio Ficino* (1943), quotes the following from a work of Ficino:

> The entire effort of our Soul is to become God. This effort is as natural to man as that of flying is to birds. For it is inherent in all men, everywhere and always; therefore it does not follow the incidental quality of some man, but the nature of the species itself.

This radical divinization of man was followed by the Hermeticists' divinization of nature. Giordano Bruno devoted himself to a type of magic that sought to give new power to man through the magical renewal of the world, the resolution of the contradictions in reality. Bruno believed that man could evoke the good nature of the gods by magic and in consequence improve the fortunes of the world and nature itself. Frances Yates, in *Giordano Bruno and the Hermetic Tradition* (1964), correctly noted the revolutionary attitude embodied in Hermetic magic:

> What has changed is Man, now no longer only the pious spectator of God's wonders in the creation, and

> the worshipper of God himself above the creation, but Man the operator, Man who seeks to draw power from the divine and natural order.

The great civilizational change in the West embodied in this desire to manipulate reality by means of the speculative imagination was visible to the fountainheads of modern political theory. Machiavelli, Hobbes, Locke, and Rousseau realized that a fundamental transformation in the intellectual order had occurred and grappled with the political consequences that this transformation created. They saw that a new sacred tradition would be necessary to replace the Christian civil theology that no longer claimed the allegiance of intellectual culture. And they met the decline of traditional order, captured in the title of Huizinga's book *The Waning of the Middle Ages* (1937), with a call for a fully secular political religion. The theorists of modern civil religion gave us new gods—the state and its rulers.

Machiavelli is representative. His call for a prince to unify Italy was couched, of course, in the "realistic" vocabulary of power politics for which he is well known. But the attentive reader of his *Prince* (1512–13) will note that the leader who will lead the Italian people into a condition of political unity is also seen as a "redeemer," a Moses, leading not the children of Israel, but a new Israel, Italy, into a new Jerusalem, the Italian nation. As Felix Gilbert noted in his *Machiavelli and Guicciardini* (1965), this new secularism begun by Machiavelli yielded political fruit when, in 1527, the Florentine republic was restored by a coalition of practitioners of power politics, and the chiliastic adepts around Savonarola. On the level of political religion, those who rejected reason in the voluntaristic dependence on the will of God in the affairs of man had much in common with those who allowed their love of power to push aside the love of reason. Machiavelli's prince *was* a "demi-god," as Bernard Crick has pointed out.

Thomas Hobbes, who wrote when his beloved English order had been destroyed by the Puritan attempt to make over English politics and culture to conform to the will of God, also saw hope for peace in a "mortal god," a sovereign, omnipotent state. In that regime the sovereign would define the terms of worship beyond which there was no appeal. Even the rationalist John Locke, much admired by America's founding generation, created a civil religion. The sons of Cromwell's Roundheads, no doubt tired of the political results of too much concern for religion, could read John Locke and find replacements for the theological symbols that had evoked so much enthusiasm in the past. Theorists such as Locke replaced the garden of Eden with a state of nature, the Fall and Satan's evil with the invention of money, which compelled prepolitical man to leave the state of nature. And is not salvation, in the end, to be found in the acquisition of private property; good government but a church, perhaps even better now that it is based on consent rather than sacramental grace. Instead of the Bible, that blessed book from which so much evil sprang, Locke's generation adopted a safer, more reliable book, none other than Locke's *Two Treatises on Government.* Whether Locke consciously created a system that could perform the role of a civil religion is beyond the scope of this inquiry. He was followed, however, by one who clearly intended precisely that.

Jean-Jacques Rousseau attacked orthodox Christianity because its emphasis on a kingdom of God after earthly life undermined the unity of the state. How could a citizen be absolutely loyal to the state if he constantly gave his ultimate loyalty to something beyond it? Since Christ's teachings diminished political power, Rousseau accused the son of God of setting up a kingdom here and now, i.e., the Church, and thus of malevolently and permanently dividing political obligation between the earthly Church and the state. As a replacement for this condition of disunity, Rousseau prescribed a civil religion that would make no distinction between divine and positive law. Such a civil religion, he wrote in the *Social Contract* (1762), "makes the fatherland the object of the citizens' adoration, and so teaches them that service to the state and service to the state's tutelary deity are one and the same thing." The dogmas of his civil religion would be established by the state, and would be rigidly applied as a test of good citizenship. Those who failed to honor them would be banished. Rousseau wrote in the *Social Contract*:

> These would not be, strictly speaking, dogmas of a religious character, but rather sentiments . . . for which no man can be either a good citizen or a loyal subject.

In the 19th century, the theorists of civil religion, particularly those students of Hegel called the "Left-Hegelians," who utilized his concepts to wage an attack on traditional culture and authority, gave the concept a new significance. They accepted the purpose of civil religion to promote social unity, advance society to its stated secular goals, and replace sacred tradition with new secular ones. Their mixture of the concept of civil religion with the immanent eschatology of heretical millennialism, however, fashioned a formidable weapon for revolutionary change. They envisioned a future society in which a totally desacralized life would be lived by men shaped by critical and, as it was formulated by Marx, revolutionary consciousness.

Ludwig Feuerbach called this new epoch the epoch of the downfall of Christianity, in which

> the place of belief has been taken by unbelief and that of the Bible by reason. Similarly, religion and the Church have been replaced by politics, the heaven by earth, prayer by work, hell by material need, and the Christian by man.

Feuerbach argued that men must once again become religious "if politics is to be our religion." The god of this new religion was man, paradise was in this world, and Marx added to this atheist humanism a superbly constructed revolutionary ideology that sought to bring paradise into this world by a revolution impelled by the laws of history.

Political or civil religion is to be found in the United States as well. Here, too, some thinkers have transformed Christian faith in a future unity with God *after* death into a certainty that history is leading to a fortuitous transfigured culmination *in* time. The belief that America was especially chosen to bring mankind to its final state of earthly happiness is very common in American thought. Less common, but of increasingly greater significance, is the aspiration to be saved by means of political action, and the rejection of the present condition of society in the certain belief that well-motivated state power can transform the nature of man.

3/American Public Philosophers: Niemeyer, Novak, Nisbet

THOUGH PUBLIC PHILOSOPHY RUNS against the grain of the civil religion of modern secular intellectual culture, men such as Robert A. Nisbet, Irving Kristol, Michael Novak, Gerhart Niemeyer, Walter Lippmann, and Fr. John Courtney Murray have attempted to restore it. Perhaps the best systematic statement of public philosophy in this century can be found in the late Fr. Murray's *We Hold These Truths* (1960), in which he examined this symbolic mode by which Western community coheres, explored the content of the American public philosophy, and set forth the epistemological ground on which any public philosophy stands. Another interesting endeavor in this mode is Robert Nisbet's *The Quest for Community* (1953), in which he analyzed the eclipse of traditional community and called for the restoration of voluntary groups and associations without which the totalitarian impulse in civil religion will dominate. Michael Novak, another public philosopher, brings to virtually every subject he treats keen insight into the ontological ground of our public symbols, social life, and political practice. Gerhart Niemeyer, the only professional political theorist among the public philosophers I have mentioned, has, in numerous works, reexamined the theory of political community. In the following pages I shall examine the contributions of three of these men, Niemeyer, Novak, and Nisbet, to the recovery of public philosophy.

The Nature of the Realm

Gerhart Niemeyer's *Between Nothingness and Paradise* (1971) asks upon what philosophical basis one may defend political order against those who reject order itself in their quest for a this-worldly paradise. Significantly, he turns to an examination of the public myths by which society coheres. By "public myth"

Niemeyer means a "set of symbols through which a multitude of people, living together symbolically secure the transparency of life and awareness of participation in the divine ground." What are some of the myths by which Americans become conscious of the theological aspect of their existence in history? Niemeyer writes:

> The average American, for instance, takes for granted that each "individual" has a soul, a claim to personal dignity, and an independent mind; he distinguishes "time" from "eternity"; he attributes authority to "the people" but also to "the law"; he believes in an enduring "Constitution"; he pledges allegiance to a "nation under God," all this in the uncritical ways of myths. If it were not for the myths, the mutual comprehensibility of actions and language symbols among the "parts" would atrophy after a while, and in place of familiarity and confident communication there would arise the universal assumption of hostility which prevails.

In this enumeration of some American myths Niemeyer finds the essential theological dimension of our existence in society. But since the Western concept "society" does not adequately express this theological dimension, Niemeyer suggests the use of the concept of a political "realm" to articulate this aspect of political order. Niemeyer prefers this concept because it forces us to understand that a political "community" includes commonly held theological truths, the public myths, and, below the mythic level, the "mores" or ethical customs, habits, and prejudices of the citizens of the "realm." Society is not merely a biological, economic, or ethnic phenomenon. By emphasizing these aspects of community existence, Niemeyer is able to focus upon the consequences when the public myths cease effectively to represent the common ethical and theological life of the "realm," when the people become alienated from the "realm," and cease to be the bearers of the truth of the "realm."

Niemeyer indicates this public truth of the "realm" is historical. Consciousness of the past, Niemeyer writes, is the only form of a society's identity. For a human being, the past is the memory of the endurance of his identity through the changes of a lifetime. Thus his identity is discovered in reflection upon the history of personal events in past time, events that shape his identity in the present. A society however, is not a biological organism, and is not fitted with an organ in which the events of its collective experience are stored. Nor would the totality of these events constitute its history, since an historical past for a community, as with the individual person, is composed of selected events, meaningful because they represent important aspects of the development of the person's, and the community's, identity. These meaningful events are not arbitrarily determined, however. We do not constitute our personal history on the basis of the remembered food we have consumed over a lifetime, nor does the identity of the community in time consist of the history of its commercial-economic development. Niemeyer writes, for example, that "Aristotle's list of associations evolving toward the polis includes man-wife, family, village, but not business partnerships, athletic teams, or crews of sailors." When we look for those historical constructions that constitute the public past, therefore, we must look for the ontological ground of our consciousness of history.

In ancient societies ordered by cosmological myths, this ontological ground had been symbolized in cosmogonies and theogonies. Rituals celebrated the original creation through myths that evoked the creation, and ritually returned the community to that past moment of creation. Modern Western societies, however, find the ground of being through philosophy as a mode of openness to transcendent divine reality. The recognition of the Lord of history of Israel and Christianity as the fundamental fact of personal and public history has substantially added to our understanding of human existence in time.

Our consciousness of history includes, Niemeyer writes, "an irrevocable and eternal past, an informed but yet unknowable hopeful future, a present responsibility before a time-transcending God whose will appears in an apodictic law." The past is "eternal" because the special moments of past time are manifestations of God's presence that have occurred once, left their indelible imprint, and will not occur again. In the history of Israel, the Exodus from Egypt constitutes what Niemeyer calls a "single event" theophany, an event in time that cannot be converted into the present by ritual reenactment. In Christianity, such an event is the Incarnation, death, and Resurrection of Christ. Indeed, St. Augustine rejected the Stoics' notion of eternal return with the simple observation in his *City of God* that

Christ died once, will return, but not to die, rather to judge the world and bring an end to history. In the ancient Near East, on the other hand, Niemeyer writes,

> time appeared capable of regeneration and its regeneration was deemed to wipe out the past. In this order man's existence was experienced not as a movement from past through present into future but rather as relatively timeless oscillation between order, fluidity, and again order; birth, death, and rebirth; impairment and restoration; being, chaos, and reconstituted being.

Our concept of history contains, on the contrary, an "eternal past" "constituted by God's breaking into time."

Another aspect is the concept of a yet unknowable hopeful future, an eschatological dimension that is so substantial that even though the theological dimension has been rejected by modern civil religion the concept of linear time leading toward a final end remains the most formidable element of secular political religions. At the core of Israel's consciousness of history was the breaking into time of Yahweh, who chose the Hebrew clans as his people. Israel was constituted, therefore, as a political community existing in the present under God. The presence of God with his people was the source of their hope for the future in which God would intervene. "The lord of time," Niemeyer writes,

> is then also the judge of human action in time, as well as the savior whose help in affliction redeems a mankind that can no longer count on cultic osmosis with divinity through a series of sacred times. Human existence in time is therefore an existence in autonomous human responsibility under God, as well as an existence that ultimately depends on divine saving action.

Niemeyer shows that this historical consciousness that informs our understanding of our political existence in time has itself been perverted by civil religion. The hope for the future has become a hope dependent on human political action. The expectation of a final end *beyond* time has been converted into an expectation of some event *in* time.

Civil religion's immanentization of history can thus be seen as a part of the often-noted secularization of religion in America. James Madison and Thomas Jefferson began a movement for the separation of church and state in 18th-century Virginia that culminated in the 20th century with the secularizing interpretations of the First Amendment by the Supreme Court after World War II. Sir James Fitzjames Stephen foresaw the consequences of this movement and lamented them in his *Liberty, Equality, Fraternity* (1873). Stephen believed that secular elements in the United States could succeed in separating church and state only partially. And in the process they would do much harm. The separation of church and state cuts life in two, he wrote, and degrades and reduces the function of the state to mere police functions. The fundamental doctrines of religion and civic morals and virtue, he thought, stand or fall together. He doubted whether, in a democracy especially, where the maintenance of civic virtue is central to moderation, any long-run benefits could result from a rigid policy of disestablishment. Stephen's analysis should be extended further. The absence of a public philosophy or of a civil theology interpreted by an established church creates a vacuum in which the theological dimensions of human social existence are allowed to die from lack of public articulation. This leads in turn to the imaginative creation of a civil religion that perverts the theological realm with immanentist religious interpretations of national life. This is a perversion, but it can hardly be expected *not* to occur when the relation between public order and a higher order is not adequately articulated by any public institutions or by an authoritative public philosophy.

Toward A Creative Social Theology

If an experience of the sacred no longer informs our public life, what will create and nourish our community loyalties? We are driven to live extreme private lives because political community no longer mediates our experience of participation in a higher order, but our experience cannot be denied. Where is it transferred? If our public institutions cease to speak with authority about ultimate truth, our lives nevertheless must be informed about the constants of life and order, of those sacred paradigms of existence that speak to us about our participation in transcendent order. In *Choosing Our King* (1974), Michael Novak comments on this problem as follows:

> Resources in the national self-understanding now lie fallow and untended. It is as though the nation is bottled up, imprisoned in too constricted a form of its own self-understanding. Its experiences seethe, the skins of old symbol systems are not sufficient to contain them. The inner pressure is intense. We struggle to find even a small escape hatch, to imagine a more ample and more accurate symbolic channel for our communal life. Consciously or not, we labor *toward a creative social theology*—not merely an economic game plan or a social scheme, but a set of symbols that will liberate the energies of the heart. [Emphasis added.]

I have argued that a public philosophy, not civil religion, should be the primary vehicle by which the American nation's self-understanding of its ultimate meaning is articulated. This ultimate meaning, as Novak suggests, is not merely economic or material, but touches upon profound theological truths. Much in the same spirit, Irving Kristol has written that the decline in the belief in immortality is the most important *political* fact of the last hundred years. The truths of the American public philosophy, or of any public philosophy, are not grounded merely in the common valuing of some goods over others. The mere common sharing of a preference, though having the utility of holding people together so long as the preference endures, is not the basis of a public philosophy. Commonly shared beliefs must be ontologically oriented, grounded in reality, and must reflect an experience of a higher order of goods than the material.

Aristotle observed that one could distinguish between types of friendship and men. There are those who love money, and the friendship among persons working together to accumulate wealth, the friendship of those who seek honor, but best of all is the friendship of those who love the good. Their friendship endures longest. The agreement among persons living in a political community may constitute a consensus, but unless that consensus includes the highest ethical and theological truths, it will not last. John Courtney Murray called such a consensus "a heritage of an essential truth, a tradition of rational belief, that sustains the structure of the City and furnishes the substance of civil life."

In this context, the importance of Michael Novak's concept of a "social theology" should be noted. Most importantly, it distinguishes the public myths of the American "realm" from civil religion. The public myths of a civil or a social "theology" are godward in direction whereas civil religion is not, as witness the Marxian civil religion. Fr. Murray, for example, calls to our attention such theological concepts of the public philosophy as the "sovereignty of God," the "virtuous people," by which he means a people whose public lives are informed by theological truth, and, lastly, the natural law. All these are godward aspects of our "social theology."

And yet it would be foolish to ignore the visible signs that our public philosophy is in decline. In *The Joy of Sports* (1976), for example, Michael Novak examines the theological dimension of sports in American life. Though he does not make the argument that sports are endowed with great importance *because* we live in a vacuum of public theological truths, his thesis that sports presently perform a valuable public, as opposed to a private, function, suggests that argument.

Absent an authoritative public philosophy, our fellow citizens invest sports with the spiritual and symbolic value that their public lives ought to have. Sports do, after all, mediate and make public our experience of a higher order. Isn't the perfection of a well-executed pass a revelation of virtue? Isn't the memory of a pitcher's perfect game a recollection of a sacred moment in time that is "godward" in direction? When an aging star successfully battles against his own weakness as an older man engaged in battle with younger men, can't we say that we've experienced a moment of the eternal? The spirit of a George Blanda, Joe Namath, or Johnny Unitas creates for us moments that are sacred in contrast to the profane moments of normal life. In this sense, Novak writes, "sports already are in end time. Participation in sports is a foretaste of the eschaton."

This, Novak believes, explains our unfilled appetite for sports. We see a glimpse of perfection, a future life, a convergence of body and soul in perfect unity, and wish ourselves to be a part of that end goal. The highest principles of sports are theological. And it is on that level that I believe Novak's analysis helps us to understand public philosophy.

The community that sports create is a community of shared experience of excellence. It is not the highest excellence, of course; the order of the soul and of society must take priority. But sports evoke an experience of community similar to life in political community. Consider this passage in which Novak reflects on the experience of community in sports:

> The human race itself is not merely an aggregate of individuals; thus, images of human unity excite some hidden longing in the heart, some long-forgotten memory or expectation. For those who have participated on a team that has known the click of communality, the experience is unforgettable, like that of having attained, for a while at least, a higher level of existence: existence as it ought to be.
>
> There is, I think, nothing mystical or anti-individual in this high form of community. It is not a community that diminishes each individual, or demands the submersion of the individual. Quite the contrary. Each feels himself to be acting at his very best, better than his individual best; and not submerged but uplifted, beyond the limits of the single self. It is true that the fellow who tends to shoot a lot, or perhaps to be a prima donna, has to find a different mode of action; and the change may be painful, its proper vein difficult to locate. Some tensions, sulking, disappointments, battles, and frustrations may be necessary. But the new mode, once discovered, does not feel like subjection; it feels like liberation. One's defenses no longer need to be held high; one can give and receive easily, ebb and flow with the rhythms of the team; and one finds new capacities, new energies.

By analogy, the experience of community of sports fans has its equivalent in the civic virtue of the citizenry. Irving Kristol writes that civic virtue allows the individual citizen to forsake his own private interest for the sake of the common good. A public philosophy fosters such public morality; in our case a unique republican morality, which gives vital answers to questions any citizen will ask. Like a well-knit team, a community with a public philosophy will respond to charges of illegitimacy that are made against the community and its representatives. When public philosophy is absent, when, in effect, there is no agreement about ends, no answer will appear, or appear authoritative. By the same token, a sports team that does not play as a team, though individual players may excel, will lose. In political existence, it is public philosophy that holds a community together and wards off defeat. But in the American political community, like a disorganized sports team, though these individual public philosophers have called attention to the need for public philosophy, the community has experienced what I call the decline of the realm.

The Decline of the Realm

The first signs of the dissolution of a realm can be found in the decline of authority. The state's monopoly of legitimate coercion is based on practical *and* moral considerations. We pay our taxes because we are compelled *and* because we are obliged. To the degree this consciousness of moral obligation informs the body politic, evokes an experience of duty and political obligation, the political realm is healthy. That element of health, however, Robert Nisbet argues, is presently missing in contemporary Western political community. The centralized state is not the recipient of patriotism and piety, nor is it capable of evoking an experience of the sacred participation of community in a higher order. The problem, as Nisbet sees it, is twofold: on the one hand there has occurred the decline of intermediate religious, kinship, tribal, and familial groups. The retreat of these authoritative institutions has, on the other hand, been followed by the growth of the centralized state which, though it can execute and administer power, can compel compulsion, cannot, absent a public philosophy, evoke the authoritative experience of obligation necessary for the maintenance of community. The functions performed by intermediate institutions that previously supported the national life are now replaced by a bureaucratic state apparatus that is efficient, but not human, powerful, but not evocative of respect, all-encompassing, yet peculiarly remote. Nisbet writes in *Twilight of Authority* (1975) that

> Centuries of gradual secularization of human belief have been followed in our time by an acceleration of secular tendencies beyond anything the West has before known. Mechanization and bureaucratization crowd out those ritual commemorations of the social bond which are the central elements of sacred experience everywhere. Christmas, Easter, Halloween are today but impoverished reminders of a time when the year was rich in celebrations of the seasons—and, far more important, of humanity and its relation to the forces of nature. If it were solely a matter of loss of these ritual experiences—through commercialization, rootlessness, and general disenchantment, the product in large part of rationalization of life—the matter would not be as grave. But even, and perhaps especially, in the smaller areas of society, in family, neighborhood, and church, a conspicuous erosion of the sense of the sacred is to be seen, also witnessed by the loss of ritual expressions in so many lives.

The chief element in our twilight age is the decline of the realm. When the experience of the realm's participation in a higher order is lost, the community becomes a lesser form of association, a "state." Nisbet has observed, moreover, that not only has the transition from community to centralized state marked our twilight age, the subsequent decline of authority has in fact led to the decline of the state itself. Just as the modern era commenced when men grew disillusioned with the Church in the 15th century, so the twilight of our era is marked by disillusionment with the state. Having taken upon itself enormous functions that government never before sought to fulfill, the state now finds itself unable to maintain public order. The loss of authority that all institutions have experienced, including the state, has made it all but impossible to provide the basic elements of social order without resorting to intolerable coercion.

The distinguishing mark of the American civil religion is its capacity to enlist state coercion not for the purpose of holding society together, but for reconstitution of society in a new utopian form. At the very moment in the development of Western political community when the realm has been transformed into a "state," the American civil religion has enlisted the "state" in the religious pursuit of a utopian order.

4/Origins of the American Civil Religion

THE UTOPIAN IMPULSE IN the American civil religion draws its inspiration from a vast source of materials. It finds expression in the theoretical development of civil religion by the modern political thinkers, and in the eschatological expectation of salvation *in* history of New England Puritanism and 19th-century ideology. It evokes experiences that are basic to man, and perhaps especially to *homo Americanus,* such as the desire for certainty and the quest for salvation now. As a result, the American civil religion has proven its capacity to inspire political loyalty, to rally the nation, and to commit national resources to particular ideological projects. As a religion, it has its gods, its saints, church, rituals, vestments, and clergy. But that is the American civil religion in its full-blown development. Let us examine its parts before examining the fully functioning system.

At its roots, the American civil religion is a type of Idealism, indeed, it is the logical development of the merger of 19th-century Liberalism and philosophical Idealism. This linkage between Liberalism and Idealism was an important development, though it seems not to have attracted the attention it deserves.[1] It represents a massive shift in orientation. Once it had occurred, however, no one seemed to notice, or to give it a second thought. It carried with it a sense of natural development, as if what happened was only right.

In general outline, the origins of Liberalism can be traced to the Social Contract theorists and, especially American Liberalism, to the thought of John Locke. His emphasis upon the community as unnatural, the artifice of persons reluctantly compelled to leave a state of nature, typifies the hesitant attitude of Liberalism toward political authority. He seems to say that atomic, isolated individuals make community by their individual choice. Consequently, man's nature is best understood in terms of individuals essentially unconnected with one another in a

[1] See my essay on this development, "Thomas Hill Green's Political Philosophy," *Political Science Reviewer,* vol. IV (Fall 1974), pp. 29–53.

hypothetical, presocial state of nature. It is as if Locke were arguing, by analogy to Christian theology, that man's nature, to be understood correctly, should be the nature of man before the Fall. Some writers have pointed out another analogy. The state of nature for Locke is equivalent to his concept of the mind as a blank tablet on which are written the experiences and reflections of the senses. The unadorned individual exercising free choice absent of political restraints is the nucleus of political community. Liberalism in this original sense emphasized the individual as the basic social unit, and thus replaced the Classical emphasis upon the priority of community. If man's nature is apolitical, then what pertains to the individual is not a proper object of governmental scrutiny. But Locke and the other Social Contract thinkers went beyond this. Man was not merely apolitical, but essentially amoral. That is, every man had the unalienable right to do whatever was convenient to him, i.e., whatever was conducive to satiation of his appetites. According to this view political community exists to realize this nature to perfection. To be sure, they interpreted these appetites differently. Hobbes saw the controlling appetite in the fear of death, Locke in the desire to protect property, and Rousseau in the quest for a legitimate order in which man exercises his natural freedom in civil society. But together they stand contrary to the Classical emphasis upon government as an agent for creating virtuous citizens, and upon political community as something most natural to man, something which rather than fostering, helps to curb men's appetites.

Though two types of individualism develop from this Liberal view of man, economic and social, it is the latter that merged with philosophic Idealism. The classic statement of social individualism is John Stuart Mill's *On Liberty* (1859). Mill argued that free scope should be given to different experiments of living and the types of character each represented. Thus he defended the Mormons' practice of polygamy. We should not be limited, he thought, in the cultivation of what is individual in ourselves; because the end for man is the fullest development of his individual capacities. There are, therefore, areas of privacy, areas that concern only ourselves, which should not be limited. These inward areas of conscience, of taste and pursuits, and freedom of association in outline, delineated what the state should not restrain. Only a society that respects these liberties, he thought, is by definition free. One individual (or society) may interfere with the liberty of another only for self-protection. In matters concerning only the individual, one's independence is absolute. For that reason Mill opposed the prohibition of alcoholic beverages, and state monopoly of education.

Mill's views were finally rejected by the very people to whom they had originally appealed, the Liberal educated elite. Toward the end of the 19th century, English individualism was overrun by those in English universities who championed an English type of philosophical Idealism. This movement was as effective as it was partly because it represented a formidable intellectual attack on the individualist tradition. What, English Idealists asked, should we do if people do not cultivate themselves when left to themselves? Is freedom to be valued when people persist in using it unreasonably, though not to the jeopardy of society at large? If they fail to use their freedom to develop their individual capacities to the fullest, then the end for man is not realized. Faced to a large extent with the social problem of alcoholism and the disintegration of the family in the wake of industrialization, these Idealists arrived at a theory of political obligation that found radical individualism to be almost unpatriotic. The Idealists did not hesitate to answer that it may be necessary to force people to realize their humanity, to actualize their potential to the fullest capacity.

English Idealism was taken almost wholly from the German Idealist movement, whose principal advocates were G. W. F. Hegel, Friedrich Schelling, and Johann Gottlieb Fichte. They believed that history was the canvas upon which God developed himself and the world. This self-development of God operated in the field of human consciousness too, and was manifest in the ideas in men's minds. The chief English Idealist, T. H. Green, influenced an entire generation of England's leaders from his chair at Oxford where he formulated an all-encompassing organic view of community according to the highest aspirations of individualism. For Green, man was not an isolated atomic individual, but rather was primarily social by nature. Green could accept that the end for man is the actualization of his nature, the fulfillment of his highest capacities. The end for man, Green thought, is the perfection of himself, his will, and of his kind. He believed this perfection actually occurs in history, which is directed toward the perfection of life. This perfect life was an Ideal, but also, in the philosophic sense, a reality. Like Plato, philosophic Idealism found reality in ideas, with the difference that Plato would not have called the perfection of the human race an *idea*. More likely than not, he would have called it an "opinion" (Soxa).

Green was quite clear that though the Ideal of human perfection was not represented in experience at this moment, nevertheless political reformers had to have such an Ideal in view so that they might bring it about by political action. This attempt to develop humanity, Green wrote, is an attempt "to enact God in the world." Idealism at that stage of its development still carried quasi-Biblical connotations, which have since evaporated. The American civil religion, for example, no longer seeks to "enact God in the world," but rather aspires to the secular equivalent. The new God is man, and the fulfillment of his will in the world is brought about by state action. The nucleus of such an Idealism was fully formulated by Green in the following passage from his *Prolegomena to Ethics*:

> No one doubts that a man who improves the current morality of his time must be something of an Idealist. He must have an idea, which moves him to seek its realization, of a better order of life than he finds about him. *That idea cannot represent any experienced reality.* If it did, the reformer's labour would be superfluous; the order of life which he seeks to bring about would be already in existence. It is an idea to which nothing real as yet corresponds, but which, as actuating the reformer, tends to bring into being a reality corresponding to itself. [Emphasis added.]

To the extent that reality is a given, which man apprehends, it is not made. Thomas Hill Green based his Idealism, however, upon the expectation that a presently nonexistent Ideal, the perfection of mankind, could be brought into existence by political action.

Let us compare Green's view of politics with the political science of Aristotle. In the *Nichomachean Ethics,* Book Six, Aristotle distinguished political science, which he saw as the reasoned capacity to act, from art, which is a technique of making of things the origin of which is in the maker or artist, not nature. To act means to act within a reality of ends that are given in experience, not made. Thus political science is an order of action within a cosmos not made by man. For T. H. Green, however, politics is conceived as a massive project for the making of realities that are not grounded in any experienced order, but rest upon the imaginative capacity of the theorist. Here in the contest between the magical or speculative imagination and political science lies the primary difference between civil religion and public philosophy. The former attempts to manipulate reality, casting it into any mold suitable to the imagination, while the latter seeks a course of prudent action aimed at attaining the common good.

The Idealist view that politics should be devoted to bringing hitherto unattainable ideals into reality merged quickly with the American persuasion that America has been chosen by God to perform heroic deeds. Ernest Lee Tuveson's *Redeemer Nation: The Idea of America's Millennial Role* (1968) contains a quotation from Albert J. Beveridge that illustrates this feature of the American civil religion:

> God has not been preparing the English-speaking and Teutonic peoples for a thousand years for nothing but vain and idle self-contemplation and self-admiration. No. He made us master organizers of the world to establish system where chaos reigned. He has given us the spirit of progress to overwhelm the forces of reaction throughout the earth. He has made us adept in government that we may administer government among savage and senile peoples. Were it not for such a force as this the world would relapse into barbarism and night. And of all our race He has marked the American people as His chosen nation to finally lead in the *redemption of the world.* [Emphasis added.]

Woodrow Wilson also spoke in this spirit when he characterized the role of American forces in Europe during World War I as redemptive. Those who turned their backs upon the League of Nations, which Wilson saw as an extension of their salvatory work, in effect turned their backs upon "the liberation and salvation of the world." A world without wars becomes the goal of politics, not in the pragmatic sense as the end to immediate hostilities, but in the redemptive sense it now comes to have.

Woodrow Wilson was not a heretic by the standards of the American civil religion. He was its completion. America, Tuveson demonstrates, had always been seen as a nation endowed with a special mission. America was innocence, the home of God's friends. In such a context, wars have always had an apocalyptic significance, as means by which the contradictions of existence can be replaced with a world free of evil, inequality, injustice, war, or whatever the fancy of the moment is.

The Civil War, for example, fit the apocalyptic mold, and that flavor was captured by the "Battle Hymn of the Republic." The bloody events of the Civil War provide the American public an opportunity to see Christ coming. This is a war that is hastening the Second Coming. But it is a secular Christ whose coming is imminent. His redemptive mission has been transformed into the secular mission of the antislavery movement to "make men free" as Christ "died to make men holy." Significantly the individual salvation promised by the Gospels is now provided wholesale to the American nation—salvation becomes collective.

5/A Critique of the American Civil Religion

PERHAPS NO OTHER TOPIC is more important for the recovery of health of the American political community than the problem of the contest between civil religion and public philosophy for the authoritative interpretation of the American political tradition. So divided has the American psyche become as a result of this conflict that Irving Kristol has concluded that there are in fact two traditions that inform our idea of democracy. One is the "constitutional-legal" tradition of the Founders, manifest in the *Federalist.* The other tradition is what he calls the "prophetic-utopian" tradition. The analysis of the contest between these two traditions constitutes the form of Irving Kristol's critique of the American civil religion.

The "constitutional-legal" tradition of democracy, Kristol argues in *On the Democratic Idea in America* (1972), was not a commitment to mere democratic procedures, but to higher ends in the light of which democratic government is only a means, albeit the only politically acceptable means. This concept of democracy cared for the "quality of life," for civic virtue, the moral quality of political and intellectual culture. Indeed, the Founders saw that democratic government under our constitutional arrangements was best suited to bringing the best persons to positions of influence in government.

Federalist Number 10 makes this argument most clearly. James Madison wrote that "each representative will be chosen by a greater number of citizens in the large than in the small republic." With a larger pool from which to draw, "unworthy candidates" will be readily detected, and men will more likely be elected "who possess the most attractive merit and the most diffusive and established characters." In an extended republic, where more interests, economic, religious, and social are to be found, it is less likely that a majority will repress the civil rights of other citizens. The Founders sought representation of the people by those "whose enlightened views and virtuous sentiments render them superior to local prejudices and to schemes of injustice." These "fit characters," it was expected, would seek "the public good." Their "wisdom," to use Madison's terms, would enable them to "best discern the true interest of their country." And their "patriotism and love of justice" will be least likely sacrificed by factious motives.

The Founders' consideration of the type of government we should have was informed not merely by popular opinion, but by a concern for the substantive goods that political community can bring, such as justice and the public good. They were persuaded that the common good could be discovered by men disposed by good character to seek it out. For these reasons, Kristol observes that, to the Founders, the question of democracy was one of political philosophy. Robert Nisbet also notes, in his *Twilight of Authority* (1975), the Founders' respect "for such cultural and social values as objective reason, the discipline of language, self-restraint, the work ethic, and, far from least, the culture that had taken root in classical civilization and grown, with rare interruptions, ever since." Our public documents and the official statements of our elected officials accordingly reflected a high level of discourse absent of cant, demagogy, and bombast. Needless to say, this has changed. Kristol believes that the change occurred around the turn of the century under the impact of the Progressive and Populist movements. Underlying this change in discourse was a more powerful transformation of our intellectual attitudes from one of philosophy, Kristol argues, to one of faith:

> . . . once upon a time, in this country, the question of democracy *was* a matter for political philosophy, rather than for faith. And the way in which a democratic political philosophy was gradually and inexorably transformed into a democratic faith seems to me to be perhaps the most important problem in American intellectual—and ultimately political—history.

Let us follow Kristol's criticism as far as he has taken it. Kristol is persuaded that the civil religion is an attitude of mind carried by a special section or class within Western democratic society, the intellectual class. He believes that the "masses of the people tend to be more 'reasonable' . . . in their political judgments and political expectations than are our intellectuals." Robert Nisbet has similarly argued that our intellectual class constitutes a "clerisy of power" imbued with a sense of "redemptive passion." The chief vehicle by which they wish to redeem American society is the state, and thus Nisbet believes that it is proper to say that they "have made the political state the temple, so to speak, of their devotion." Michael Novak similarly speaks of the "superculture" and its commitments to the values of modernity—science, technology, industry.

Kristol is also persuaded that the "redemptive" passion of our clerisy of power is a heritage of the millenarian or millennial elements in Western civilization. John Courtney Murray called this "utopianism" a Christian heresy. As we saw in Chapter Four, at the roots of the American civil religion lies the lust to replace reality as it is given with conditions more acceptable to its tastes. As such, it constitutes a radical shift of focus from a view of the limited state of the Founders. Now we have a view of an essentially unlimited state whose function is to provide for the creation of the only real heaven, the one here and now. That this runs contrary to the public philosophy of the Founders, who saw that men were limited by their natural tendency to be vicious, and the Founders' fear of an unlimited state, suggests the revolutionary change in attitude accomplished by civil religion in the American context. But it is also revolutionary in a general sense. If the state is to become the "kingdom of God," Kristol writes, then any regime that does not approximate the virtues of that city is unacceptable. Only the best regime, from this perspective, is legitimate. Thus the adversary stance by our clerisy of power toward the organic institutions of the American political community, and, we must add, their disillusionment with politics. Politics requires the adjustment of conflicting interests, and an attitude of mind that seeks the good in the particular. This is an unacceptably dull process to those who seek in politics a field for the actualization of their private visions. Nisbet suggests that the rise of non-Party movements, and the decline of our political parties is a part of this attitudinal development. To the degree that pragmatic politics is rejected, we also find an all-encompassing politicization of the mind. All problems are now seen to be capable of being resolved by the application of arbitrary power in a good cause, and the grander the scope of involvement of state power, the more hope there is for the realization of utopian visions.

Nevertheless, like any religion, the American civil religion will experience backsliding, a defection from the "cause." The expectation of Jonathan Edwards that the "new heaven and new earth" prophesied in Revelation would occur in America eventually met with resistance by a generation for whom Revelation no longer provided socially acceptable symbols. In this context, it is interesting to recall John C. Miller's *Sam Adams: Pioneer in Propaganda* (1936) in which it is shown that the Massachusetts revolutionary patriot was motivated to mob action in Boston by his religious belief that separation from the mother country was necessary if Puritanism was to flourish again, not by political philosophy. Few shared Adams' desire to bring Puritanism back or desired as early as he to precipitate a revolution. Milier portrays a picture of Adams as a revolutionary before there was reason for revolution, suggesting that his political views were founded on a basically fanatical and irrational faith. Later, almost alone among his American contemporaries, Adams supported the Jacobin revolution.

Adams' call for revolution as the vehicle to overcome backsliding has its modern equivalent in Robert N. Bellah's more recent call for a secular spiritual rebirth in *The Broken Convenant* (1975):

> If we are to transcend the limitations of American culture and society it can only be on the basis of an imaginative vision that can generate an experience of inner conversion and lead to a new form of covenant. Liberation without any sense of constitution will surely be self-defeating. The perils of late 20th-century America will not be overcome by everyone doing his or her "own thing," but through the discovery of cultural and social forms that can give the disciplined basis for a new degree of moral freedom.

For this cleric of American civil religion, a call for a collective "inner conversion" and a "new covenant," though using the symbols of the old-time religion, is actually a call for the revival of atheist humanism. Who will be the "God" of the "new covenant" (other than ourselves), anointed by our own "imaginative vision," and baptized in the waters of our own "experience of inner conversion"? Political community in Bellah's mind is an autonomous entity, independent of a higher order, except one created by ourselves, composed of autonomous men who give moral freedom to themselves by covenanting with their own will. The new god in Bellah's civil religion is man, whose will will be done by collective action. Who are the leaders of this rebirth? In *Beyond Belief* (1970), Bellah sees hope in the prophetic voice of Senator Fulbright, and we would be remiss, of course, not to include Bellah's own voice among the prophets.

Bellah correctly points out, however, that America has been the object of eschatological hopes since it was discovered in the 15th century. America was the new Eden, a paradise, it was thought, in contrast to the hopelessly degenerate Old World. John Locke pointed to America and the Indians as examples of his idyllic "state of nature," a condition that all societies had reluctantly left. For others, America was perceived as existing now in the condition toward which all mankind would eventually progress: America, the new Israel, chosen by God as he once chose the ancient Hebrews. The endurance of this immanent eschatological phantasizing has played a large part in the demise of public philosophy. But it has never been more effective than when secularized and fashioned into a political ideology, first by Abraham Lincoln, and then in the 20th century by the Progressives Herbert Croly and Woodrow Wilson.

Abraham Lincoln is both a central and a transitional figure in American civil religion. Much of the Biblical symbolism in his public speeches clothes genuine political insights. However, immanent eschatology of the American civil religion runs like a strong stream through much of his public teaching. Lincoln spoke of and for a community of believers in the millennial destiny of America. Their language was his language too. And yet the full-blown political religion of the "Battle Hymn of the Republic" is only hinted at here and there in Lincoln's House Divided speech, Gettysburg Address, Second Inaugural Address, and other public pronouncements. While Woodrow Wilson's political religion is full-blown for all to see, the light of Lincoln's political religion winks at you like a meteor, far distant, but approaching at a rapid speed.

Consider Lincoln's Second Inaugural (March 4, 1865), in which he touches upon several eschatological aspects of America's civil religion. The address concludes with a call to charity and absence of malice while holding firmly to "the right," "as God gives us to see the right." Melvin Bradford has correctly pointed out that this emphasis on the right is not action in accordance with reason, but a special kind of apocalyptic power to see God's revelation.[1] It is the revelatory "right" that is given and withheld in inscrutable ways. Lincoln's ethics are a voluntaristic ethics rooted in the condition of mind that seeks "God's will" as opposed to a rational choice of action. The nation is led by a man who Lincoln himself implied spoke for God, in the language of the Good Book. After his death the claim was made more directly. Reading the Gettysburg Address in 1868, Edwin M. Stanton said, "That is the voice of God speaking through the lips of Abraham Lincoln. . . . You hear the voice of Father Abraham here tonight. Did he die in vain?" Ernest Lee Tuveson also has called attention to certain other perplexing aspects of the Second Inaugural:

> The Almighty has His own purposes. "Woe unto the world because of offenses; for it must needs be that offenses come, but woe to that man by whom the offense cometh." If we shall suppose that American slavery is one of those offenses which, in the providence of God, must needs come, but which, having continued through his appointed time, He now wills to remove. . . .

This central passage evokes, Tuveson reflects, "an idea of history as having an apocalyptic program." The offenses or evil of the world are due not only to men, but to the "Almighty" who "has His own purposes." History then is a divine plan into which evil comes as a matter of plan. The "appointed time" for the removal of the particular world historic evil of slavery has come. But why, Tuveson asks? Was Lincoln suggesting that these are the final days that will usher in the millennium? The passage "He now wills to remove. . . ." suggests Revelation 17:17 in which God is said to lead men to give over their affairs to the "beast" for a time until "the words of God shall be fulfilled."

The nature of the Lincolnian millennium is one of a "new birth of freedom." The liberty of the original Founders established on this continent is seemingly to be replaced by Lincoln with a new freedom. But what is the nature of the new freedom and equality that were consecrated, hallowed, and dedicated by the men who died at Gettysburg? Is it the absolute freedom to

[1] Melvin E. Bradford, "The Heresy of Equality: Bradford Replies to Jaffa," *Modern Age*, vol. 20, no. 1 (Winter 1976), pp. 62–77.

do whatever you want, and the equality that commits the state to projects designed to assure that though we may not all start out equally in the race of life, we will all end it as equals? Or is it simply the equal protection of the laws, that no man will be treated differently at the bar of justice, and the common-law freedom to live in peace? If so, then what is "new"? The former is consistent with the aspirations of America's civil religion, the latter with its public philosophy. The former is revolutionary, bent upon overturning the established order in the pursuit of a reality reconstituted, the latter is conservative, seeking to assure liberty and equal protection of the law, but not license or leveling egalitarianism. Though the legacy of Abraham Lincoln raises legitimate doubts about the intention of his rhetoric, the same cannot be said for Woodrow Wilson and Herbert Croly.

Both Herbert Croly and Woodrow Wilson were Idealists in the tradition of T. H. Green. Both represented the merger of English Idealism and Liberalism, both shared the eschatological aspirations of the American millennial tradition, and both left an indelible impression on American intellectual culture. Herbert Croly's *The Promise of American Life* (1909) and, later, the journal *The New Republic* that he founded and edited performed a role in shaping the political attitudes of America's intellectual elite, a role that Woodrow Wilson complemented by shaping the popular attitudes of Americans toward democracy, the nature of peace, and America's destiny.

The promise of American life, indeed the solution to the social problems of American community existence, can be found, Croly thought, in the assertion of a new "democratic social ideal." This ideal was to give cohesion to a society tending to fall apart.

> The solidarity which it would impart to American society would have its basis in feeling and its results in good fellowship; but it must always remain a promise and constructive ideal rather than a finished performance.

This new "creed" could not be a new version of traditional American beliefs, because they embody nothing more than a concept of government by drift. Croly was critical of the Jeffersonian notion of automatic harmony of interests, individual freedom, and equal rights. As an alternative he offered a reconstituted Hamiltonianism, by which he meant a more open attitude to state regulation of social life motivated by "thoroughly democratic" political principles. This policy is required if "progressive national ideas" are to be actualized. Croly was persuaded that any danger to democracy from the state would be held in check by democratic principles that make up the "formative idea" of American national life, an ineluctably moving national spirit, the forerunner of things to come. And what is to come? For one thing, the fulfillment of the promise of American life, "the gradual creation of a higher type of individual and associated life." Croly believed we are impelled toward a condition of human perfection. In the *Promise of American Life* he wrote: "For better or worse, democracy cannot be disentangled from an aspiration toward human perfectibility, and hence from the adoption of measures looking in the direction of realizing such an aspiration." That aspiration would be realized primarily by those "exceptional fellow-countrymen" of his, the American intellectuals for whom he wrote:

> The common citizen can become something of a saint and something of a hero, not by growing to heroic proportions in his own person, but by the sincere and enthusiastic imitation of heroes and saints, and whether or not he will ever come to such imitation will depend upon the ability of his exceptional fellow-countrymen to offer him acceptable examples of heroism and saintliness.

The secular saints who lead the common mass, Croly speculated, will not necessarily be conservators of the American political tradition. He speculated that the realization of the promise of American life will sometimes require a "partial renunciation" of the American past and of present interests, if necessary, to contribute to the "national purpose." There may even occur a sudden transfiguration by "an outburst of enthusiasm":

> If such a moment ever arrives, it will be partly the creation of some democratic evangelist—some imitator of Jesus who will reveal to men the path whereby they may enter into spiritual possession of their individual and social achievements, and immeasurably increase them by virtue of personal regeneration.

Let us reassemble the parts of Herbert Croly's political religion before examining the political evangelism of Woodrow Wilson. Dominating his civil religion is the view of a national purpose to be realized in public affairs. The job requires secular saints, themselves led by a messiah who will reveal the true path. This transfiguration will come because the American nation itself is formed by a democratic ideal that is working its way in time toward full realization. But in order to begin, this democratic ideal, always a promise, must be fully articulated, its creed formulated now, so that the American people may believe once again in the promise of American life.

A critique of Croly's civil religion requires that we return to basics. Politics is a science requiring rational judgments informed by an awareness of circumstances, by a proper assessment of the limits of government and potential abuses of state power, by a concern for institutions that limit power, and by the prudent knowledge of the common good. But Croly's call for secular saints who will conduct us into a condition of reconstituted and transfigured reality has less to do with political science than with prophecy, enthusiasm, and magic. The national life is indeed informed by an idea, by public myths that articulate the commonly shared beliefs of society's members. But that idea does not exist independently nor is it working its way in human events toward a logical fulfillment. The national life exists in the souls of its public philosophers who apprehend the common good. But that national life can expire, change its form, become something altogether different, not by means of the twists and turns of a world spirit, but by the weakening or collapse of civic virtue and of political judgment. How swiftly such a collapse can occur, and how vulnerable the American political system is to such collapse, is visible in the influence of Woodrow Wilson's political religion.

The political religion of Woodrow Wilson can be analyzed in terms of his immanentist eschatology; the presence of an engendering spirit to destroy existing political conditions; his will to attain the utopian vision of a world order never yet attained; his glorification of violence in the pursuit of that phantasm, and his view of politics as a field of action requiring "vision" as opposed to reason.

Dominating Wilson's political religion is a view of history quite similar to Croly's. History, Wilson believed, moves according to a plan in which America plays a major role. His view of history is one of a progressive development, moving slowly but inexorably to a condition of reconstituted reality. Speaking at the dedication of a synagogue in Newark, New Jersey on September 7, 1911, Wilson said:

> Look at the splendid progress of mankind. Look at the gracious providence of God which has brought more and more light unto the world, more and more judgment, more and more recognition of the rights of all races of people. The greatest brotherhood of mankind has made great strides within the short reaches of recorded history and there is approaching upon our modern times a sort of expectation of still greater days to come, when every man may lift his eyes with hope to the horizon, when there has come a day of peace and righteousness—when the nations shall be glad in the presence of God.

Similarly, in an address in Pittsburgh, Pennsylvania, at a Y.M.C.A. celebration on October 24, 1914, he said:

> . . . no man can look at the past of the history of this world without seeing a vision of the future of the history of this world; and when you think of the accumulated moral forces that have made one age better than another age in the progress of mankind, then you can open your eyes to the vision. You can see that age by age, though with a blind struggle in the dust of the road, though often mistaking the path and losing its way in the mire, mankind is yet—sometimes with bloody hands and battered knees—nevertheless struggling step after step up the slow stages to the day when he shall live in the full light which shines upon the uplands, where all the light that illumines mankind shines direct from the face of God.

The role of America in this plan of history, Wilson was persuaded, was shaped and directed by God from the beginning. This, he declared on one occasion, is a nation God built with our hands. To what end? In an address before Confederate veterans of the Civil War on June 5, 1917, Wilson declared that "we are to be an instrument in the hands of God to see that liberty is made secure for mankind."

Wilson's view of history, in which America and mankind were moving to a world-immanent transfiguration of the human condition, was not an isolated facet of the thought of an otherwise pragmatic man of affairs. It was an integral aspect of his attitude toward life, and the skills required if political life was to be governed rightly. Politics, for Wilson, required "vision," and vision for Wilson meant knowledge of God's purpose in history.

However, Wilson himself associated visions with "facts." Throughout his career, Wilson repeated Carlyle's view that the "facts" of the universe are inescapable. But by "facts" both Carlyle and Wilson meant something beyond ordinary human knowledge. Perhaps it is no coincidence, therefore, that in Wilson's first inaugural address he proclaimed a vision of a "new age of right":

> At last a vision has been vouchsafed us of life as a whole. We see the bad with the good, the debased and decadent with the sound and vital. With this vision we approach new affairs.
>
> . . . .
>
> The feelings with which we face this new age of right and opportunity sweep across our heartstrings like some air out of God's own presence, where justice and mercy are reconciled and the judge and brother are one. We know our task to be no mere task of politics but a task which will search us through and through, whether we be able to understand our time and the need of our people, whether we be indeed their spokesmen and interpreters, whether we have the pure heart to comprehend and the rectified will to choose our high course of action.

Wilson was speaking of his own visionary view of politics when he described his task as "no mere task of politics." The politics Wilson proclaimed was not "mere politics"; it was the capacity to announce the imminence of a new age certified by the political leader who experienced a special revelation. But this was not blasphemy in Wilson's eyes or in the eyes of his co-religionists of the American civil religion. After all, Herbert Croly proclaimed the coming of a "democratic evangelist" who was an "imitator of Jesus" and indeed looked forward to the event. Wilson, moreover, felt this nation was so blessed among nations that, as a whole, it had seen such visions. In a speech in Los Angeles on September 20, 1919, he said:

> America is great because of the purposes she has set herself to achieve. America is great because she has seen visions that other nations have not seen, and the one enterprise that does engage the steadfast loyalty and support of the United States is an enterprise for the liberty of mankind.

Not only had our nation seen visions, but the immigrants who came to America had a vision much like the three Magi who came searching for the king born in Bethlehem. In a speech at Des Moines, Iowa, on September 6, 1919, Wilson said that the immigrants

> saw this star in the west rising over the peoples of the world, and they said, "That is the star of hope and the star of salvation. We will set our footsteps towards the west and join that great body of men whom God has blessed with the vision of liberty."

America, for Woodrow Wilson, was a nation ordained to play a mighty role in history, and it is only fitting that Americans should be perceived as different from the rest of the peoples of the world. We, for example, entered World War I "for no selfish advantage." Our troops were "the armies of God." Accordingly, America undertook missions of redemption. At St. Louis, Missouri, September 5, 1919, Wilson observed that America

> has said to mankind at her birth: "We have come to redeem the world by giving it liberty and justice." Now we are called upon before the tribunal of mankind to redeem that immortal pledge.

Wilson was an Idealist in the sense of T. H. Green's definition of an Idealist as one who sought to "enact God in the world" by the pursuit of ideals not given in experience. The revolutionary character of this ideology lies in its unwillingness to accept the conditions of reality; in the case of Wilson, world politics as it is practiced. Wilson was committed to the vision of a world absent of war, a world he believed was within the grasp of the civilized world. And America's entry into World War I was largely motivated by the desire to attain such an ideal. That it was to be accomplished by violence did not dismay Wilson. It excited him. It is important to realize that Wilson's desire to involve us in World War I was grounded in his will to destroy the system of world politics as it had been practiced since the beginning of time. Wilson's often repeated assertion that America had no selfish interest to be satisfied by her entry into the war, that we sought no territory, no concessions, was his way of expressing utter contempt for balance-of-power politics, and his desire to destroy it utterly. On July 10, 1919, in his address to the Senate presenting the treaty of peace with Germany, Wilson proclaimed that

> Every true heart in the world, and every enlightened judgment demanded that, at whatever cost of independent action, every government that took thought for its people or for justice or for ordered freedom would lend itself to a new purpose and utterly destroy the old order of international politics.

Wilson's desire to "utterly destroy" the reality of the balance of powers was yoked with his desire to destroy "autocratic authority." He was persuaded that only governments governed by majority rule, not by autocratic minorities, could truly seek peace. As a consequence, he sought to destroy autocratic governments, in the present instance the government of Kaiser Wilhelm. In such a "good cause" Wilson believed that the maximum use of force was acceptable. Wilson saw a "halo" around the musket over the mantel of the soldier who fought to redeem the world, and around the returning troops. Force apparently was not to be disdained when exercised by the "armies of God." Wilson was searching for a "cause" in which to destroy the existing world order, and he found it.

Wilson found this cause in "the terrible war for democracy and human rights." The war was "terrible" no doubt in part because, Wilson said, the winner of the conflict, "the only people in the world who are going to reap the harvest of the future are the people who can entertain ideals, who can follow ideals to the death." But the war would be "terrible" also because Wilson saw the war in apocalyptic terms. This war had eschatological significance. He called the war a "final contest" that would bring about a "final emancipation." And if America did not join the League of Nations he foresaw another "final war," for surely there would be war again, he said, and that one would bring the evil policies of the powers of this world to a close. Oliver Cromwell has been called "God's Englishman." There is little doubt that the title "God's American" aptly describes Woodrow Wilson. Looking at history as a progressive movement toward a transfigured condition of peace and justice, Wilson saw himself as living in the last days when heroic acts were necessary to bring history to fruition.

The tragedy of Woodrow Wilson is magnified since it was shared by the people of the United States. His distortion of theological truths about history, politics, and peace have become aspects of America's self-interpretation of itself. To the degree that his view of history has saturated our political consciousness, it can be said that we have experienced a loss of history.

Gerhart Niemeyer writes in his *Between Nothingness and Paradise* (1971) that "the problem of human order is to relate men and their purposes to that which is." Political existence has ultimate meaning grounded in the constitution of being, and unless that relationship of community and being is articulated, the community will commence to decay. The mystery of being in which community shares, and which its public myths must articulate, evokes an experience of history: that the origins of political community are providential; that community exists under the sovereignty of God and serves some purpose; that man, society, and God are participants in the movement of being, are all theological dimensions of the Western concept of history. The public past, the history of the collective life of the nation, must express the truth of this mystery, or its public myths will become distorted. All Americans will readily admit, for example, that our history has been particularly fortunate. Since 1775 only 650,000 Americans have been killed in war, a figure, Richard Pipes has recently indicated,[2] fewer than the number of Russians killed during the 900-day siege of Leningrad in World War II. The mystery of why we have been so fortunate should yield the balanced judgment that God's providence cannot be understood completely. From the perspective of Wilson's civil religion, however, Americans are a chosen people, spared the holocaust for

[2] Richard Pipes, "Why the Soviet Union Thinks It Could Fight and Win a Nuclear War," *Commentary*, July 1977, p. 34.

some great event to come in the future that will bring to an end, once and for all, the suffering of all mankind. History is given an ersatz interpretation, a pseudohistory is created, and national consciousness is distorted by an arrogance, for which, unfortunately, Americans have been too well known.

It is also well known that Woodrow Wilson suffered a disabling stroke toward the end of a national tour in which he attempted to bring pressure upon the Senate to ratify the Covenant of the League of Nations. During those waning days of his tour, days filled with train stops and multiple speeches in American cities, Wilson repeated the theme that more than 55,000 Americans died to save the world in a war to end all wars, and that if the Covenant was not ratified by the United States those men died in vain. Why, he asked, should mothers of sons killed in the war come to see him and speak to him during his trip? After all, he said, he sent them to their deaths.

The visionary politics of a politician for whom politics is a religion, for whom politics is a field in which to attempt to realize an ideal that is not given in reality to be attained, is the crippling bane of American politics. Recall the following passage from the Inaugural Address of John F. Kennedy:

> Let every nation know, whether it wishes us well or ill, that we shall pay any price, bear any burden, meet any hardship, support any friend, oppose any foe to assure the survival and the success of liberty.

The difficulty that this ideal presents has often been commented upon after the toll of deaths of Americans in Vietnam had been counted. First, it is not the liberty of the American political community that is to be defended, but liberty in general. Second, our friends are put on notice that they will be judged by the standards of an ideal liberty evoked by the president. Our relationship will be based not on mutual interest, but their willingness to impose uniquely Anglo-American concepts of civil liberty upon their own societies. Third, it overestimates the capacity of America to pay "any" price, "any" hardship, and bear "any" burden. In the economy of real possibilities, such an aspiration is pernicious and potentially dangerous. It also fosters a cynicism about politics, because such ideals are never attainable, and vast dislocations in civil society are brought about in the attempt to realize them. The population eventually becomes skeptical of the claims of all politicians. In turn, some politicans—Richard Nixon is the prime example—overreact by pursuing a ruthless, supposedly "realistic," politics. Policies that seek to maintain a balance of power in world politics, or more immediately seek to preserve our national interests, have to be promoted within an Idealist framework (the policy of détente is an example) in order to avoid the rebuke that we are selfish, and untrue to American tradition. Lastly, the failure of the symbolism of such policies leads to a general revulsion against all politics, and the search for the nonpolitician, the outsider, the uncorrupted one to lead the national life. He in turn will reassert the Idealism of the "true" American tradition, the pursuit of policies because they are right (to the exclusion of ones in our national interest), and the cycle of ideological rejection of political reality beings anew.

6/What Is *the* American Political Tradition?

As Irving Kristol has suggested, there are two political traditions in America, each vying to be recognized as *the* American political tradition. The "constitutional-legal" tradition, associated with the common law and interpreters thereof such as John Marshall, Joseph Story, Felix Frankfurter, has been, for the most part, a legal tradition. The difficulty is that our common-law tradition does not exist from time immemorial, as was once popularly believed of the unwritten law of the English constitution. The precedents on which it is based are the work of human hands in historical memory. Tracing an existing order's genesis by an unbroken line of succession from the beginning of time, gives stability to a political order. Our tradition, our law, and our constitution, however, have a beginning in time. Moreover, that beginning was itself a revolutionary event. Leo Strauss took pleasure in pointing out that the most conservative voluntary association in the United States called itself the Daughters of the American Revolution, so it should not come as a shock to discover that the "prophetic-utopian" interpreters of the American political tradition legitimately wrap their calls for a continuing social revolution in the symbolism of the American political tradition.

Within the political tradition of the American republic exists a tension between a utopian commitment to justice and a philosophic emphasis upon order. Perhaps the following constructions can express that tension. The first attempts to state the nature of the American political tradition from the "constitutional-legal" perspective, the other from the "prophetic-utopian."

"Constitutional-Legal" View of American Political Tradition

The institution of civil society on the American continent was an act of Providence, and we as a people must remember with gratitude our debt to the

Creator who bestowed his blessings on this land. The end of political community is order, and the preservation and protection of life, with as much justice as circumstances will permit. The means by which this can best be attained in the American political community is by representative institutions of government. These institutions should reflect the will of the majority, and express the changes in public opinion that occur from time to time in the development of political life.

We believe also that all who reside in this political community should have the same liberties. Our customs and political traditions, our heritage, have given us insight into those liberties most conducive to political order with justice. They are uniquely political liberties, derivative of our political culture. They are not prepolitical or natural rights. Thus they can be limited or even abrogated, if necessary, for the protection of the community as a whole. But they can be limited only by our elected representatives. Among these liberties we count the following: freedom of press, speech, religion, trial by jury, the protection from cruel and unusual punishment, double jeopardy, habeas corpus. All may be found in the Constitution of the United States. The democratic procedures outlined in that document constitute the channel through which the political life of the country flows. These same procedures require compromise, for that is the nature of political life.

"*Prophetic-Utopian*" *View of American Political Tradition*

All men are equal, having unalienable rights. These rights are not political rights. They are natural rights, self-evident to all men regardless of nationality. They stand as general principles to which we as a people are committed, and by which our community must be judged. Governments are founded to secure these rights. If government does not impose them on the

community, then that government is evil. Only the corrupt would not seek to make all Americans more free and equal. When that failure occurs, then we the people must strike down our government by revolutionary means, and form a new one.

As the above rendition of the "prophetic-utopian" view suggests, the principal document to which all priests of the American civil religion refer is the Declaration of Independence. To them, this is the founding document of America's commitment to the inalienable rights of mankind: absolute equality and freedom. In a direct attempt to contradict that argument, two political scientists, the late Willmoore Kendall and George Carey, challenged the document's paramountcy. Their *Basic Symbols of the American Political Tradition* (1970) traces the origins of the political tradition not to the Declaration but to the pre-Lockean "Mayflower Compact" (1620). The thrust of their argument is that *the* American political tradition is not a utopian tradition, but a tradition of self-government. In this perspective, the Revolution begun in 1776 was not a radical revolution along the lines of the Idealism that came to dominate our politics in the presidency of Woodrow Wilson, but was a supremely conservative attempt to protect uniquely American institutions of self-government that had developed over a period of more than 150 years. The Revolution was fought not for the rights of mankind or of Englishmen, but for uniquely American civil liberties. Kendall and Carey point to the interesting fact that the Constitution of the United States, which, unlike the Declaration, is the *governing* document in our tradition, contains no "natural rights" language, and that, in fact, when the Constitutional Convention had an opportunity to vote upon the motion that the Constitution contain a Bill of Rights, that motion was voted down. Though prior to the writing of the Declaration, Leveller-like sentiment, which motivated the urban mobs of Boston and proclaimed the "inalienable rights" of the colonists, is an inescapable part of the historical record of the times, in the 11 years from 1776 to 1787, when the Constitutional Convention met, this rhetoric began to disappear. Kendall and Carey imply that soberer, more prudent men, trained in the common law and the philosophical natural law tradition, took charge of the nation's political life. To emphasize their point, Kendall and Carey sug-

gest a comparison of the Mayflower Compact and the Preamble to the Constitution.

In the Mayflower Compact the colonists committed themselves to virtue, the glory of God, the common good, and the advancement of the Christian faith. The colonists promise "due" submission and obedience to whatever governmental machinery is necessary, inclusive of just and equal laws, to accomplish these ends, and the preservation of the community. In the Preamble we find the following:

> We the People of the United States, in Order to form a more perfect Union, establish Justice, insure domestic Tranquility, provide for the common defense, promote the general Welfare, and secure the Blessings of Liberty to ourselves and our posterity, do ordain and establish this Constitution for the United States of America.

There is no statement in the Preamble of any commitment by the people to absolute individual rights, to the liberation of mankind from the shackles of feudalism, or even to the rights of man. But it does contain a commitment to order and justice. A commitment to civic virtue is also implicit in the statement of interest in domestic tranquility. What then is to be made of the language of the Declaration of Independence? Kendall and Carey, Melvin Bradford, and others suggest that we read the *entire* document. After the first few ringing sentences the Declaration is a lawyer's brief, itemizing the grounds that justify the action about to be taken. Willmoore Kendall took great pleasure in pointing out that the bill of indictment contained not one instance of a violation of an inalienable right, but rather the citation of numerous violations of the principle of representative government, and of violation of the principle of separation of power, interlaced with statements of outrage against the violation of the moral sensibility of a virtuous, and hitherto loyal, people. But what about those first few sentences? There, too, the critics of the prophetic-utopian interpretation of our basic documents contend that the *entire* document, including Jefferson's original draft *and* the revisions it underwent, suggests the work of careful statesmen quite uninfected by the fervor of political religion.

Three Drafts of the Declaration of Independence[1]

JEFFERSON'S FIRST DRAFT

A Declaration by the Representatives of the United States of America in general Congress assembled.

When in the Course of human Events it becomes necessary for a People to advance from that Subordination, in which they have hitherto remained and to assume among the Powers of the Earth, the equal and independent Station to which the Laws of Nature and of Nature's God entitle them, a decent Respect to the opinions of Mankind requires that they should declare the Causes, which impell them to the Change.

We hold these Truths to be self evident; that all Men are created equal and independent; that from that equal Creation they derive Rights inherent and unalienable; among which are the Preservation of Life, and Liberty, and the Pursuit of Happiness.

DRAFT REPORTED BY COMMITTEE TO CONGRESS

A Declaration by the Representatives of the UNITED STATES OF AMERICA in General Congress assembled.

When in the course of human events it becomes necessary for one people to dissolve the political bands which have connected them with another and to assume among the powers of the earth the separate and equal station to which the laws of nature and of nature's God entitle them, a decent respect to the opinions of mankind requires that they should declare the causes which impel them to separation.

We hold these truths to be self-evident that all men are created equal; that they are endowed by their creator with inherent & inalienable rights, that among these are life, liberty, and the pursuit of happiness.

[1] The manuscript drafts of the Declaration can be found in *The Writings of Thomas Jefferson,* ed. Paul Leicester Ford, (New York, 1893), Vol. II, pp. 42–58.

ENGROSSED COPY

In Congress, July 4, 1776. The Unanimous Declaration of the thirteen United States of America.

When in the Course of human events, it becomes necessary for one people to dissolve the political bands which have connected them with another, and to assume among the powers of the earth, the separate and equal station to which the Laws of Nature and of Nature's God entitle them, a decent respect to the opinions of mankind requires that they should declare the causes which impel them to the separation.

We hold these truths to be self-evident, that all men are created equal, that they are endowed by their Creator with certain inalienable rights, that among these are Life, Liberty, and the pursuit of Happiness.

Consider, for example, the sentence, "We hold these truths to be self-evident, that all men are created equal. . . ." When Jefferson originally wrote "created equal and independent," he was probably following the Social Contract thinkers. For these men, the state of nature was a prepolitical condition in which men lived isolated and necessarily "independent" lives, more or less thrown upon their own resources to survive or die. Man, in the state of Nature, was seen to be independent, asocial, autonomous. But Congress struck the word "independent" from Jefferson's draft, suggesting that the "men" they believed "free" were by nature political or social animals. That, I suggest, is the minimal meaning of this excision. But Congress' action also implies the notion, which clearly dominated the Constitutional Convention, that rights are powers. Unlimited rights are unlimited powers, powers to do whatever one wants. Thus for community life to prevail, unlimited but competing rights and powers had to be limited. Unlimited rights like unlimited powers were not consistent with the concept of political community of the Founders.

Consider also the statement in the Declaration that all men "are created equal, that they are endowed by their Creator with certain inalienable rights." Jefferson had originally written that "all Men are created equal and independent; that from that equal Creation they derive Rights inherent and unalienable."

These lines are sometimes counted as the historical basis for programs of government that seek equality of condition, as opposed to equality before the law. Questions such as the following are often answered by reference to the original meaning of the Declaration of Independence: Is the proper function of the American government to equalize the conditions in which its citizens conduct their daily lives? Should some children have greater access to educational resources merely because by accident of birth they were raised in a family willing and able to make them available? Should the government discriminate against members of heretofore privileged classes of citizens because heretofore conditions discriminated against other classes? Had Jefferson's original words prevailed, pregnant as they were with the ideological Idealist tradition, then the claims for such action by the government would have at least historical legitimacy. One could then argue that, right or wrong, Affirmative Action programs, busing of children to schools to achieve racial balance, the right of women to obtain abortions, or a policy of hostility to pro-Western authoritarian regimes are part of the American political faith.

But what did Congress, which amended and approved the language, mean by the phrase "all men are created equal"? Well, literally it meant that men have certain "inalienable rights." But Congress specified that men get these rights because so "endowed by their Creator." These very important words distinguish between the tradition in which Jefferson stood and the one generally held by the Congress. In Jefferson's view men derive unalienable Rights from an equal Creation. There is no mention here of God, but of a derivation of rights from an impersonal creation. Absent in Jefferson's language is the Judaeo-Christian personal God before whom all men are equal. The creation of which he writes does not evoke the dependent relationship of man to God that is found in Congress' term "Creator." Man stands before his Creator as in the book of Genesis we are told that man is made in the image of God. If man is made in His image, all men have in common their consciousness of their immortality though they are mortals, and thus must deal with one another equally. Men are obliged to God to treat every other man with justice. This does not say that we should ignore rational differences in ability, inheritance, and character. Men are quite unequal in those terms. It merely says that we must be just to one another because we are all equally obliged by God in whose image we are made. The concept of "inalienable rights" of the Declaration, therefore, speaks of the integrity of the human person, an integrity informed by the history of philosophy of the Classical-Christian tradition.

The language of Jefferson, however, ignores the nuances of Congress' phrase, "endowed by their Creator." Perhaps his language evokes a biological equality, the physical equality of all men that Thomas Hobbes spoke of, and suggests a biological concept of rights. But he must also have meant that the unalienable rights of man are the rights of man *qua* man, not man *qua* American. The rights man possesses, he possesses independently of the political community. Does that mean that he may exercise them to the destruction of the community that protects him? Because Jefferson's language of unalienable rights of man does not evoke a concomitant unalienable moral obligation; *his* language, but not the Declaration's, leads to the political *cul-de-sac* of the prophetic-utopian interpretation. It envisions essentially autonomous men whose rights must be honored by the political community, and if they are not, then the community must be deemed to be evil, corrupt, and the fitting object of revolution. No political community can long survive, of course, and continually be subject to the attacks of citizens who find that it does not quite meet their standards of righteousness. The Puritan revolution in England that led to the murder of Charles Stuart is the best example of what will occur to a community indicted in such a manner. To a large degree the social malaise of the American political community, the civil disorder, the general loss of authority that our community has experienced, the disdain that its intellectuals have toward it, is the outgrowth of such an attitude. Some, like Robert Bellah, have called for a revival of the American civil religion as the antidote. In truth, the antidote is a recovery of public philosophy.

Part II:

Selected Readings in the Public Philosophy

7/American Civil Religion

A Foolish American Ism—Utopianism*

Irving Kristol

LET US SUPPOSE THAT we have provided the President of the United States with two imaginary speeches, both of which he is dutifully prepared to deliver. They deal, in a highly general way, with the goals of American foreign policy. The first speech goes somewhat as follows:

> Our American nation, ever since its foundation, has pursued the ideal of a world without war. This ideal—the abolition of war—has been the ultimate foundation of our foreign policy, despite all circumstantial changes of strategy and tactics. The ideal is as alive today, in our hearts and minds, as it ever was. This Administration is dedicated to pursuing it with the utmost vigor, and with all the patience and skill that is necessary. We seek, by our policies, to create a world in which man's inhumanity to man will become but a horrible memory, in which men will, under the conditions of a just and secure peace, live harmoniously and creatively together. We seek a world without war, without bloodshed, without poverty, without oppression or discrimination. Such a world, I am convinced, is within our reach if only the statesmen of all nations are sufficiently farsighted to seize the opportunity. I am confident, moreover, that

* From *New York Times Magazine,* November 14, 1971.

> they will display such farsightedness, and will not let the opportunity for a universal and enduring peace slip from their grasp. The people of the world—the people of all nations—demand such a peace. We shall betray their aspirations, and shall certainly be held to account, if we fail to resolve our quarrels and conflicts so as to make man's dream of permanent peace a reality in our own time.

What would happen if the President gave this speech (in a considerably lengthier version, of course)? It is fair to predict—it is indeed absolutely certain—that nothing would happen. It is a perfectly conventional speech, of a kind that many Presidents have given many times. The press corps would yawn over the familiar clichés; the citizenry would scan the headline ("President Reaffirms Goal of World Peace") and then turn to the sports or financial pages; the heads of all nations would formally indicate their approval of these noble sentiments; and "informed sources" in Washington would explain that it is too early to tell what significance, if any, the speech had for any particular area of American foreign policy. As I said: nothing would happen.

Now, let us have the President deliver a rather different speech—our second version. And let it proceed somewhat as follows:

> This American nation, ever since its foundation, has for the most part pursued its national interests in a moderate and prudent way. This Administration is determined to continue on this path of moderation and prudence. However, we are well aware that there is no guaranteed path to peace with justice. True, men have always dreamed of perpetual peace, and presumably always will. This dream is a noble one, and a man must be deficient in humanity not to have felt its appeal. But let us remember: It is a dream, whereas we live out our lives in a real and material world that is governed, not by dreams, but by limited possibilities. In this real and material world, conflict between men and war between nations appear to be permanent features of the human condition. It has always been so; we must, if we are to be responsible

> statesmen, assume that it always will be so. I shall strive to minimize our chances of experiencing war; if war is unavoidable. I shall do my best to limit its extent and the mischief it is bound to create; and whether I am able to limit it or not, I shall always do my utmost to ensure that the war we shall be engaged in will be a just war, and will be justly conducted. I cannot promise you a world without war, for such a promise is inherently fraudulent. But I can promise that we shall conduct our foreign affairs in a responsible and honorable fashion, that we shall make every effort to achieve a reasonable compromise of our differences with other nations, and that whatever calamities befall us will be as little as possible of our own making.

What would happen if the President gave *this* speech? One's imagination is inadequate to the prospect. It is fair to predict, however, that after a shorter or longer period of stunned silence, a storm of censure would gather round the President's head. The press corps would explode with moral indignation, and the headlines this time would be eye-catching ("President Denounces Peace as Impossible Dream"); the citizenry would be alarmed; the heads of all nations would express concern at "the new American belligerency"; only the "informed sources" in Washington would remain steady, explaining that it is too early to tell what significance, if any, the speech had for any particular area of American foreign policy.

And yet—what is wrong with the second speech? I submit that there is nothing wrong with it. It is, in every respect, superior to the meaningless banalities of the first speech. It reads 5,000 years of human experience truthfully and sagaciously, and it announces the results of this reading with a pleasing directness and candor. It is a statesman's speech—whereas the first version was nothing more than a politician's speech. True, it is an American statesman's speech; not everyone would agree that this nation's foreign policy has always displayed such moderation and prudence. But that sort of bias is comprehensible, easily discountable and even justifiable—after all, Presidents of the United States are not supposed to be objective and neutral political philosophers.

So the question arises: If the second speech is so much superior to the first, why is it that no President would ever dare to make it? Why is it that, if the President were to say that no reasonable man can expect enduring peace on earth until the day that our Redeemer cometh, this would be regarded as a terrible, cynical blasphemy—even though it is recognizably one of the most venerable platitudes of the Judaeo-Christian tradition? What is it about our political condition that constrains our leaders to define politics as the pursuit of impossible dreams? Are we the most high-minded people who ever lived, or the most hypocritical?

To that last question, the answer is: If you are extraordinarily high-minded in your political pronouncements, you are bound in the nature of things to be more than ordinarily hypocritical. But it is only in the last half century or so that high-minded hypocrisy has completely driven statesmanlike reasonableness out of the American public forum. The point is important and not at all self-evident to our smog-beclouded eyes, so it is worth a bit of elaboration.

II

The United States has always had, by historical standards, quite ambitious ideological ends of a timeless and universal nature. George Santayana, echoing the worldly wisdom of Old Europe, could dismiss the Declaration of Independence as "a salad of illusions." But these "illusions" represented a deep emotional commitment by a new national community to the idea that government—all government, everywhere—should be subservient to the citizen's individual life, his personal liberty, and his pursuit of happiness. True, and inevitably, this fundamental document of the American credo was involved in hypocrisy from the outset: It carefully refrained from saying anything about "the peculiar institution" of slavery which then flourished in this country. Nevertheless, one cannot begin to understand the American people and its history unless one appreciates the extent to which our literature, our journalism, our philosophy, our politics were shaped by this powerful ideological commitment. One does not exaggerate when one calls it a kind of Messianic commitment to a redemptive mission: The United States was to be "a city . . . set on a hill," "a light unto the nations," exemplifying the blessings of liberty to the common man in less fortunate countries, and encouraging him to establish a liberal and democratic regime like unto ours.

So, in a sense, the United States can be said to be the most ideological of all nations—far more ideological than the Soviet Union, for instance, whose official political orthodoxy has never been able to sink deep roots, has never become a popular civil religion, a consensual orthodoxy, as has happened here. But, in another sense, the United States can also be said to have been one of the least ideological of nations. For, in addition to the philosophy of the Englightenment, as incarnated in the Declaration of Independence, there was another and, for a long time, equally powerful political tradition that prevailed in the United States. This political tradition, rooted in centuries of British political experience and in British constitutional-juridical thought, found expression in the Constitution—a document that (unlike the contemporary French Revolutionary constitutions) was far more a lawyer's job of work than a social philosopher's. There is nothing particularly grand or visionary or utopian in the language of the Constitution. Its eloquence, where it exists, is the eloquence of British jurists as carried over and preserved in American legal education. And it proceeds to establish a mundane government based on a very prosaic estimate of men's capacities to subordinate passion to reason, prejudice to benevolence, self-interest to the public good.

For more than a century, these two traditions coexisted amiably if uneasily in American life. The exultant prophetic-utopian tradition was always the more popular; it represented, as it were, the vernacular of American political discourse. It was, and is, the natural rhetoric of the journalist and the political candidate, both of whom instinctively seek to touch the deepest springs of American sentiment. In contrast, the constitutional-legal tradition supplied the rhetoric for official occasions and for the official business of government—for Presidential messages, debates in Congress, Supreme Court decisions, and the like.

Andrew Jackson, for example, was a radical populist in his time, and when he vetoed the bank bill in 1832, his followers celebrated this as "driving the money changers from the temple." He himself, however, in sending his message to the Senate, began it as follows:

> The bill "to modify and continue" the act entitled "An Act to Incorporate the Subscribers to the Bank" was presented to me on the 4th July instant. Having considered it with that solemn regard to the principles of the Constitution which the day was calculated to inspire, and come to the conclusion that it ought not to become a law, I herewith return it to the Senate, in which it originated, with my objections.
>
> A bank of the United States is in many respects convenient for the Government and useful to the people. Entertaining this opinion, and deeply impressed with the belief that some of the powers and privileges possessed by the existing bank are unauthorized by the Constitution, subversive of the rights of the states, and dangerous to the liberties of the people, I felt it my duty at an early period of my Administration to call the attention of Congress to the practicability of organizing an institution continuing all its advantages and obviating these objections. I sincerely regret that in the act before me I can perceive none of those modifications of the bank charter which are necessary, in my opinion, to make it compatible with justice, with sound policy, or with the Constitution of our country.

This "high" mode of discourse—without cant, without demagogy, without bombast—was then thought to be the normal way in which the American government should engage in public conversation with its own people or with the world at large. Concurrently, the political vernacular was infused with a declamatory passion. John L. O'Sullivan, a Jacksonian Democrat journalist who subsequently became a leading popular exponent of the United States' "Manifest Destiny" to expand over the entire continent, composed an endless stream of demagogic-prophetic editorials. They are perfect specimens of their type. Thus he wrote in 1839:

> The far-reaching, the boundless future, will be the era of American greatness. In its magnificent domain of space and time, the nation of many nations is destined to manifest to mankind the excellence of divine principles, to establish on earth the noblest temple

> ever dedicated to the worship of the Most High—the Sacred and the True. Its floor shall be a hemisphere. . . .

And so on and so forth. The public lapped it up, and the Fourth of July orations continued to serve it up. But if one turns to the official statements of American foreign policy—statements by Presidents and Secretaries of State—one finds almost nothing of this sort. From George Washington to William McKinley, practically all such statements are sober and measured formulations of "sound policy," composed by constitutional lawyers who felt the need to argue the merits of their cases before the bar of rational and informed opinion. It is rare for any kind of breathless utopian or shrill prophetic notes to be sounded. Even at the outbreak of the Spanish-American War, when jingoistic rhetoric was deafening in its persistence and intensity, President McKinley's War Message to Congress was a lawyer's brief, arguing the legality of American actions, emphasizing their moderate and prudent qualities, outlining the material issues involved, and offering only a minimum of that "high idealism" that has since become obligatory in Presidential prose.

Sometime around the turn of the century, the impact of the Populist and Progressive movements combined to establish the vernacular utopian-prophetic rhetoric as the official rhetoric of American statesmen. It happened gradually, and it was not until the 1930s that the victory of the vernacular was complete and unchallengeable. But it also happened with a kind of irresistible momentum, as the egalitarian, "democratic" temper of the American people remorselessly destroyed the last vestiges of the neo-Whiggish, "republican" cast of mind. By now, we no longer find it in any way odd that American Presidents should sound like demagogic journalists of yesteryear. Indeed, we would take alarm and regard them as eccentric if they sounded like anything else.

III

The effects of this transformation have been momentous, though not much noticed or commented upon. High-flown doubletalk has become the normal jargon of American government. This flatters and soothes the citizenry, but at the same time engenders a permanent credibility gap; instead of paying attention to what the government literally says—a waste of anyone's time—we expend much energy trying to figure out what the government really means. Official or quasi-official state documents, for the historian of today, have become trivial, superficial, and unreliable sources of information. No historian of Abraham Lincoln's period would dare minimize the importance of what he said during his debates with Douglas or in his two inaugural addresses; no historian of the 1960s would bother paying nearly as close attention to the public words of John F. Kennedy, Lyndon B. Johnson, or Richard M. Nixon. Our public rhetoric has become largely ritualistic—resounding utopian clichés that obfuscate a presumed "inside story" our reporters are always snuffling after.

The kinds of dangers this situation creates in the area of American foreign policy have been noted by some critics. Hans J. Morgenthau has pointed out that the closer we get to the founding fathers, the more sensible, the more forthright, the more realistic are our official statements of foreign policy. Conversely, the more we approach the present, the windier and more meaningless they become. Even our vocabulary becomes corrupted. The countries of Asia and Africa and South America used to be "poor"; in the course of the past twenty years they become first "underdeveloped," and now "less developed." Plain language that accords with reality has become positively offensive to our sensibilities.

The corruption of plain language has been accompanied by—one might even say it has resulted in—the corruption of plain speaking. No Secretary of State can today describe the governments of Greece or Peru or Bolivia or Spain or Argentina or Egypt as what they obviously are: military dictatorships. It would cause a diplomatic row; these nations have become so accustomed to our hypocritical doubletalk that they would sense some sinister intentions in any deviation from it. Similarly, no Secretary of State could ever say that a particular regime—for example, the Communist government of China—is abhorrent to our own political values but that we are nevertheless prepared to have diplomatic relations with it and to do business with it, since it suits our national interests at this time to do so. No, he has to announce the dawn of a new diplomatic era, a giant step to world peace, and all the rest of that nonsense. It is nonsense because he has no grounds whatever for believing this, and it is altogether possible that a United States-China *rapprochement* could heighten the possibility of war in some parts of the world—on the Russian-Chinese border, for instance, or the India-Pakistan frontier.

A particularly striking instance of how impossible it is for simple and incontestable truths to be uttered in high places is provided by the rhetoric in which our foreign-aid programs are cocooned. Never mind, for the moment, whether these programs are good or bad, overly generous or terribly niggardly. The one certain fact about these programs is that they cannot even begin to do what they promise: namely, in our lifetime to bring the standard of living of the "less developed" countries closer to the American-West European standard. *Nothing* can do that. If we allow that India's economy might grow at an uninterruptedly rapid rate (say, 10 percent) for the next 29 years, and assume that the American growth rate will sustain itself at the modest level of 5 percent during that period, then—because of the initial huge disparity—by the magic year 2000 the gap between the Indian and American per capita income will, in absolute terms, be *greater* than it is today. The notion, therefore, that any significant portion of the "third world" can even begin to "catch up" to the West in the next generation is an absurdity. Indeed, given the fact that "less developed" countries are dependent on fairly high growth rates in the United States and Europe for their own economic growth, the probability is that they will not "catch up" anytime in the next several generations, and there is a good chance they may never "catch up" at all.

Yet who can say this? No United States government official can—he would be denounced as a sour pessimist and driven from office. No official or political leader in a "less developed" country can—he would be denounced as a traitor and driven from office. So, no one says it. Instead we talk grandly about "economic development" in a deceitful and misleading way. The inevitable result is that the economic growth which does take place in poorer lands—and many of them are doing quite well, by historical standards—is universally denounced as "inadequate." A more perfect recipe for permanent political instability in these nations cannot be imagined.

Worst of all, the corruption of language and speech results in the corruption of thought. One has only to observe the hearings before the Senate or House Foreign Relations Committees to realize that, once you surrender the liberty to speak plainly, you lose the capacity to think clearly. Sustained hypocrisy is one of the most intolerable regimens for the mind: In the end, you find yourself believing yourself and taking your own empty rhetoric seriously.

Thus, it is one of the oldest and truest proverbs in international relations that, under certain circumstances, the enemy of your enemy becomes your friend—even if, had you a freer choice, you would never want such a friend at all. All nations operate on this essential principle, and the United States is no exception. Yet one can read the testimony of government officials and "expert witnesses" for years on end without coming across a clear enunciation of it as the rationale for some aspect of American policy. We have a terrible time explaining to ourselves that, while we have an instinctive, democratic (and healthy) dislike for dictatorships, we have precious little control over the way other peoples govern or misgovern themselves. Our relations with other nations, and theirs with us, are determined for the most part by calculations of mutual advantage. One gets the distinct impression that our government is not only ashamed to admit it engages in such calculations—it actually is reluctant to engage in them, except under the random pressure of necessity which it then perceives as an "emergency." We have been telling ourselves for so long that our foreign policy proceeds on quite other principles that we have lost the art and skill of coping with the principles that do, in fact, prevail. Our statesmen are always reacting to reality as an "emergency," in an *ad hoc* fashion, and having at the same time to invent a fancy, "idealistic" motive for the most prosaic and practical actions.

Witness the typically American fuss and furor in recent months over whether the elections in South Vietnam were truly democratic—and if they were not, what we should then be doing about it. The assumption seems to be that the original purpose of our intervention in Vietnam was to establish parliamentary government there, and that the absence of such government presents us with a crisis. But this is a childish assumption. We did not intervene for any such purpose. (At least I hope we didn't—I can't bring myself to believe that the men who make our foreign policy were quite that idiotic.) Our intervention was to help establish a friendly, relatively stable regime which could coexist peacefully with the other nations of Southeast Asia. If such a regime prefers corrupt elections to the kind of overt military dictatorship that more usually prevails in that part of the world, this is its own affair. It constitutes no problem for us—any more than does the fact that Communist China prefers to manage with no elections at all. Our relations with both of these Asian nations are based mainly on considerations of international stability—on maintaining a version of international stability acceptable to us—not on how they go about governing themselves.

To be sure, being an American I am keenly aware of the merits of representative government, and I do hope that the Vietnamese (South *and* North) will at some time recognize these merits. But I am also aware that these merits do not automatically commend themselves to all nations, at all times, everywhere. Our foreign relations, therefore, must of necessity be more concerned with the external policies of any particular nation than with its internal form of government. This is as true for South Vietnam as it is for China or Russia or Cuba. We are perfectly free, as Americans, to be critical of, or even to have contempt for, their systems of government. But, as Americans, we are also free not to live there, and we are therefore bound to be more interested in their behavior to others than in their behavior to themselves. I think most Americans would subscribe to this common-sense proposition. But it is not a proposition we would permit our spokesman at the United Nations to enunciate. And there do seem to be many eminent Americans—notably, an entire class of liberal journalists—who have been utterly bewitched by our official platitudes. These men and women, after traveling freely throughout South Vietnam, heap scorn upon its "corrupt" democracy. They then make a strictly guided tour of China to return aglow with admiration! One can only assume that such men and women think it natural to judge our allies by quite utopian standards, but are ready to give unfriendly nations the benefit of every possible doubt.

IV

But it is not only in foreign affairs that our government proceeds by utopian promises of future benefits and hypocritical explanations of actual performance. Our entire domestic policy is suffused with this same self-defeating duality. Thus, as a domestic counterpart to a "war to end all wars," we have in the past decade launched a "war to end poverty." The very title of that crusade reveals a mindless enthusiasm which could only lead to bitter disillusionment.

There are two ways of defining poverty: in absolute terms or relative terms. The absolute definition, involving estimates by government agencies of an adequate diet, adequate shelter, adequate clothing for an average family, is relatively easy to make. It is also largely meaningless in a context of "the abolition of poverty." To see just how meaningless it is, one has only to report that the majority of welfare families in New York City are now above the officially determined "poverty line." Have we ceased regarding them—have they ceased regarding themselves—as poor? Of course not. If you take a family with an annual income of $3,800 and, one way or another, increase this income to $4,500, you have helped them somewhat—but you certainly have not abolished their poverty, as grandly promised. The consequence is that the modest but real improvement is obliterated by an exacerbated sense of "relative deprivation."

Most people, when they hear talk of "abolishing poverty," inevitably and immediately have in mind a substantial relative improvement, not merely a modest absolute one. They think in terms of elevating all those below the United States median family income—approximately $9,500 a year—to the vicinity of this level. That does not *look* like such an unreasonable goal. After all, families that make $9,500 a year have to watch their nickels and dimes if they are to make ends meet. (Ask them, and they'll tell you—and they'll be telling the truth.) But this is one of those cases where appearances are deceptive, and what looks like a reasonable goal is in fact utopian. To achieve it would require either the creation of new income or the redistribution of existing income to the tune of perhaps $200 billion a year.[1] This is simply impossible; there is no policy, however "radical," that

[1] One must remember: If you establish a guaranteed minimum family income of, say, $8,000 a year, you are then faced with the problems of those who work to earn $9,000 or $10,000. Are they to labor for a measly $1,000 or $2,000 a year? You cannot ask that, and they would not tolerate it if you did. So you have to make some kind of supplementary payments to these families, too. And *then* you are faced with the problem of those who work to earn $12,000 a year—and so on, and on. It is this "ripple effect" that makes the guaranteed income, at any level above a ludicrously low one, such a fantastically expensive proposition.

could come close to accomplishing this. We may be an "affluent" society by historical standards, but we are not nearly that affluent. (Total corporate profits last year, after taxes, were well under $50 billion). Yet who dares to say so? Instead, our politicians (and our journalists and professors, too) persist in holding up this impossible ideal, with the quite predictable effect of making people intensely dissatisfied with social policies that achieve (though never easily) smaller increments to their income or smaller improvements of their condition.

The upshot of this state of affairs is that any American who, today, passes his working life in moving from $4,000 a year to an ultimate $9,500 is regarded as a pathetic victim of circumstances, a prisoner in a "dead-end job." Yet just about half of all Americans pass their working lives in this way, and are going to do so regardless of anything said or done in Washington. All that our utopian rhetoric can do is to convince them that the normal working-class experience—the *inevitable* working-class experience, which would be as common in a socialist United States as in a capitalist United States—is a fate akin to degradation.

V

Or take our "welfare problem." Welfare policy in the United States is based on a very simple—and enormously flattering—thesis about American human nature. The thesis consists of the following propositions: (1) all Americans are highly motivated to work as a means of improving their material condition; (2) those Americans who seem not to be so motivated are suffering from temporary "psychological deprivation" as a result of poverty, bad housing, bad health, and so on; (3) improve their material environment and the "normal" impulse to self-betterment will automatically assert itself. It is a plausible thesis to our American ears. Moreover, there is enough historical experience behind it to suggest it is not entirely false. Only, when applied indiscriminately, it turns out to be more false than true. Some people, whether in the United States or elsewhere, respond according to this formula. A great many others, however, do not. It turns out there are lots of people in this world, including a great many Americans, who do not fill the American prescription for "human nature."

Once you think about it, this is not really surprising. For what our high expectations and our high-flown rhetoric overlook—are bound to overlook, because they are so high-flying—is that we are for the most part talking about motivation directed toward *small* improvements. You can motivate almost anyone to become a millionaire, if the possibility is offered; but that possibility rarely is. And it is another thing entirely to motivate people to move from a badly paying situation (say, casual laborer) to a slightly better-paying but also more arduous one (say, laundry worker or drill-press operator). That is the kind of grim motivation you need to get "self-sustained" economic growth, whether among nations or among individuals. Not all human beings are born with this kind of grim motivation—which is just as well, I'd say, since the earth would then be a pretty dreary, if industrious, place.

In the absence of such ingrained motivation, the usual way we motivate people—even in America—has been by adding the spur of necessity to the offer of modest opportunity. That small improvement has to make a real difference: the difference between squalor and poverty, or between poverty and minimum comfort. These "little" differences—almost invisible to the middle-class eye, and never taken seriously by middle-class reformers—are absolutely crucial to the self-discipline and self-respect of ordinary working people. They need to be very much aware of the costs of not achieving them, if the achievement is to have any merit or meaning in their eyes.

I suspect that all of this sounds petty, and sordid, and mean-spirited. We are accustomed to thinking about poor people, and about ways of helping poor people, in more elevated terms than these. And so we introduce something like our present welfare policies. These policies, at one swoop, abolish all those important little differences in achievement. They generously offer all poor people more in the way of welfare than they can get for their unskilled labor on the open market—more, often, than they would earn at the legal minimum wage. Naturally, these people, not being fanatics about work, move onto the welfare rolls in very large numbers. To be precise, their wives and children are pushed onto welfare. The men themselves drift away from their homes, demoralized by the knowledge that their function as breadwinner has been preempted by welfare. These men then merge into the shadows of street-corner society—superfluous men, subsisting by casual labor or casual crime, men whose families are materially no worse off for their absence and would be no better off for their presence. Has there ever been a more ingenious formula for the destruction of poor families? Indeed, one can fairly speculate how many middle-class families would hang together if the family suffered no financial inconvenience as a result of the husband's vanishing.

Welfare is wreaking devastation on the American poor—making the child fatherless, the wife husbandless, the husband useless. We see this "welfare explosion" happening and, disconcerted, turn this calamity of our own creation into an indictment of our social order

Once you have put people on welfare, it is a nasty business getting them off. You can either (1) cut welfare rates so as to make it distinctly worth their while to go to work, or (2) keep welfare rates high for those truly unable to work—the aged, the sick, the disabled, the unemployed—but have a severe, suspicious welfare bureaucracy that defines its mission as getting as many of the rest off the rolls as is possible. Neither alternative is attractive, though the latter seems to me considerably more humane. (Its social consequences are also likely to be beneficial, since we know that families on welfare tend to develop social pathologies: they produce relatively more criminals, drug addicts, alcoholics, illegitimate children, etc.). But the second option does involve our taking a more realistic view of human nature and of human motivation—and this we are most unlikely to do. So we shall either veer toward the first course, indiscriminately penalizing all welfare recipients in the name of "economy," or, more probably, we shall simply stagger on until some kind of social explosion takes place.

It really is a curious phenomenon we are witnessing: a nation preferring to live under a perpetual, self-inflicted indictment of "social injustice," and amidst an ever swelling and ever more demoralized population on the dole, rather than revise its utterly fanciful and utopian idea of human nature. There cannot have been many instances in history of such high-minded masochism. We may even be the first.

VI

What is true of welfare is even more blatantly true of our other social problems. Our utopian illusions always are preferred to realistic assessments of human beings, and to the world in which real human beings live.

In no area are the ravages of American utopianism more visible than in education. Here intellectual fads and fashions reign supreme, all of them exultant in promise, all of them negligible in accomplishment. Our professional educators today are perpetually and enthusiastically engaged in deception and self-deception, in part out of necessity, in part because they actually feel this is their "responsibility." We know a great deal about the relation between schools and academic achievement. But it is the rare educator who dares to say what we know, to challenge the sovereign platitudes as to what a school can do to the young people who enter it.

We know from the Coleman Report and other studies, for instance, that there is practically no correlation between the physical plant of our schools and the academic achievement of our students. We may desire new, well-equipped schools for all sorts of reasons. They may be good reasons; they may even, in some vague sense, qualify as "educational" reasons; but they are not academic reasons. Students learn as well in old, decrepit school buildings as in new, shiny ones; or they learn as little in the latter as in the former. Middle-class parents who think they are improving their children's academic potential by sending them to a brand-new school with a fine library, a sumptuous gymnasium, a lovely lunchroom are kidding themselves. So are slum parents who think that their children's academic potential is weakened by old buildings, cramped gymnasiums (or no gymnasium), shabby lunchrooms, paltry libraries (or no library). What determines a child's academic achievement is his genetic endowment plus the values and motivation he acquires at home. All the rest may have significant consequences for a child's life style, his appearance, perhaps (and I myself regard this as the most important function of schools) what we call his "character." But it will have little to do with his academic achievement.

Even class size turns out to have nothing to do with academic achievement. There are, in my view, good reasons—having to do with the role of the teacher as an "adult model" in the process of "character formation"—for preferring smaller classes to larger ones. But they are not academic reasons. Whether a class has twenty pupils or thirty or even forty simply doesn't matter. Students who do well in small classes will do well in large ones. Students who do poorly in large classes will do no better in small ones. This subject has been studied to death by generations of educational researchers, and the results are conclusive.

Nevertheless, the educator who dares to utter these truths publicly is instantly classified as, at best, an eccentric. His opinions are marked as "controversial"—though they are not—whereas an educator who stresses the academic importance of new schools and small classes is simply seen as tediously "sound." Every year, in New York City, a furious debate breaks out when the statistics on the reading levels in the city schools are made available. These statistics always show that the average reading levels in New York's schools are lower than the national average—and they usually show that, with each year, they are steadily falling further below the national average. The publication of these figures always shocks, always provokes front-page news stories. But far from being shocking, these statistics aren't even newsworthy, since they are perfectly predictable. The reason that reading scores in New York's schools are falling away from the national average is that an ever-increasing percentage of our students come from very low-income families that are also broken, transient, and generally problem-ridden families. The children in these families show low academic aptitude. We insist that our schools "do something" about increasing the academic ability of these youngsters, and our educational leaders furiously institute every gimmick they can think of with the assurance that this time they will turn the trick.

Our insistence is as unreasonable as their assurances are worthless. The schools cannot perform this sociological miracle—which, if it is to take place at all, will happen in the family, at home, over a period of time that is rarely shorter than a couple of generations. As such poor families move up the economic and social ladder, as their home life becomes more stable and the family concern for education becomes more emphatic, the student's academic performance improves. In individual cases, "miracles" do certainly occur. But in the mass, statistical probability reigns supreme—and the schools play no role in the calculations. If you want to estimate the chances of a student doing well or badly in school, give him a physical examination, look at his home, and give him an intelligence test. But don't bother him with questions about his school—it is of no importance for *this* purpose.

And how do we react to this fact? With furious indignation, usually. So, as the school's impotence to satisfy our unrealistic demands becomes ever more clear, we shall—it is already beginning to happen—abolish reading scores and reading tests on the grounds that they are irrelevant to eventual academic achievement. This monumental act of self-deception will, of course, fool nobody and change nothing. But it will certainly be hailed by professional educators as a marvelous innovation.

Of late, many educators have waxed enthusiastic over the educational possibilities of small mixed classes, with the older students helping to instruct the younger, and with every student proceeding "at his own pace." This is, of course, exactly what used to happen in the "little red schoolhouse." I have always been fond of the little red schoolhouse and was unhappy that, after a determined campaign over many decades, our professional educators succeeded in outlawing it. If they now wish to reinstitute it, I certainly have no objections. But I find it more than a little nauseating that they should now present it as a brilliant educational innovation which will solve all our educational problems. And I find it unconscionable that these educators can be so easy in mind and spirit about their newest fad when the huge educational parks which—only yesterday—they insisted were absolutely necessary, are just now coming into existence.

A good principal can always make a *small* difference in the academic power of a school—and a small difference is surely better than none at all. A dedicated teacher may make a big difference to *a few* students—and this difference is to be treasured. But none of this satisfies us. We insist that our schools fulfill impossible dreams—and so they pretend to be able to do this (given a larger budget, of course). As a result, the world of American education is at the moment suffused with charlatanism, and anyone with a sober word to say is encouraged to go elsewhere.

VII

The consequence of this public insistence on a utopian vision of man, history, and society is that our public life is shot through with a permanent streak of hysteria. We are constantly indicting ourselves, denouncing our nation, lamenting our fate. Indeed, an entire profession has emerged—we call it "the media"—which has taken upon itself the responsibility for leading this chorus. Just imagine what our TV commentators and "news analysts" would do with a man who sought elected office with the promise that, during his tenure, he hoped to effect some small improvements in our condition. They would ridicule him into oblivion. In contrast, they are very fond of someone like John Lindsay, who will settle for only the finest and most glowing goals. Public figures in our society get credit for their utopian rhetoric—for their "charisma," as we now say—and only demerits if they emphasize their (necessarily modest) achievements.

Every society needs ideals and self-criticism and some prophetic admonition. It needs these to correct its "natural" tendency toward smugness, inertia, and parochial self-satisfaction. But when the countertendency toward insistent self-dissatisfaction becomes overwhelming, then such a society is in grave trouble. The capacity for contentment is atrophied. So is the willingness to see things as they really are, and then to improve them in a matter-of-fact way. We certainly do have it in our power to make improvements in the human estate. But to think we have it in our power to change people so as to make the human estate radically better than it is, radically different from what it is, and in very short order, is to assume that this generation of Americans can do what no other generation in all of human history could accomplish. American though I be, I cannot bring myself to accept this arrogant assumption. I think, rather, that by acting upon this assumption we shall surely end up making our world worse than it need have been.

The Nation with the Soul of a Church*

Michael Novak

G. K. CHESTERTON ONCE described America as "a nation with the soul of a church." It is a nation "founded on a creed," committed to values no nation can fully achieve. Our basic national scriptures are texts to which after errant wanderings we return again and again in order to renew ourselves. Right and Left try to prove that the other is betraying the nation's fundamental convictions. Each tries to prove it loves the "true" nation more. Thus Norman Mailer brooded about what he saw in Miami in 1972:

> *In America, the country was the religion.* And all the religions of the land were fed from that first religion which was *the country itself,* and if the other religions were now full of mutation and staggering across deserts of faith, it was because the country had been false and ill and corrupt for years, corrupt not in the age-old human proportions of failure and evil, but corrupt to the point of terminal disease, like a great religion foundering. [Emphasis added.]

The religion of America is not Christianity. It is not Judaism. There are many theories about what it is. Professor Sidney Mead calls it "the religion of the Republic." It is, Robert Bellah says,

* From *Choosing Our King: Powerful Symbols in Presidential Politics.*

"the civil religion"; or John Dewey, "the common faith"; Will Herberg, "the American way of life"; John E. Smylie, "the nation itself." Conrad Cherry has collected some basic documents of this national religion in *God's New Israel* (1971).

The country as the religion—the theme is an old one. Walt Whitman wrote of it in the preface to the 1872 edition of *Leaves of Grass,* a hundred years before *The Greening of America*:

> The time has certainly come to begin to discharge the idea of Religion, in the United States, from mere ecclesiasticism, and from Sundays and churches and church-going. . . . The people, especially the young men and women of America, must begin to learn that Religion . . . is something far, far, different from what they supposed. It is, indeed, too important to the power and perpetuity of the New World to be consigned any longer to the churches old or new, Catholic or Protestant—Saint this, or Saint that. . . . It must be consigned henceforth to Democracy *en masse,* and to Literature. It must enter into the Poems of the Nation. It must make the Nation.

Most Americans do not take America's corruption, evil, or powerlessness as simple matters of fact, as inevitable. Most are shocked and they protest when life in America is not morally beautiful. America is a vessel of salvation, the bearer of transcendent hopes, as for Italians Italy, say, is not. Foreign observers such as Gunnar Mydral frequently comment:

> America, relative to all the other branches of Western civilization, is moralistic and "moral conscious." The ordinary American is the opposite of a cynic. He is on the average more of a believer and a defender of the faith in humanity than the rest of the Occidentals. It is a relatively important matter to him to be true to his own ideals and to carry them out in actual life. . . . Compared with members of other nations of Western civilization, the ordinary American is a rationalistic being. . . . These generalizations might seem venturesome and questionable to the reflective American himself. . . . But to the stranger it is obvious and even striking.

In order to describe the anomaly of racism in America, Myrdal had first of all to isolate the American creed. If that creed were racist, there would be no anomaly. He found its tenets more "explicitly expressed" than in any other nation of the world.

> The schools teach them, the churches preach them. The courts pronounce their judicial decisions in their terms. They permeate editorials with a pattern of idealism so ingrained that the writers could scarcely free themselves from it even if they tried. . . . Even the stranger, when he has to appear before an American audience . . . finds himself espousing the national Creed, as this is the only means by which a speaker can obtain human response from the people to whom he talks.

After a visit to America, G. K. Chesterton tried to answer for himself, "What makes America peculiar?" His answer: "America is the only nation in the world that is founded on a creed. That creed is set forth with dogmatic and even theological lucidity in the Declaration of Independence. . . . It enunciates that all men are equal in their claim to justice, and that governments exist to give them that justice, and that their authority is for that reason just." These are staggering notions. The United States thought of itself, Chesterton divined, as a "home for the homeless." It had the unique idea of "making a new nation literally out of any old nation that comes along." America even aspired to offer a pattern for "a new world" and to make of each raw human individual of the rest of the race "a new man."

No one church was allowed to become the official guardian of the central symbols of the United States. Instead, the nation itself began to fill the vacuum where in many cultures a church would be. The nation became its own unifying symbol system, the chief bestower of identity and purpose.

A candidate for the presidency of the United States does well to recognize that he is running for a religious office. The national religion is, to be sure, quite pragmatic and secular. His concerns will be power, vested interests, money, jobs, and other utterly mundane affairs. Still, America conducts itself like a religion. A candidate had better understand that.

There are those, of course, who say that the religion is weakening. Some young blacks, for example, have become defiant. In 1968 at the Olympics, two raised clenched fists during the playing of "The Star-Spangled Banner," and in 1972, two others chatted casually, as though that anthem were not *their* symbol and the usual forms of respect not *their* form. A white housewife in San Jose told the *New York Times* that she now hates to say the pledge to the flag, it "means nothing" to her, what it says "isn't true," especially "those words about justice for all." "Above all else," President Nixon intoned during his second Inaugural Address in 1973, "the time has come for us to renew our faith in America. In recent years, that faith has been doubted."

Isn't the language of "faith" an odd language for a wholly secular, managerial state? Such a state, more than any other, requires faith. For unless they believe in something, invest their dreams in it, how will people be led to make sacrifices for it? The weaker the churches become as symbol systems, the heavier the symbolic weight that must be taken up by the state. In the twentieth century, nations are everywhere becoming politically religious; politics is regarded as a means of salvation. Words once used for religious matters—"commitment," "dedication," "purpose," "principle," "conscience," "witness," "sacrifice," and "prophecy"—are now used frequently in reference to political behavior. Many altogether secular and agnostic persons reveal in their political pursuits both the kind of passion and the intensity of passion one used to think of as religious. One wonders whether politics can support such hopes, what will happen when disillusionment descends. "If you desire a purpose in life," Prime Minister Heath told some of his idealistic constituents, "don't come to me. Kindly call on your archbishop."

In America, belief in the nation is especially deep. On the dollar bill appear the words, *Novus ordo seclorum*: "The new order of the ages." We dreamt here of a "new world," separated by oceans from the Machiavellian corruptions of Europe and Asia and Africa and Latin America. *We* were "the last best hope of mankind." *We* were charged with "setting an example for the world." *We* were a "good, generous, compassionate people." We thought of ourselves (not quite consciously, which would have been arrogant, but just below the threshold of consciousness) as unusually candid, clear-eyed, innocent, good-willed, young, strong, brave, true. The tall cowboy with the white hat. *Foreigners* were the untrustworthy ones.

Today even our cynics manifest the reverse side of the same

faith. Few are the black militants or youthful revolutionaries or middle-aged radicals who accept racism, militarism, corruption, or official lying as matter of course. True cynics, by contrast, do not expect government to be trustworthy. They do not expect justice in society. Of empire they do not ask sensitivity. Calm in their cynicism, they feel no excess of emotion, no bitterness, no anger. Our cynics are not true cynics, but more intense believers than the rest of us. Our doubters are disappointed lovers.

A social system is easy to take for granted. One wants it to be personal, just, warm, compassionate, liberating. But society is not a loving father, nor does the state offer a loving God. (The price true religion asks for such gifts is that one live in the thin air of the transcendent.)

In June 1940, when Nazi armies had overrun Paris with ease and were massing for assault on England, Walter Lippmann told his Harvard class reunion: "You took the good things for granted. Now you must earn them again. It is written: For every right that you cherish, you have a duty which you must fulfill. For every hope that you entertain, you have a task you must perform. For every good that you wish to preserve, you will have to sacrifice your comfort and your ease. There is nothing for nothing any longer."

In those days, the threat was external. Today America is a land without adequate symbols. The experiences of its people and the aspirations many feel find no legitimate public outlet. The faith of many is narrow, naive, immature. Want of means and resources is not our dilemma. Our own imagination is our enemy.

We need to reconstruct our national project. Having conquered the frontier, worldwide enemies, space, we must at last face what we have spent so long avoiding: we must face each other.

8/What is Public Philosophy?

The Definition of Public Philosophy: Lippmann and Murray*

Robert F. Cuervo

IF THE INTELLECTUAL LIFE of America at mid-century may justly be called an era of self-reflection and reassessment, that circumstance is in part due to the attempt to recover public philosophy. Among the first indications that such a recovery was underway was an essay entitled, "The Problem of Pluralism in America," by John Courtney Murray, S.J., published in the Fordham University quarterly review *Thought* in 1954, and Walter Lippmann's *Essays in the Public Philosophy* in 1955. Also, in 1960, Murray expanded his doctrines in *We Hold These Truths: Catholic Reflections on the American Proposition.* These public philosophers argued that the political regime needs a consensus of common truths that should be reflected in the state's public orthodoxy and institutions. This is not simply a consensus about democratic procedures, because a consensus concerning justice, integrity, and human dignity must underlie any agreement about how to proceed (as opposed to self-interested, transitory bargains). Further, public philosophy is not an attempt to impose a rigid orthodoxy on the democratic community. Public philosophy best endures by synthesizing traditional truths *and* new circumstances. It places a high priority on the discussion and deliberation of contemporary issues, but it demands that norms of discussion and deference to basic truths be observed.

Walter Lippmann offered a twofold thesis about the public philosophy: (1) "that free institutions and democracy were conceived by men who adhered to a public philosophy" and (2) that modern democracies have abandoned the principles, precepts, and "manner of thinking" that constitute the public philosophy. This latter phenomenon distinguishes us from the men of the 17th and 18th centuries, who would have denied that a community could do without a general public philosophy. What the public philosophy is, Lippmann thought, could be seen in the answer to the question, "Is there a body of positive principles and precepts that a good citizen cannot deny or ignore?" Lippmann answered that the public philosophy is *natural law*: legal and moral principles that "fixed the boundaries past which the sovereign—the King, the Parliament, the Congress, the voters—were forbidden to go." Without a public philosophy of natural law (transcendent principles of right, wrong, and the rule of law) it is impossible to operate successfully such basic democratic institutions as popular elections, majority rule, civil liberties, private property, corporations, and voluntary associations.

John Courtney Murray's approach to public philosophy, which he called the *public consensus,* is similar to Lippmann's. Like Lippmann, he believed that the American public consensus is being severely questioned, even lost, and "what is at stake is America's understanding of itself." Public philosophy is that part of the "public argument" which deals with the "constitutional consensus" that gives a people its identity, gives society its vital form, and organizes a community for action in history. Murray traced this idea back to Cicero, who said in his *De Republica* that a republic is not just any assembly. A true republic presupposes a people *juris consensu et utilitatis communione sociatus*—a people united by a common agreement about law and rights and a desire for mutual advantage. United by the idea of law, the public consensus is "an ensemble of substantive truths, a structure of basic public knowledge, an order of elementary affirmations that reflect realities inherent in the order of existence."

To civilize, this consensus must be considered real; it must not be eroded by doubt or relativism. We must be able to say that there *are* truths and that *we* hold them. Further, although the public philosophy is a patrimony, it will continue to civilize only if it has a "growing end" that synthesizes new developments.

For Murray, the previous American consensus acknowledged that America was a nation under God and that our founders believed in natural law, as Lippmann noted earlier. There was also a belief in governing with the consent of the governed, based not only on Locke but also on the entire British constitutional tradition. Consent of the governed necessitated democratic institutions like free elections and free speech and press, through which government submits that a free people stays free by being a *virtuous people,* not living hedonistically, but by acknowledging a universal moral order. Thus the order required by civil society "flowers" almost spontaneously. Finally, human rights are *natural*; they are not mere creatures of the state. Nor are they simply the rights of an atomistic state of nature but the product of the Christian concept of human moral obligation.

Both Lippmann and Murray believed that the loss of the public philosophy had caused a profound political malaise in democratic society. According to Lippmann, the loss of public philosophy resulted in an abstract form of democracy that required national executives to please the people in matters of war and peace. The consequences included the bloody doctrine of unconditional surrender and the Versailles Treaty, which produced Hitler. Also, an individual freedom separated from ancestral constraints produced *mass men* who were lonely for a sense of community. Thus, when public order broke down after World War I, people looked to men like Mussolini and Hitler for a feeling of community.

What are the basic causes of the decline of public philosophy? Lippmann said that one reason was the French political theorist Rousseau's view of man. Since man is born naturally good, according to Rousseau, his education should develop only his faculties and vocational skills. Since goodness is inborn and since man naturally loves justice and order, it becomes unnecessary and even harmful for education to inculcate a public philosophy.

Lippmann also argued that when the founders of our free institutions removed the state from the "sovereignty and proprietorship" of the public philosophy, they were not acting as relativists. They did so merely because they feared that political power would corrupt the public philosophy. However, this precaution itself was corrupted into the notion that ideas were private and that moral ultimates were not in the public domain. When the Rousseauan faith failed to produce a "new man" and the passing of "fine Victorian weather" gave way to postwar disorder, harder alternatives (the methods of the dictators) prevailed.

Murray believed that the public consensus was declining for several reasons. First, with the exception of Catholic education, the tradition of natural law was no longer taught in American universities. Second, the loss of natural law, the great transcendent law open to *reason,* led to another "idiom," the "voluntarist idea" that law is will. This idea, Murray indicates, is the basis of nontranscendent "empirical" approaches to political issues.

The idea of law as the will of the state rather than the product of rational deliberation corresponds to the type of political liberalism that calls for a secular "integrity of the political order" in which the state is the sole enforcer (and sometimes the only source) of human rights. Under this view, the Church, religion, and natural law are replaced as protectors of human rights by a "law of nature" that asserts the inviolability of the human conscience. As Lippmann indicated, the individual right to conscience has often failed to withstand the assaults of tyranny in the absence of a strong constitutional tradition based on transcendent values.

Since both Lippmann and Murray believed that public philosophy was the necessary foundation of free institutions, they both wished to see it revived. They both warned, however, that any attempt at revival would encounter serious objections and difficulties. Lippmann warned that rationalism had severely weakened Western man's "capacity to believe." As a result of the long and wearing attack on religion and metaphysics, modern men, to whom the public philosophy is addressed, "have a low capacity to believe the invisible, the intangible, and the imponderable." For decades, man has regarded truth as personal and private. Accordingly,

> in the prevailing popular culture, all philosophies are the instrument of some man's purpose. . . . All principles are the rationalization of some special interest. There is no public criterion of true and false. . . .

Further, the great classics of political philosophy that support our traditions of civility are regarded as outmoded, since they do not answer today's "immediate and concrete questions." Lippmann believed that the classics of the Western tradition of civility are not outmoded but have been neglected by generations of teachers who fail to show the relevance of philosophical standards to public affairs. After all, when the public philosophy was lost in the fall of Rome, medieval and modern thinkers revived public philosophy, restored it, and used it as the basis for the great modern constitutional orders.

Teachers must blow the dust off the classics and rediscover their relevance. We must learn once again that power belongs under contract to a public philosophy. Finally, if men are to differ constructively, they must share a "language of accommodation" on such fundamentals as natural law, human nature, and the possibility of objective truth. As Murray has written,

> Barbarism threatens when men cease to talk together according to reasonable laws. . . . Argument ceases to be civil when it is dominated by passion and prejudice; when its vocabulary becomes solipsist . . . when dialogue gives way to a series of monologues. . . . Civility dies with the death of dialogue.

To Murray himself, there are two cases for the public philosophy—one that fails and one that may succeed. The "case that fails" simply offers the tenets of the traditional (and now questioned) American consensus. This approach exposes the advocate of public philosophy to the full range of positivist, pragmatist, relativist, and antiorthodox arguments that have always been raised, and the "case that fails" cannot rise above them. This is because a simple repetition of what has been held in the past cannot answer for what is held at present or for why the traditional consensus should have been held in the first place.

The case that fails argues that we have a public philosophy. The "case that may succeed" argues that we *need* a public philosophy and that we should recover the public consensus if we have lost it, since public philosophy is required for the vitality of our free institutions. According to Murray,

> If public affairs today are going badly, the basic reason is the absence of a public philosophy. In other words, it is not true to say that America does not need a public philosophy, for the fundamental reason that this assertion will fail to work. It is daily proving its own falsity. The further conclusion will be that there

> is today a need for a new moral act of purpose and a new act of intellectual affirmation, comparable to those which launched the American constitutional commonwealth, that will newly put us in possession of the public philosophy, the basic consensus that we need.

For example, Murray argued that our goal in the Cold War was usually "survival," not a set of moral alternatives to Soviet Communist doctrine. The result of this narrow goal has been insecurity and anxiety about our position in the world. Unless we can "utter" that there are truths and that *we hold them,* there will be a paralyzing, confusing vacuum in the minds of both citizens and policy makers. In today's world, even "survival" requires a public philosophy.

Once the necessity for a revival is demonstrated (provided the argument that may succeed does succeed), Murray believes that the "ultimate warrant" or "authority" of the consensus will come (as it always has) from natural law, especially from what St. Thomas Aquinas calls the *secondary principles* of natural law. These secondary, "remote" principles are derived from the primary principles of natural law (which are readily intelligible to all men), but, unlike the primary principles, the secondary principles are more complex. They are generally discovered by "the wise," and accordingly, Murray believes that the university must be the key institution for rediscovering and reviving the public consensus.

In summary, Lippmann and Murray believed that (1) the public philosophy exists; (2) it is basically the idea of natural law; (3) this public philosophy has been lost or is being lost due to extreme empiricism, subjectivism, and misconceptions about democracy; (4) public philosophy must be revived, since it is a necessary ingredient of workable democratic institutions; (5) its loss will cause disruption in society; and (6) the revival of public philosophy is possible if thinkers of light and learning will lead the way. Revival, however, will be difficult because positivist-subjectivist ideas are so dominant at present.

Two Cases for the Public Consensus*

John Courtney Murray, S.J.

PREVIOUS CHAPTERS HAVE RAISED the issue of the American consensus, or, what comes to the same thing, the public philosophy of America. (I shall use the terms pretty much synonymously, though there is a nuance of meaning. The term "public philosophy" emphasizes an objectivity of content; the term "consensus" emphasizes a subjectivity of persuasion.) There is no doubt that the issue is today alive in the American mind, in itself and in its relation to broad public problems, notably that of the "national purpose." However, from some experience on lecture platforms and in conversations I have found that the very notion of an American consensus or public philosophy meets considerable opposition.

There are two possible approaches to the subject. First, one can raise the question, does the United States have a public philosophy, or not? When the question is put in this way, it has been my experience that the argument tends to run out in futility. I am therefore inclined to think that the form of the question should be altered. One should ask whether the United States needs a public philosophy or not. If the question is asked in this way, there may be the possibility of constructive argument.

* From *We Hold These Truths: Catholic Reflections on the American Proposition,* (New York: Sheed and Ward).

The Case That Fails

The affirmative case on the question, as put in its first form, can be made in four steps. I shall run through them briefly, since some of the materials of argument have been stated already. The starting point, as I have indicated, is the forthright statement of the Declaration of Independence: "We hold these truths. . . ." That is to say, we have a public philosophy; as a people, we have come to a consensus. This philosophy is the foundation of our public life; by coming to this consensus we have come to be a people, possessed of an identity.

The truths we hold, as a people, belong to the order of philosophical and political truth. (Here I presume that God Himself belongs to the order of reason, in the sense that His existence and sovereignty as the Author of the universe are not inaccessible to human reason.) The truths are the product of reason reflecting on human experience. They are not simply a codification or registration of experience; they are reached by an act of abstraction from experience, which carries the mind of man above the level of experience. Hence the affirmation of these truths pretends to and possesses a certain universal validity. Not only do *we* hold these truths; they are human truths of a sort that man as such is bound to hold.

The second step is to explain the three-fold function of the ensemble of truths that make up the public consensus or philosophy. The first function is to determine the broad purposes of our nation, as a political unity organized for action in history. This determination of purposes is, as always, a moral act. Second, the public philosophy furnishes the standards according to which judgment is to be passed on the means that the nation adopts to further its purposes. These means, in general, are what is called policy. Third, the consensus or public philosophy furnishes the basis of communication between government and the people and among the people themselves. It furnishes a common universe of discourse in which public issues can be intelligibly stated and intelligently argued.

The third step would be to indicate the ideas that form the object of the consensus, the content of the public philosophy. Since the consensus is constitutional, its focal concept is the idea of law. We hold in common a concept of the nature of law and its relations to reason and to will, to social fact and to political purpose. We understand the complex relation between law and freedom. We have an idea of the relation between the order of law and the order of morals. We also have an idea of the uses of force in support of law. We have criteria of good law, norms of jurisprudence that judge the necessity of law and determine the limits of its usefulness. We have an idea of justice, which is at once the basis of law and its goal. We have an ideal of social equality and of social unity and of the value of law for the achievement of both. We believe in the principle of consent, in terms of which the order of coercive law makes contact with the freedom of the public conscience. We distinguish between state and society, between the relatively narrow order of law as such and the wider order of the total public good. We understand the relation between law and social progress; we grasp the notion of law as a force for orderly change as well as for social stability. We understand the value of law as a means of educating the public conscience to higher viewpoints on matters of public morality. All these ideas, and others too, of which there will be question in a later chapter, form the essential contents of the consensus.

The argument here should be made to include the notion that the whole consensus has its ultimate root in the idea of the sacredness of man, *res sacra homo.* Man has a sacredness of personal dignity which commands the respect of society in all its laws and institutions. His sacredness guarantees him certain immunities and it also endows him with certain empowerments. He may make certain demands upon society and the state which require action in their support, and he may also utter certain prohibitions in the face of society and state. He may validly claim assistance, and with equal validity he may claim to be let alone.

In its fourth step the case reaches the question of dissent from the consensus. Here the essential point is that the consensus does not "exterminate" dissent, in the ancient sense of the word, *scil.,* by putting dissent or the dissenter beyond the pale of social or civil rights. On the contrary, the consensus supposes and implies dissent. But it remains the function of the consensus to identify dissent as dissent. As for dissent, its function is not to destroy or undermine the consensus but to solidify it and make it more conscious and articulate. This has always been the historical function of error, to contribute to the development of truth. Dissent from the public philosophy serves to stimulate public argument about the philosophy and thus keep the philosophy alive, bring it to refinement, and maintain it in its vital contact with new questions that are always arising under the pressure of constant social change.

These then are the four essential points I should develop in making the affirmative case on the question: Is there or is there not an American consensus, a public philosophy on which the whole order of the Republic rests? The case is only outlined here; these bones would need to be clothed with flesh. And the full case would have to be made both by philosophical and by historical argument.

I have tried to take this affirmative case on more than one public occasion. What is usually the result? Briefly, when the result is not simply a blank stare, it is emphatic negation. The sort of thing that happens may be indicated as follows.

Someone is sure to rise with this question: Sir, you refer to "these truths" as the product of reason; the question is, whose reason? I reply that it is not a question of whose reason but of right reason. But, says the questioner, whose reason is right? And with that question the whole footing is cut from under any discussion of the public philosophy. For the implication is that there can be no philosophy which is public. Philosophy, like religion, is a purely private affair. Indeed, there is no philosophy; there are only philosophies, or better, philosophers. And for all anyone knows or could possibly tell, any of them may be right, or none of them.

Someone else then rises to say that all talk of a public philosophy in America is idle and irrelevant. The argument is that ours is an industrial and technological society; it acknowledges only one value in the end; that value is success; and success in this society can only be defined and measured in material terms. Therefore, let there be no talk of philosophy. Such problems as confront us were created by technology, and they are to be solved by technology, either by more technology or by less. The business of America is business, and philosophy has nothing to do with it.

Then a more sophisticated form of resistance is manifested. There are truths and we hold them? Well, yes, says the positivist, provided you understand clearly what "truth" is and how it is to be "held." There is no other truth but scientific truth, reached by the methods of science, whether classical or statistical. And one holds truths only tentatively; one is never committed to them. Such commitment spells the death of the free mind. Your public philosophy—it may be myth of fancy, poetry, or symbol; but, as described, it cannot pretend to be permanent truth.

The pragmatist will also join the argument. If there is to be talk of ideas, he says, you must remember that all ideas were born free and equal; that all of them are to be thrown into the competition of the market place; that the ideas which are bought are true, or the ideas that work are true, or at least the ideas that survive are true. But the ideas in your public philosophy are no longer bought; they are no longer operative; they have not even survived. The forces of history have made a vacuum where once there was a public philosophy, if indeed there ever was a public philosophy. Why then bother to talk about it?

Since the word "morality" was used in making the affirmative case, another speaker will rise to say that there may indeed be an American morality, but it is hardly more than tribal, a matter of the national mores, having no greater warrant than custom or fashion or the necessity of convention and even hypocrisy in any manner of social life. If the speaker is a philosopher, his proposition will be that all morality is contextualistic. Or he may choose to say that all morality is existentialist, a situation-ethics, a problem of individual decisions in whose making no appeal may be made to a moral order, since there is no moral order. In a word, the argument about the public philosophy gets involved in all the confusions about the idea of morality that are today current.

In the end, someone will surely advance the view that the American consensus contains only one tenet—an agreement to disagree. With this agreement all agreement ends; and this agreement is hardly sufficient to constitute a philosophy.

Against these varied but converging lines of argument I customarily fall back on an historical point, that no society in history has ever achieved and maintained an identity and a vigor in action unless it has had some substance, unless it has been sustained and directed by some body of substantive beliefs. The rejoinder is that we are a new kind of society, a "free society," a democracy. And the consensus proper to this kind of society is purely procedural. It involves no agreement on the premises and purposes of political life and legal institutions; it is solely an agreement with regard to the method of making decisions and getting things done, whatever the things may be. The substance of American society is our "democratic institutions," conceived as purely formal categories. These institutions have no content; they are simply channels through which any kind of content may flow. In the end, the only life-or-death question for American society is that it should live or die under punctilious regard for correct democratic procedures.

My experience has been that the foregoing represents the general range of response that one gets to the affirmation that there is an American public philosophy. This sort of response is pitched on the intellectual level. There is, of course, a more heated response on the level of emotion. Usually, the outcry is raised: But this is orthodoxy! Thus the great word of anathema is hurled. The limits of tolerance have been reached. We will tolerate all kinds of ideas, however pernicious; but we will not tolerate the idea of an orthodoxy. That is, we refuse to say, as a people: There are truths, and we hold them, and these are the truths.

So the argument runs down and out. It ends in negation. On the question as put, is there an American public philosophy? the Noes will have it. I have about come to the conclusion that they do have it. Their negation of a public philosophy seems to be valid on the two levels on which the question itself is validly asked.

First, there is the level of the people at large. On this popular level the public philosophy would appear as a wisdom, possessed almost intuitively, in the form of a simple faith rather than an articulate philosophy. To this wisdom the people are heir by tradition; it is their patrimony. It gives them an identity as a people by relating them to their own history within which their identity was shaped. Even in simple form this wisdom would be adequate to its function, which is to enable the people to "judge, direct, and correct" the moral bearing of courses of government (I use the famous three words of medieval political theory). The ancient example from the field of religious faith is valid here. The simple people of Alexandria caught the resonances of heresy in the preaching of Arius before the clerics caught them, entangled as these latter were in the subtleties of emanationist theory that confused the simple issue: The Word of God—is He God or not? Analogously, the body politic by reason of its patrimony of political wisdom should be able to sense in some instinctive fashion the basic errors in governmental policy, even when the politicians themselves get lost in their technical arguments and partisan feelings.

Second, there is the level of the "clerks," the intellectuals. I mean, of course, not only the academicians—the professional students of philosophy, politics, economics, history, etc.—but also the politicians, the writers, the journalists, the clergy, the whole range of men and women equipped by formal education and training to take an intelligent interest in public affairs, in the *res publica.* These are the people who are supposed to be in conscious possession of the public philosophy as a philosophy; for them it would be a personal acquisition and not simply a patrimony.

On both these levels I am inclined to think that the Noes have it. Say there is no public philosophy in America. By one cause or another it has been eroded. And the sign of the vacuum, especially on the intellectual level, is the futility of argument on the question as put in its first form, whether there is a public philosophy or not.

The Case That May Succeed

Nonetheless, I am unwilling to relinquish the argument. But the form of the question must be changed to read: Do we or do we not need a public philosophy? Can we or can we not achieve a successful conduct of our national affairs, foreign and domestic, in the absence of a consensus that will set our purposes, furnish a standard of judgment on policies, and establish the proper conditions for political dialogue?

To argue the question in this form I would recur to the truth that lies at the heart of the philosophical error of pragmatism. It is false to say that what works is true. But it is an altogether sound proposition that what is not true will somehow fail to work. I think it is possible to prove America's present need of a public philosophy by using this principle as the key to the method of demonstration. The demonstration would be concrete; the materials for it would be drawn from the facts concerning public affairs.

Briefly, the argument would be that, if public affairs today are going badly, the basic reason is the absence of a public philosophy. In other words, it is not true to say that America does not need a public philosophy, for the fundamental reason that this assertion will fail to work. It is failing to work; it is daily proving its own falsity. The further conclusion will be that there is today a need for a new moral act of purpose and a new act of intellectual affirmation, comparable to those which launched the American constitutional commonwealth, that will newly put us in possession of the public philosophy, the basic consensus that we need.

Obviously, this kind of demonstration cannot be undertaken here. But I might make a rapid statement of the lines along which it would proceed.

The starting point is the obvious fact that the United States is doing badly in this moment of historical crisis. I would myself accept the view of Mr. Max Ways, for instance, as stated in his book *Beyond Survival,* that America today is more insecure than it has ever been in its history—more insecure than in the darkest days of the Civil War, more insecure than in the perilous time that followed Pearl Harbor. These were moments of crisis. But at least a goal was clear before us in both of them—a victory to be won, whose symbol would be the capture of a place, Richmond, Berlin, Tokyo. Today what is the goal, the victory to be won? Surely it has no such simple symbol. So baffling has the problem of our national purpose become that it is now the fashion to say that our purpose is simply "survival." The statement, I think, indicates the depth of our political bankruptcy. This is not a purpose worthy of the world's most powerful nation. It utterly fails to measure the meaning of the historical moment or to estimate the opportunities for greatness inherent in the moment. Worst of all, if we pursue only the small-souled purpose of survival, we shall not even achieve survival.

From this comment on our current insecurity I should go on to say that the reason for the insecurity is not Communism, whether as an external threat or (much less) as an internal threat. I would not be misunderstood. If the menace of Communism is properly understood, it would be almost impossible to exaggerate it, so massive is it, and so fundamental. Moreover, if the menace is not understood, it becomes all the greater. And this, I fear, is the current situation. However, postponing to a later chapter an analysis of the exact nature of the Communist challenge, I would here maintain that Communism is not the basic cause of our present confusions, uncertainties, insecurities, falterings, and failures of purpose. I would go so far as to maintain that, if the Communist empire were to fall apart tomorrow, and if Communist ideology were to distintegrate with it, our problems would not be solved. In fact, they would be worse in many ways.

I can here suggest only one general reason for this assertion. Having finally, and much too slowly, reached a consensus that Communism is an evil thing, we have resolved to be "against" it. We reject the Communist idea of world order; we object to a Communist organization of the world. The trouble is that, after you have rejected the Communist order, you are still stuck with the sheer fact of the world's disorder. It is the fact of the century. Communism did not create the fact, though it exploits it. The disorder would persist, or be rendered even more chaotic, if Communist ideas and power vanished into thin air this very moment. Facing the massive fact of world disorder, the United States faces the question: What kind of order in the world do you want? What are its premises and principles? What is to be the form of its institutions—political, legal, economic? How do you propose to help organize this disorganized world? Or do you propose not to help? Or do you perhaps think an order of peace, freedom, justice, and prosperity will come about in the world simply by accident, or by sheer undirected technological progress, or by the power of prayer, or by what? Order is, by definition, the work of the wise man: *sapientis est ordinare*. It is the work of men and peoples who are able to say: There are truths and we hold them. Hence the disordered state of the world itself puts to America the question: What are your truths? With a decent respect to the opinions of a mankind that is groping for a civilized order, speak these truths.

Cicero and the Politics of the Public Orthodoxy*

Frederick D. Wilhelmsen
Willmoore Kendall

OUR IMMEDIATE TOPIC: the meaning of what we shall call "public orthodoxy" in the political philosophy of Marcus Tullius Cicero. Our objective: to throw light on the meaning of public orthodoxy in political philosophy in general. We shall investigate Cicero's position on the issue, that is to say, with an eye primarily to its possible usefulness in the resurrection and reconstruction of politics as *scientia,* which is rendered necessary today by the theoretical decay into which that science has fallen under insistent pressures from positivism.

Positivism denies to the concept of public orthodoxy, in effect, any theoretical meaning at all. It reduces public orthodoxy to a factual *datum*; one, morever, which cannot be penetrated scientifically because it is based upon an irrational *charisma*—the study of which, we are told, belongs properly to the sociology of religion or to the psychology of the collective unconscious. Clarification and defense of the concept of public orthodoxy as a concept pertaining integrally to politics as science, we shall contend, is crucial both to an understanding of Cicero's teaching and to an understanding of the very meaning of political science.

Let us provisionally define the public orthodoxy as that tissue

* From the *Intercollegiate Review,* vol. 5; no. 2 (Winter 1968–69).

of judgments, defining the good life and indicating the meaning of human existence, which is held commonly by the members of any given society, who see in it the charter of their way of life and the ultimate justification of their society.

This provisional definition, it might be objected, raises more problems than it solves. Our reply must be that this is the classical role of a provisional definition within Western logic: to *name* a reality simply by pointing at it, in order that that reality may be brought within the scope of the human intelligence for the sake of scrutiny and ultimate clarification. By pointing at a thing, we make that thing a *subject* of a future judgment, a judgment potentially scientific in nature. And the present essay proposes, *inter alia,* to give to the subject "public orthodoxy" a predicate—a predicate distilled by the Roman experience as understood and thought through by Cicero. That predicate will by no means exhaust the issue at hand; but it will, we think, make it more intelligible to the student of political philosophy.

Let us notice, to begin with, that there can be a purely *legal* "orthodoxy," in terms of which the members of a community merely agree upon the political instruments that are to govern them—for example, the formal orthodoxy that unites most members of the Conservative and Labour parties in Great Britain today, which is a set of common convictions concerning the "goodness" of a bicameral parliamentary system under a ceremonial and symbolic monarch. Such a legal "orthodoxy" is certainly a constituent part of the "way of life" of most societies; but it cannot be simply *identified* with that way of life, and it is, therefore, a more restricted topic than ours. As Professor Leo Strauss puts it, "way of life" is a rough translation of the Greek *politeia,* which means the "character" or tone of a community, and is itself dependent upon "what the society regards as most respectable or most worthy of admiration."[1] In classical political philosophy an aristocratic republic, tempered by monarchical and democratic elements, was considered the best form of government because the urban *gentleman,* whose wealth rested on the land, was considered, for purposes of government, the highest type of human being. The excellence of the urban gentleman, in turn, was both measured and created by his allegiance to the institutions of the City, the highest of which were the

[1] Leo Strauss, *Natural Right and History* (Chicago, 1953), p. 137.

religious rites that propitiated the gods and thus guaranteed their continued providence over the *politeia.* The aristocratic values enshrined in this class were regarded, accordingly, as the ideals of the *politeia* at large, and acceptance of these "values," and the commitments they involved, constituted the public orthodoxy of the classical society.

Hilaire Belloc detailed a similar public orthodoxy for the England that emerged from the Whig triumph over the Stuart kings and that endured well into the present century—that is, the public acceptance of the *gentleman* as the standard of excellence and as the embodiment of what Britain stood for.[2] As Belloc argued, with his characteristic irony, a cad might in the long run stand a better chance for salvation than a gentleman, but to suggest that this theological consideration ought to alter the fabric of English society would be unthinkable. Writing far earlier than Belloc, in a vein that might shock those who find "Machiavellianism" in every blunt statement of political ends, Lord Bolingbroke—in his famous letter to Sir William Wyndham justifying his political role in the months preceding and following the death of Queen Anne—candidly stated that he and his men, representing as they did the "landed party" of the country gentry, the still powerful yeomanry, the older aristocracy, and the Church of England, considered it only "natural" that they should seize power and exercise it for their own ends against the new financial and commercial aristocracy represented by the Bank of England.[3] When Bolingbroke wrote, the English *politeia* was still rural and aristocratic, rather than urban and aristocratic; still agrarian and Christian, rather than commercial and latitudinarian; and the defense of the existent *politeia* seemed to Bolingbroke as absolute and unavoidable a duty as the defense of England itself: England and its *politeia* or way of life, were, for him, one and the same thing. That Bolingbroke himself was neither Christian nor "rural" illuminates rather than obscures his grasp of the meaning of the public orthodoxy as defined here, of a standard of values maintained publicly as ideals even if often sinned against in practice.

[2] Hilaire Belloc, *The Nature of Contemporary England* (London and New York, 1936), *passim.*

[3] *The Works of the Late Right Honourable Henry St. John, Lord Viscount Bolingbroke* (London, 1809), vol. I, pp. 8–11.

The *politeia,* then, is something more fundamental than "the Laws." Cicero locates the study of "the Laws" in a hierarchy of science which *first* answers the question as to the best regime—as Cicero does by identifying it concretely with the Roman Republic. The laws must fit the *politeia,* not the *politeia* the laws: what is just in the best society might be highly unjust in a less perfect society; what is just for a free man might well be crying injustice if done to a slave. Because it is the source of all laws, though capable of being articulated in law and governmental institutions, the *politeia* raises issues that are prior to those of law and governmental institutions. To what we, following Professor Strauss,[4] call "regime," T. S. Eliot applies the term "culture"—as when he writes that if bishops and darts do not belong equally to British culture, they nonetheless equally belong![5] What we "point" to, in a word, is that matrix of convictions, usually enshrined in custom and "folkways," often articulated formally and solemnly in charter and constitution, occasionally summed up in the creed of a church or the testament of a philosopher, that makes a society. The Thing it is and that divides it from other societies as, in human thought, one thing is divided always from another.

That is why we may (and do) speak intelligibly of a Greek, a Roman, or an American "way of life." The nominalism that would deny meaning to these phrases might conceivably be defensible, to be sure, if it restricted itself to borderline cases, such as, say, the Bavarian and the Austrian way of life. But it renders itself absurd when it attempts to deny any essential distinction between, for example, societies like the Chinese and the British, because the denial then becomes a denial of what is *evidently* true. The serious political philosopher simply cannot converse with the nominalist on this primitive level; all the less because there is no way in which we can prove the evident, no way in which we can demonstrate strictly that what is evident *is* evident. What replaces argument on this level is the ability, pure and simple, to see what is *there* to be seen. We must, therefore, draw a distinction between the scientific elaboration of the social disciplines and that intuitive grasp of a cultural complexity which itself precedes all science and, in truth, makes science possible.

[4] Strauss, *Natural Right and History,* pp. 136–37.

[5] T. S. Eliot, *Notes towards a Definition of Culture* (New York, 1949), p. 30.

In fine, the denial of meaning, of intelligibility, to the terms *regime, politeia,* "way of life," culture, cannot be refuted rationally because the source of the denial is an intelligence and a sensibility blunted to the historically and socially given; and if the principle of contradiction is the unquestioned point of departure for metaphysics, then the existence of the *politeia* is the unquestioned point of departure for political philosophy.

Should it be objected here that we are laboring the obvious, our reply must be that laboring the obvious is necessary because the *denial* of the obvious regarding these points has been and is labored constantly elsewhere, in the political literature inspired by positivism, which refuses to touch the question of the *politeia* because the *politeia* enshrines an orthodoxy, and because an orthodoxy is composed of what the positivists call "value judgments," which are precisely what the positivists tell us that political science is *not* about.

The issue may be elucidated further as follows: the *politeia,* in the terminology of Eric Voegelin, is a "cosmion" of meaning illuminated from within by and for the members of a society. Enshrining as it does convictions concerning the existence of God or of the gods, the good life, and the destiny of man and of society, the *politeia* can ultimately be defined only in ontological terms, be they strictly religious, strictly metaphysical, or a combination of the two. These convictions can be understood, therefore, only on their own terms, terms that are by definition theological and metaphysical. Thus positivism's refusal to admit within the temple of political science judgments of a philosophical and theological nature prevents it from coming to grips with any *politeia* whatsoever. In order to understand a *politeia,* we must think through its ultimate philosophical presuppositions; and the thinking must be *thinking,* not mere reporting. If, therefore, we are denied the right to exercise our philosophical and theological intelligence when functioning as political scientists, the unavoidable result is that while we can understand a *politeia* in our capacity as philosophers or theologians, we can never do so in our capacity as political scientists. In short, a *polis* can never be understood by the *science* of politics!

The positivist tries to escape from the horns of this dilemma, but his maneuver only succeeds in goring him the more. I can, he insists, understand a public orthodoxy as "fact," but I cannot criticize it as "value"; to attempt the latter would be to fall into "subjectivism." What he fails to see is that if the phenomenon in question *be* a judgment of value, a judgment that bears integrally upon the meaning and destiny of human life, then the understanding (for every critique presupposes understanding of the criticized) of that judgment *as it objectively is* involves understanding it *as value*. And the so-called refusal to fall into "subjectivism" is itself subjectivism because it converts what is in fact value into disemboweled "fact," and so blocks on principle that which it originally sets out to do—namely, to understand the judgment as objectively *there*, as "fact." There is something radically wrong with the use currently being made of the distinction between judgments of "fact" and judgments of "value," an epistemological blunder which has prevented contemporary political science from coming to terms with the first indisputable principle of its own discipline—that is, the existence of the *politeia* as a cosmion of meaning ultimately metaphysical and theological in structure—the existence, in short, of the public orthodoxy. If, then, Cicero can help us understand the meaning of a public orthodoxy, he can do so only if we are prepared to *philosophize* with him. Which we can do only if we exorcize the notion that "value judgments" are never "scientific."

In classical and medieval philosophy, the *subject* is nothing more than—merely—the thing presented to the intelligence; the *object* is the intelligible light under which the subject is understood—that is, the subject as "objectified" in this or that fashion. There is, in other words, no "split" between subject and object: what we have, rather, is an intelligible relation between (in Aristotelian terms) a *potency* and its *act*: the subject is *potentially* "objectifiable" in any given number of ways; it is *actually* "objectified" in single judgments, in each of which the intellect predicates meaning or intelligibility of the subject—that is, asserts that what it understands of the subject actually *exists in* the subject.[6] The contemporary use of the terms "subject" and "object" is, in consequence, far removed from the classical usage and the doctrine that underlies it—so far, that we can fairly speak of the meanings as having been reversed. The objective, in the classical and medieval sense, is not only "subjective" in the modern sense, but *more* subjective in the modern sense than the "subject" itself in the classical and medieval sense. The

[6] For further treatment of this point, see Frederick D. Wilhelmsen, *Man's Knowledge of Reality* (New York, 1956), pp. 101–57.

"objective" belongs properly to the *mind*; it is the subject *as thought* in this or that way. Similarly, the "subject" in the classical and medieval sense is more "objective" in the modern sense than is the objective in the classical and medieval sense. For the "subject" is the *thing* "extramentally existing,"—that is, in independence of the mind.

Now, the separation of subject and object, which begins as early as the 14th century, reaches its apotheosis in German idealism. For it, the human spirit is the sole *subject* in a world of *objects,* and brings out of its own depths *values,* proper to itself, that are duly imprinted upon the world like seals upon wax. But the decay of idealism did not restore the *status quo ante*; rather, it left intact the subject-object dichotomy, and so prepared the way for what we know today as the positivist banishment of values to an interior and irrational world, the Freudian cave of the psyche, a reservoir of demonic and charismatic forces that has nothing to do with the daylight world of "facts"—a world that belongs properly to "science," which enumerates the facts and classifies them.

In classical and medieval philosophy, the political depends on the metaphysical, as we may see most clearly in Aquinas. For Aquinas, the "ought" is consubstantial with the fullness of the "is"; it is the Good *proper* to man. The Good, viewed most broadly, is that which can *perfect*; that which can perfect, however, can do so only to the degree to which it is perfect in itself; things are perfect in themselves to the degree to which they are in act, and things are in act to the degree to which they are, because existence (*esse*) is the act of all acts and the perfection of all perfections.[7] It follows that the Good is rooted in being itself, and is, in truth, the fullness of being, of existence. Thus, Aquinas can go on and say that the *ratio boni* belongs to the *ratio esse*: not only is there no discrepancy between the Good and the Is; the Good is, we repeat, the *fullness* of the Is, its flowering into perfection—into an actuality fully perfective and desirable, lovable. Obligation, be it personal or social, is not the command of a *deus ex machina,* but is the in-built dynamic push towards perfection which is man's act of existing and within which is inscribed his humanity. And his humanity is itself the structural limit and therefore the determination of his existential act.

[7] St. Thomas' most celebrated passages dealing with existence are to be found in *De Potentia Dei,* Q. 7, a. 2, ad. 9. The *hoc quod dico esse* clearly shows the importance that he attaches to it.

We recapitulate: the root of all intelligibility is being; the act of being is existence; the Good is the fullness of existence. Therefore, the Good is eminently knowable, and from knowledge of the Good there can flow, given a will rectified in the good proper to a man, the life of virtue itself.[8] That is the beginning of wisdom in the order of politics, and it has been lost to positivism because the latter has not given itself the pains to master the inheritance that it presumes, out of its ignorance, to supplant.

We have, up to now, fixed attention on the positivist objection to scientific penetration of the public orthodoxy. We could equally well have discussed the issue, however, from the standpoint of either historicism or existentialism. With respect to the public orthodoxy the three doctrines coincide materially, for all that they move from distinct theoretical positions. The denial of a properly theoretical dimension to the public orthodoxy—this is the point towards which we have been moving—reduces itself, on the one hand, to a positivism that must accept any old orthodoxy on the grounds that it is politically viable, that it is simply given. But that denial may reduce itself, similarly, to a system that identifies transcendent meaning with *historical* factuality, even if this factuality be only an irrational charisma. And it may reduce itself, finally, to a position that justifies the public orthodoxy on the grounds of its *brute* factuality. Theoretically speaking, positivism, historicism, and existentialism come here to one and the same thing, and if we tend to ignore this it is because the three are the existential representatives of three distinct dynamisms within history: positivism, today the ally of liberal democracy in America and yesterday, through the pen of Maurras, the ally of absolutism; historicism, the ally of the marriage of idealism and nationalism within the Germanies and of its progeny; and existentialism, the ally of the counter-revolution against the bankruptcy of 19th-century rationalism and liberalism in all its forms.

In sum, the denial that propositions concerning the good life and the end of man have a trans-immanent validity leads to the identification of the content of those propositions with a factual

[8] Etienne Gilson, *Le realisme methodique* (Paris, 1935) This, Gilson's *vade mecum* for any youth aspiring to philosophical realism, lays down the following as a cardinal principle: Never speak of "values," speak always of "goods" or of "the Good."

datum, a given, whose meaning and justification does *not* transcend its factuality. And this is equally true whether the factuality be termed "the useful" (as in pragmatism), "the historic" (as in historicism), or "the national inheritance" (as in German existentialism's flirtation with National Socialism); in each case justice and law are conjured away in the name of the relevant factuality, and the ontological must be subordinated, theoretically, to the political—with, in all three cases, the same existential consequences: subordination of both church and intellectual freedom to the state; reduction of transcendent truth to existential truth; the pressing of God into the service of man.

Now, this three-headed refusal to face the issue of a public orthodoxy on properly theoretical grounds, however interesting historically, would lack a properly philosophical interest but for this: the three positions—positions that dominate in varying degrees the academic world within the West—do possess a theoretical dimension, do represent an attempt to come to grips philosophically with a genuine political problem. The no-longer-tacit assertion that the public orthodoxy is the central *fact* around which a society's greatness and even existence must be organized, be that "fact" the American myth of democracy (which is capable of being exploited rationally and scientifically, as in Dewey) or be it the French myth of the *ancien regime* (which can be exploited rationally and scientifically by a Maurras), points to a profound truth, as disturbing as it is unavoidable: *the public orthodoxy* is, after all, *useful.* Not only can society not avoid having a public orthodoxy; even when it rejects an old orthodoxy in the name of "enlightenment," "progress," "the pluralist society," "the open society," and the like, it invents, however subtly, a new orthodoxy with which to replace the old one. As Aristotle is always at hand to remind us, only gods and beasts can live alone—man, by nature, is a political animal—whose very political life demands a *politeia* that involves an at least implicit code of manners and a tacit agreement on the meaning of the good life and, therefore, on the meaning of man within the total economy of existence. Without this political orthodoxy—itself involving both a metaphysics (and we must never forget that the denial of the metaphysical is itself a metaphysical proposition) and a theology sketched at least in broad outline—respect for the state withers; contracts lose their efficacy; the moral bond between citizens is loosened; the state opens itself to enemies from abroad; and the *politeia* sheds the sacral character without which it cannot long endure. The public orthodoxy implies, that is to say, a commitment to metaphysical propositions whose claim to acceptance cannot be mere political utility or historical sanction, but the very structure of things as they are in themselves. And this poses a genuine problem: to accept those propositions on existentially political grounds is not really to accept them at all; while if they are not accepted, the political order decays. And we run up hard against the paradox: the political order can be served politically only if its ultimate foundations are *not* accepted on political grounds! Is this perhaps the apparently insoluble dilemma between whose horns man has always been trying to escape?

Such a dilemma certainly faces any man who is aware both of the demands of the transcendent and of society, any man whose soul is turned out towards the truth of things as they are (that is, apart from political considerations), but also faces his responsibilities as a member within a society that incarnates a way of life involving a certain (at least apparent) commitment to the Absolute. Such a man, unable or unwilling to reduce ultimate meaning to utility or to historical factuality, must either find ultimate meaning within his society's orthodoxy, or face up to two alternatives: to seek meaning *beyond* that orthodoxy, and preach this New Truth to the citizenry—thus corrupting the bonds that have hitherto kept his society in being; or to seek meaning beyond the public orthodoxy but keep the New Truth to himself, thus living a public lie. He must choose between rebelling against his society and sinning against the light. His dilemma is terrible, since *either* choice is evil: to destroy an essentially decent society is wrong, even if that society repose upon theoretically erroneous foundations; but to fail to speak the truth when the truth demands that it be spoken is wrong, too. Whatever our hypothetical citizen-philosopher does or fails to do is, on the face of it, evil—at least within the context we have proposed, within the circle we have drawn. If political theory can break this circle it can do so only by exploring it carefully, for the circle captures the insights alike of positivism, historicism, and existentialism, along with those of the classical tradition that modernity in all its forms would jettison.

II

Now, the citizen-philosopher we have sketched above is one of the giants of the Western tradition, Cicero; and we believe that after following him as he walks around the circle we have drawn we may be able to do what we have proposed, namely: to give a predicate, a meaning, an intelligibility, to the subject of the public orthodoxy, a light that may lead us beyond the hideous dilemma with which we are confronted: betrayal of the light or betrayal of the community.

Let us speak first of the setting in which Cicero places the opening passages of his *De Legibus*:[9] a long summer day in Cicero's estate at Arpinum, that Arpinum which he considered his "second fatherland," where grew the Marian Oak, planted not by the hand of man but by the voice of poetry. The reader will remember the grave and eloquent discourse in which Cicero sets forth the doctrine that the whole universe is "one commonwealth of which both gods and men are members."[10] That which binds men to the gods, especially to the "supreme god," is reason itself, the most divine attribute "in all heaven and earth."[11] And reason, Cicero goes on, implies *right* reason: "Since right reason is Law, we must believe that men have Law also in common with the gods." Further, "those who share Law must also share Justice; and those who share these are to be regarded as members of the same commonwealth."[12] For Cicero the commonwealth is not a cosmological but an ontological reflection of the universe. The universe itself is an order of reason and law and therefore a commonwealth in its own right.[13] Seeking the roots of law and justice deep within virtue itself,[14] Cicero asserts that virtue "is nothing else than Nature perfected and developed to its highest point."[15] Penetrating further, he lays it down as a first principle that although penalties in fact often do keep men from injustice, that which ought to make them just should be nature itself. He thus attempts to disengage the concept of justice from brute factuality and to root it in the structure of nature.[16] He comes to grips, so to speak, with positivist and historicist contentions (as we know them) when he affirms that "the most fool-

[9] *Laws,* I, i (beginning).

[10] *ibid.,* I, vii (end).

[11] *ibid.,* I, vii (middle).

[12] *ibid.,* I, vii (middle).

[13] *ibid.,* I, vii (end).

[14] *ibid.,* I, viii (middle).

[15] *ibid.,* I, viii (middle).

[16] *ibid.,* I, xiv (beginning).

ish notion of all is the belief that everything is just which is found in the customs or law of nations."[17] That is, he separates the concept of justice from its historical incarnations, and holds that "Justice is one; it binds all human society, and is based on one Law, which is right reason applied to command and prohibition. Whoever knows not this Law, whether it has been recorded in writing or not, is without Justice."[18]

Let us be quite clear as to what Cicero is doing here: he is defending the *naturalness* of justice against the historicists and utilitarians and positivists of his own day. According to Cicero, the doctrines that he is attacking coincide in insisting that the sanction of history gives to the law its usefulness; that history has tested the laws and found them good, and good because useful to the preservation of the state. He is even willing to use the argument from utility *against* the utilitarians, and, by extension, against the historicists:

> But if Justice is conformity to written laws and national customs, and if, as the same persons claim, everything is to be tested by the standards of utility, then anyone who thinks it will be profitable to him will, if he is able, disregard and violate the Laws. It follows that Justice does not exist at all, if it does not exist in Nature, and if that form of it which is based on utility can be overthrown by that very utility itself.

As far as Cicero is concerned, we see clearly, the historicists and the pragmatists are one and the same crowd, at least as regards the central issue. If the former maintain that written and national custom gives the law its sanction and imposes upon us the obligation to observe the law, the latter maintain that the very existence of the law, linked with my existence under the law, makes it expedient that I obey the law. The unexpressed premise is obvious: to disobey the law would be useless to me since, willy-nilly, I find myself subject to the law. Exposing the fallacy of this argument, Cicero points to the clear and cynical truth that a man can disobey a law not profitable to him if he thinks that disobeying would be "useful" to him. Were utility itself the very ground of law, it would follow that laws not useful

[17] *ibid.,* I, xv (beginning).
[18] *ibid.,* I, xv (middle).

(read: useful *to him*) could be overthrown by the very principle that establishes them. And Cicero's conclusion is lucidly expressed: "Justice does not exist at all, if it does not exist in Nature."[19]

Now, on the surface, this argument against utilitarianism itself does seem to be utilitarian and pragmatic in structure. Justice will go down if justice is based on utility alone. Why not, then, accept the conclusion and *let* justice go down? Why *not* accept a political jungle? Cicero apparently considers the answer self-evident, though he never tells us, in so many words, why he does. But however that may be, his apparently utilitarian treatment of the issue indicates sufficiently the ontological springs of his thought. Without justice, "where will there be a place for generosity, or love of country, or loyalty, or the inclination to be of service to others or to show gratitude for favours received? For these virtues originate in our natural inclination to love our fellow-men, and this is the foundation of Justice."[20] The key word, of course, is "natural." The ground of justice is the ultimate character of nature, and a challenge to nature is a challenge to the very structure of reality. The Ciceronian call to virtue, though fundamentally Platonic, is one with the Stoic insistence that virtue is nothing other than nature itself perfected through right reason.[21].

But these same philosophical considerations, on which Cicero bases the natural foundations of justice, catch up also the religious foundations of the state. If Justice is not founded in nature, "not merely considerations of men but also rites and pious observances in honor of the gods are done away with." And he hastens to state the reason: "For I think that these ought to be maintained, not through fear, but on account of the close relationship which exists between man and God [sic]."[22] The reasoning, in other words, harks back to Cicero's opening observations on the grand community of nature, which links man and the gods together in a commonweal as broad as the universe

[19] *ibid.,* I, xv (middle).

[20] *ibid.,* I, xv (end).

[21] Paul Tillich has brilliantly demonstrated the Stoic identification of the ontological and the ethical in *The Courage to Be* (New Haven, 1952), especially pp. 9–20, 23–26. In Stoicism, he argues, the ethical imperative is one with being itself. To neglect or deny such imperative would be to fall into non-being, into Nothing, the ultimate enemy both of the human spirit and of reality itself.

[22] Cicero, *Laws,* I, xv (end).

itself. Were justice not one with that nature in which both man and the gods share, then the Laws and the customs of society would not join man to the divine in the intimate bond that is suggested by the very word "religion."

The argument thus advanced is simply a corollary of Cicero's main discourse, but this corollary leads us into the heart of the problem: it is not only that the Laws receive their sanction from nature; the religious rites of the state receive *their* sanction from nature as well. The theoretical issue could not be drawn more clearly: the religious rites, as also the public orthodoxy they enshrine, are sanctioned by the naturalness of justice; justice is necessary for the preservation of the state; whence it follows that the public orthodoxy *can* be maintained on utilitarian grounds: the law of nature demands the maintenance of the religious rites and observances *for the good of the state.* Cicero, we perceive, refuses to use the argument from utility to establish the naturalness of justice, but does not hesitate to use it to establish the naturalness of the rites. The philosophical precedence of nature and its law over religious convictions and the observances demanded by them forces us to base the latter on the former.

But why, we might and indeed must ask, are the rites of Rome so necessary to the well-being of the state? Here we reach one of those absolutes in evidence upon which all political philosophy is based. We reach here the meaning of the Roman *politeia.* The answer is one with the whole Roman tradition: belief in the gods and pious observance of the rites dedicated to them have bred in the Roman people that austerity and rectitude, that *gravitas,*[23] which has made Rome possible and which alone can assure her continued existence. But the Roman forefathers "believed" in the gods in the sense that they were convinced that the gods really exist, really guide the destiny of the city of Rome. Their belief was not a matter of calculated policy, seeking to instrumentalize a religion for the sake of the greatness or even the continued existence of a state based on justice. Rather, the gods dispense justice and providence to those who tend their rites. It is indeed useful to propitiate the gods; but the belief in their existence, which created the public cult of propitiation, is just that: a belief *not* a policy. Cicero, in deducing the utility of the rites from the harmony of nature, indicates a philosophical so-

[23] On the role of *gravitas* in Cicero's thought, see Antonio Fontan, *Artes ad Humanitatem* (Pamplona, 1957), *passim.*

phistication within Roman thought that has moved far beyond the simplicity of belief that marked the attitude of the old republic.

When Cicero speaks directly to the state in relation to the public orthodoxy, he does not hesitate, then, to give precedence to the political rather than the metaphysical or religious. In "the very beginning," he argues, we must "persuade our citizens that the gods are the lords and rulers of all things"; "what is done, is done by their will and authority."[24] The gods are "great benefactors of men" and, make no mistake about it, they "take account of the pious and the impious." (They watch each individual: the wrongs he does, the intentions and the degree of piety with which he fulfills his religious duties.)[25] If we *do* persuade the citizens' minds in this sense, they "will not fail to form true and useful opinions"; and let no one be so "foolishly proud" as to suppose that "reason and intellect exist in himself, [but] . . . do not exist in the heavens and the universe."[26] This would be tantamount to saying that *no* reason guides "those things which can hardly be reached by the highest reasoning powers of the human intellect," and that a man can remain a man and "not [be] driven to gratitude by the orderly courses of the stars, the regular alteration of day and night, the gentle progress of the seasons, and the produce of the earth brought forth for our sustenance."[27] The truth is that "all things that possess reason stand above those things which are without reason," and that "reason is inherent in nature"[28]—so that to say that anything stands above nature is "sacrilege."[29] Then the utilitarian note again: "Who will deny that such beliefs are useful when he remembers how often oaths are used to confirm agreements, how important to our well-being is the sanctity of treaties, how many persons are deterred from crime by the fear of divine punishment, and how sacred an association of citizens becomes when the immortal gods are made members of it, either as judges or as witnesses."[30]

[24] Cicero, *Laws,* II, vi (beginning).
[25] *ibid.,* II, vi (beginning).
[26] *ibid.,* II, vi (middle).
[27] *ibid.,* II, vi (middle).
[28] *ibid.,* II, vi (beginning).
[29] *ibid.,* II, vi (middle).
[30] *ibid.,* II, vi (middle).

Cicero's reasoning here is more subtle than a cursory reading of the text would suggest. The context is a discussion concerning Plato's contention that the laws ought not merely to coerce, but should win some measure of consent on the part of the citizenry.[31] Cicero attempts to locate the ground of such consent in a belief in the existence of the gods, and to this end asserts the following things: We must persuade the citizenry that the gods are the lords and guardians of all things and that they exercise a benevolent providence over all who propitiate them, because, to repeat, "minds which are imbued with such ideas will not fail to form true and useful opinions." A belief in the existence of the gods, therefore, is good because it is conducive to the formation of true and useful opinions. Cicero then discusses, one by one, the true and the useful opinions that grow from such a belief, above all this one: He who piously fulfills his duties to the gods will be moved to consider the very structure of the universe in all its orderliness and thus come to assent to the proposition that reason exists, not alone in man, but in the universe as well. In short, Cicero puts religious piety to work for the sake of philosophy, "true opinions": a religious attitude in a man, itself bred by a pious observance of the rites and by a belief in the existence of the gods, is good because it will move him to meditate carefully upon the reasoned course of the universe. True opinions here serve the common good of the polity and true philosophy serves virtue. Although Cicero formally divides his argument into reasons for the forming of both "true" and "useful" opinions, his "true" opinions are themselves at bottom based on political utility. It is not merely that he argues openly that belief in the gods is useful because it casts a sacred character over all society, which in turn deters evildoers, sanctifies treaties, and guarantees oaths; his *previous* argument is equally utilitarian: faith breeds sound philosophy and sound philosophy breeds the virtue needed to consent to the Laws and consent to the Laws breeds a sound *politeia.* And what we want, at least as political philosophers, is a sound polity!

The political expediency of the public orthodoxy, of belief in the gods, is even more nakedly expressed further on in the *Laws,* when Cicero comments on the ancient Twelve Tables and Sacred Laws, those *sacratae leges* which were thought to have been formulated in the earliest days of the Republic and which gave

[31] *ibid.,* II, vi (end). Cf. Plato, *Laws,* 718B–723D.

inviolability to the plebeian tribunes.[32] They read: "No one shall have gods to himself, either new gods or alien gods, unless recognized by the State. Privately they shall worship those gods whose worship they have duly received from their ancestors. In cities they shall have shrines; they shall have groves in the country."[33] And Cicero takes up the contention—astonishingly "modern" it must seem to us—that the divine can be worshipped not merely in temples and in shrines at designated times, but in any old place and at any old time that suits the whim of the worshiper, as witness his reference to the "Persian Magi, in accordance with whose advice Xerxes is said to have burned the temples of Greece on the ground that the Greeks shut up the gods within walls, seeing that this whole universe is their temple and home."[34] Cicero's reply is a precious text, not only because it reveals magnificently the piety and reverence of that Roman spirit of which we are all the heirs,[35] but also because it introduces us further into the heart of Roman religion and of Cicero's teaching concerning the public orthodoxy:

> The Greeks and Romans have done a better thing: for it has been our wish, to the end that we may promote piety towards the gods, that they should dwell in the cities with us. For this idea encourages a religious attitude that is useful to States, if there is truth in the saying of Pythagoras, a most learned man, that piety and religion are most prominent in our minds when we are performing religious rites, and in the saying of Thales, the wisest of the Seven, that men ought to believe that everything they see is filled with the gods, for all would then be purer, just as they feel the power of religion most deeply when they are in temples.[36]

[32] Cicero, *Laws,* II, vi (end).

[33] *ibid.,* II, viii (beginning).

[34] *ibid.,* II, x (end).

[35] For a profound and beautiful meditation on the Roman sense of *place* and its economy in the religious life of Western man, see Hilaire Belloc, *Hills and the Sea* (New York, 1906), the essay entitled "The Men of the Desert."

[36] Cicero, *Laws,* II, xi (beginning).

The psychological argument is evident: a sense of piety and reverence is more easily invoked in the atmosphere of a shrine, a *place* set aside for worship and for worship alone, than in the open air. Even the very conviction that the divine is everywhere is better bred in a man who meditates the divine in some predilected spot that bears in upon him the meaning of divinity in an especial manner. The religious argument is evident: Romans and Greeks set aside shrines and groves in order to produce a greater devotion to the gods. But the political argument is also evident and is, once again, evidently utilitarian down to its very wording: "For this idea encourages a religious attitude that is useful to States." (*Adfert enim haec opinio religionem utilem civitatibus.*)

The text would merely support our earlier conclusions did it not also, as indicated, finger the very meaning of the Roman religious experience, and thereby lead us to the center of Cicero's dilemma concerning the politics of the public orthodoxy. "It has been our wish . . . that [the gods] should dwell in our cities with us." A Christian must read this text twice in order to believe what is before his eyes, which he can do only when he understands that what we confront here is the difference between transcendence and immanence. The gods come to dwell in the City—at the wish of Rome! Which is to say: the gods can be commanded by man to dwell where man would have them. To the Christian, who believes in a God who commands and is in no sense commanded, the very notion is shocking; but not so in a society that has not yet broken through to transcendence: there, nothing could seem more natural. For the Roman world would have looked, and in fact did look upon the Christian claim to a God beyond the cosmos as blasphemy. As Cicero puts it: the contention that "anything stands above universal nature" is "sacrilege";[37] and this "sacrilege" is precisely the Christian claim, the claim to know a God who forms no part of the world but who infinitely transcends it. The classical universe was a closed universe and the gods dwelt within it as ultimate principles of order, themselves immanent to the order they established.[38] There is hence a certain equality between gods and

[37] *ibid.,* II, vi (beginning).

[38] Cf. Romano Guardini, *The End of the Modern World* (New York and London, 1956); Etienne Gilson, *God and Philosophy* (New Haven, 1939).

men, an equality that emerges at its clearest in Cicero because of the Stoic overtones in his thought: gods and men themselves share a reason more fundamental than either of them. Although man must propitiate the gods, man can in a sense call upon them to dwell in the City in order that he may the better worship them—and we must add, in order that the gods can better assure the common good of the commonwealth (which itself participates in a universal harmony that includes gods and men alike).

We can turn for assistance here to Eric Voegelin: St. Augustine, he notes, could not understand Varro when he argued that "as the painter is prior to the painting, and the architect prior to the building, so are the cities prior to the institutions of the cities."[39] And Voegelin comments: "What St. Augustine could not understand was the compactness of Roman experience, the inseparable community of gods and men in the historically concrete *civitas,* the simultaneousness of human and divine institutions of a social order."[40] Cicero, when he argues that the Twelve Tables are in accord with the law of nature, would seem to avoid the blunt and more clearly formulated Varronic conception of the Roman experience. But if we examine Cicero's text we find that "Nature" is made to justify divination, the ritual games, and the institution of soothsayers;[41] and to the objection that the House of Augurs was "invented to be of practical use to the State," Cicero can only answer vaguely that "there is no doubt that this art and science of the augurs has by now faded out of existence on account of the passage of time and men's neglect."[42] Moreover, after discussing the religious functions of the pontiffs in connection with the laws of burial and the consecration of land, Cicero tips his hand, and we see his real interest in the Roman religious observances, in the candid assertion that "we make so much of these matters" in order that "these rites shall be perserved and continuously handed down in families, and, as I said in my Law, that they *must be continued forever (perpetua sint sacra).*"[43] Here again we are in the presence of the panegyrist of the Roman State. The *Civitas* demands the rites for its preservation and grandeur. For this reason, regard-

[39] Saint Augustine, *The City of God,* vi. 4.

[40] Eric Voegelin, *The New Science of Politics* (Chicago, 1952), p. 88.

[41] Cicero, *Laws,* II, xiii.

[42] *ibid.,* II, xiii–xiv.

[43] *ibid.,* II, xix (italics ours).

less of the *religious* truth that the rites may or may not contain, they must be perpetuated and observed down to the last flourish of ritual so long as time shall be.

Eric Voegelin points up sharply the significance of the *De Natura Deorum* in the Ciceronian corpus.[44] The work of a man profoundly affected by Greek philosophy, especially in its Platonic and Stoic forms, the *De Natura Deorum* remains the exercise of a Roman who cannot really take philosophy seriously, who cannot permit philosophical conclusions concerning the meaning of things as they are and the structure of the soul to alter his inherited commitments to the Roman Order. The key figures in the drama are Cotta and Balbus. The latter represents the claims of philosophy—claims that transcend the rites of the city and the institutions of the state; the former, a *pontifex maximus,* stands for the civil *sacredness* of the old Roman orthodoxy. He insists throughout the discourse on the differing sources of authority in any discussion concerning the gods.

There are, he says, those who rest their claims upon authority, an authority inherited from the state. He, Cotta, as a pontiff, is bound by his very office to accept the authority of the state concerning the existence and nature of the gods and the rites required for their propitiation. Cotta admits the authority of Balbus ("the authority of reason, of philosophy"), as also, however, the justice of Balbus' plea that he (Cotta) remember that he is a pontiff:

> This no doubt meant that I ought to uphold the beliefs about the immortal gods which have come down to us from our ancestors and the rites and ceremonies and duties of religion. For my part I shall always uphold them and always have done so, and no eloquence of anybody, learned or unlearned, shall ever dislodge me from the belief as to the worship of the immortal gods which I have inherited from our forefathers. But on any questions of religion I am guided by the high pontiffs, Titus Coruncanius, Publius Scipio and Publius Scaevola, not by Zeno or Cleanthus or Chrysippus; and I have Gaius Laelius, who was

[44] Voegelin, *New Science,* pp. 87–91. In the following paragraphs of our text we have drawn heavily upon Professor Voegelin's analysis.

> both an augur and a philosopher, to whose discourse upon religion, in his famous oration, I would rather listen than to any leader of the Stoics. The religion of the Roman people comprises ritual, auspices, and the third additional division consisting of all such prophetic warnings as the interpretations of the Sybil or the soothsayers have derived from portents and prodigies. Well, I have always thought that none of these departments of religion was to be despised, and I have held the conviction that Romulus by his auspices and Numa by his establishment of our ritual laid the foundations of our state, which assuredly could never have been as great as it is had not the fullest measure of divine favour been obtained for it. There, Balbus, is the opinion of a Cotta and of a pontiff; now oblige me by letting me know yours. You are a philosopher, and I ought to receive from you a proof of your religion, whereas I must believe the word of our ancestors even without proof.[45]

Cotta represents the Cicero, if not always of the Platonic and Stoic meditations, at least the Cicero of the *Laws,* who lays it down as a first principle that the public orthodoxy must be preserved forever in order that Rome remain the Eternal City. Confronting the philosopher Balbus, Cotta is content to say that a "single argument would have sufficed" to convince him of the existence and nature of the gods, namely: "that it has been handed down to us by our ancestors." "But," he goes on, "you despise authority, and fight your battles with the weapon of reason."[46] On the surface, the issue seems to be quite simple: a Roman priest, representing the full authority of the civic theology of the Fathers of Rome, confronts a representative of that Greek philosophy that would meddle with matters long ago settled and agreed upon, who would meddle in the name of reason, of some authority superior to that of the *politeia.* Did not the Assembly so stand up to Socrates? And did not the eventual victory of Socrates, a victory achieved beyond his grave, mark the dissolution of the archaic Greek city-state in the name of speculation and the impieties that spawn therefrom?

[45] Cicero, *On the Nature of the Gods,* III, ii–iii.

[46] *ibid.,* iii–iv.

The issue, however, is not simple, though the critic is forced to read twice in order to understand what has *really* been said. Balbus, representing philosophy and her claims—claims that transcend allegiance to the State and to the public orthodoxy that supports it—takes his stand with the Stoics, throughout the *De Natura Deorum,* in favour of the whole pantheon of the gods, insisting that our very dreams are sent to us by Jupiter.[47] Balbus rejects authority as a safe ground for believing in the gods, asserting that their reality can be established by reason itself. Cotta, the Roman priest and avowed representative of the gods, however, advances every argument in the arsenal of the classical world *against* the existence of the gods. He heaps scorn upon the philosophical arguments marshaled by Balbus. He stoutly maintains that a meditation on the heavens can lead to disbelief as readily as to belief;[48] that awe before nature can lead to atheism;[49] that divination even if it occurs, is beside the point;[50] that the arguments of Zeno would force us to accept such absurdities as that "the world will also be an orator, and even a mathematician, a musician, and in fact an expert in every branch of learning, in fine a philosopher";[51] that the Stoic contention that a universal reason gave birth to all the arts in which man is skilled would necessitate our holding that the world was itself "a harper and a fluteplayer."[52] Admitting the irrationality of the pantheon of the gods, Cotta insists that when he reflects "upon the utterance of the Stoics," he "cannot despise the stupidity of the vulgar and the ignorant."[53] If the Stoic arguments hold that the world is god, "then why do we add a number of other gods as well? And what a crowd of them there are!" Admitting that intelligence is forced to combat superstition, the pontiff renews his attack by damning Stoicism for absorbing every god dreamed by the fevered mind of man within its system, which is itself little more than the personification of allegorized virtue.[54] Moving to the core of the classical religion, Cotta points to the belief

[47] *ibid.,* xi.
[48] *ibid.,* iii–iv.
[49] *ibid.,* v–vi.
[50] *ibid.,* vi–vii.
[51] *ibid.,* viii–ix.
[52] *ibid.,* viii–ix.
[53] *ibid.,* xv–xvi.
[54] *ibid.,* xxiii–xxiv.

in providence and in a reward for the just and a punishment for the wicked: our experience, he maintains, simply fails to show us this hoped for providence because the evil are exalted and the good are often despised and trod upon by the powers of this supposedly rational and benevolent world.[55]

Balbus, shocked by this defense of atheism, appeals to Cotta's character as a pontiff, declaring that the "habit of arguing in support of atheism, whether from conviction or in pretense, is wicked and impious."[56] Cotta replies modestly, perhaps coyly, that he only "desires to be refuted," and assures his philosopher opponent that he is "confident" that he can "easily refute" him.[57] "No doubt," sarcastically answers Velleius, the partisan of Cotta, "why, he [Balbus] thinks that even our dreams are sent to us by Jupiter—though dreams themselves are not so unsubstantial as a Stoic disquisition on the nature of the gods."[58] The book ends with Cicero's doubtful affirmation that Balbus "approximated more nearly to a semblance of the truth" than Cotta.[59]

We can marshall Cotta's arguments under five points, which follow one another in logical sequence:

1) He distinguishes between Stoicism, as such, and the *authority* advanced by Stoicism for the doctrines it maintains: an authority transcending that of society and of the State—that is, the authority of reason. Against this authority for belief in the gods Cotta—as a Roman pontiff—pits the authority of the fathers, of society, of the state. His attack must not, therefore, be read as though it were a philosopher's controversy with another philosopher. Representing as he does the authority of the state, Cotta sets himself squarely against the supposed authority of a reason that pretends to by-pass the exigencies and demands of society. Cotta is the Assembly against Socrates.

2) Cotta grants that reason might lead us to belief in, and adherence to, the gods, to the public orthodoxy; however, reason might equally *fail* to lead us to such belief and adherence. Reason might lead us into impiety and unbelief. *A priori,* before I begin to philosophize, I confront two possibilities: a confirmation of, or a destruction of, the public orthodoxy. Philosophy

[55] *ibid.,* xxx–xxxvi.

[56] *ibid.,* xxvii.

[57] *ibid.,* xxxiv–xl.

[58] *ibid.,* xl.

[59] *ibid.,* xl.

is a risk, and nobody knows where its siren call may lead him.

3) In fact, philosophy might well take a man into atheism (Cotta's whole discourse is an exercise in metaphysics aimed at revealing that very possibility).

4) Should reason lead a man into atheism—and we must remember that Cotta never says that it *must* lead a man in that direction—belief in the gods will collapse and will bring with it the eventual ruin of the state. Religion is not only eminently useful to the state; it is the very cornerstone of the *politeia.*

5) The conclusion is inexorable: the authority of the *politeia* and the public orthodoxy it enshrines must have precedence over that of reason. Should a man engage in the business of philosophizing about the origins of the universe and the ultimate truth of things, he must not do so seriously but only as though he were playing a game. And his conclusions, should they violate the public beliefs of society, must be set aside like toys.

Up until this point, Cicero speaks through Cotta, the high priest. But we must remember that Cicero is more than Cotta, that Cicero is not only a Roman statesman but a philosopher in his own right, a philosopher deeply grounded in Plato, and by no means the popularizer and rhetorician of Stoic doctrine that some commentators have made him out to be. Underneath the doctrines of Cotta, and forming a dimension of Cicero's thought, there are three Ciceronian positions, already adverted to, that buttress Cotta on *philosophical* grounds:

1) If the State collapses, justice collapses; and justice is rooted in the very fabric of universal nature. This is the central meaning of the *Laws,* which has as its heart—as we have seen earlier—the demonstration of the naturalness of justice.

2) It follows that reason itself, philosophy, dictates that we give precedence to the authority of society, to the authority of the public orthodoxy over that of private philosophical speculation. Philosophy must doff its cap to the public faith; it must even humble itself before the claims of religion, even to the extent of declaring irrational its own rationality, should that ultimate sacrifice be demanded. There is a fragment from the lost passages of the third book of the *De Natura Deorum* in which Cicero, stating the case for the Censor, makes the point in the most naked manner possible: Lactanius, filling in the lost text, writes of it: "Cicero was aware that the objects of man's worship were false. For after saying a number of things tending to sub-

vert religion, he adds nevertheless that"—and now we are given Cicero's own words—" 'these matters ought not to be discussed in public, lest much discussion destroy the established religion of the nation' " *(Non esse illa vulgo disputanda, ne susceptas publice religiones disputatio talis exstinguat)*.[60]

Cicero was, clearly, confronted with a frightening contradiction between his natural law doctrine and his public worship of the gods—a worship that his own philosophical convictions rejected on theoretical grounds, but that he freely accepted in the name of his Roman citizenship. As a philosopher committed to justice and to the naturalness of justice, as a philosopher aware of the impossibility of maintaining the state (and therefore justice) without a public adherence to a commonly accepted religious orthodoxy, Cicero was forced into what we may fairly call a public lie for the sake of a properly philosophical truth. The Ciceronian position absorbs within itself the insights of positivism and pragmatism, of historicism, and of existentialism of the political order; but the Ciceronian position transcends them all in that Cicero was philosopher enough to know that all three positions are theoretically fallacious.

The positivist and pragmatist epistemology, as indicated, reduces truth to empirical factuality and usefulness. We find the doctrine in its most articulate form in John Dewey, who held that the predicate of every judgment is nothing other than a cerebral instrument for the solution of a problem presented by the subject. Predicates belong in subjects, are "true" only when they resolve the problem of the subject, only when they are useful; and Dewey tries to resolve the problem of American society in terms of the highly elaborated predicate, "the democratic society and adjustment thereto." This predicate, when applied in government, in education, and in life, "works." Democracy is the ideal solution to the complexities of the American experience. The predicate "adjustment to a democratic society" (the myth has been expressed in any number of ways) becomes, therefore, the sole content of the American public orthodoxy, and this orthodoxy is justified exclusively in terms of its utility. John Dewey is an admirable Cotta, a high priest of an orthodoxy, of a public faith. What Dewey and his disciples call "Absolutism" could not be made to "work" in America, and—asserts Dewey—given the American experience and tempera-

[60] *ibid.*, xl.

ment, *ought* not to be made to "work." It follows that the utility of the democratic *process* (whether it be expressed mythologically or conceptually is irrelevant in this context) is its own justification to the title of public orthodoxy within 20th-century America. From this American Maurrasianism have come forth "adjustment to the community," "education for life," "the open society," "the pluralist society," and many similar myths. Nor does it matter here that pragmatists, failing to distinguish between the existential and theoretical meanings of the term, avoid the word "orthodoxy." Existentially, the "orthodoxy" they reject is the Western Christian experience as permeated by the classical inheritance. Existentially the term "orthodoxy" attaches in letters and in history to *that* doctrine; in rejecting that doctrine, positivism and pragmatism indeed reject "orthodoxy." But theoretically orthodoxy refers to any public doctrine accepted unconditionally by a community, even if the orthodoxy in question is somebody else's heresy; and the emotional reaction of positivists to the word "orthodoxy" is only one aspect of *their* orthodoxy. From a theoretical point of view the positivist and liberal myth, that is to say, is as much an orthodoxy as any other that ever has existed on this globe: an *ultimate* frame of reference, a court of doctrine and dogma before which all other doctrines and opinions must present themselves for judgment. The fact that many Christians (Catholics and Protestants alike) in America feel obliged, at least publicly and academically, if not in their hearts, to justify their Christianity in terms of its supposed affinities with democracy and liberal myths indicates, moreover, that positivism and liberalism are well on the road, in certain quarters at least, to establishing *their* orthodoxy as the public one. The main point, however, is that the positivist insight is englobed within the Ciceronian experience: the utility of the existent (or nascent) orthodoxy justifies its preservation and commands for it the assent of the citizenry. In Cicero's time that orthodoxy was the public Roman cult of the gods. Without that cult, the state would collapse. Therefore its very utility was its *laissez-passer* to the theatre of existence and meaning.

The notion (associated with the name of Dilthey) that man is his history, Cicero rejected when he spoke as a philosopher. But when he spoke as a Roman, when he spoke through the mouth of Cotta the high priest, he spoke good Dilthey. The House of Augurs may not be much good at divination nowadays, but the House of Augurs is the product of history, and history justifies its own products. The city of Rome is given us as a concrete cosmion, incarnating its own meaning in terms of its own historical experience. It stands up against nature as it stands against the forests and the mute skies above: every ultimate source of meaning must be found within the walls of the city itself. The city establishes its institutions, its own gods, insisted Varro; the city calls upon the gods to live within shrines and groves that they may better be seen and thus may better fill the hearts of the people with piety and awe, insisted Cicero. This is but a blunt way of stating the historicist thesis, of identifying meaning with its generation.

The existentialist contention that meaning is one with the brute existent, that theoretical formulation cannot look out towards a possible actualization that transcends the existent in this given moment of time, is due to the existentialist identification of existence and possibility, of actuality and potentiality. If man is nothing other than his own possibility, then possibility cannot look beyond man but *is* man, in the terrible drama of perpetual crisis. It follows that every theoretical formulation must be justified in terms of man as we find him here and now. There can be no appeal to a possibility beyond the present, itself promising a future and better actuality. All meaning is reducible to what is given because the annoying Aristotelian distinction between the possible and the actual has been rubbed away, thus leaving man a naked existence thrown into the world, an existence identical with its own possibility and therefore not the standard for a politics that transcends the immanence of the historical moment. In the political order the given is the state as we find it, society as we encounter it. Theory must be validated in terms of this given, and politics becomes a justification for a nationalist charisma or a gnostic dream simply because these happen to be the historical given. Thus with one hand Cicero rejects the existentialist thesis, but with the other accepts it. "In the debate about the best political order (*status civitatis*) . . . Scipio takes his stand against Socrates. Scipio refuses to discuss the best order in the name of the Platonic Socrates; he will not build up a 'fictitious' order before his audience, but will rather give an account of the origins of Rome."[61] What we here find thrown up against a problematic universe is Rome Herself: splendid; erect; the City Eternal. Let all political and philosophical meaning

[61] Voegelin, *New Science,* p. 90; Cicero, *Republic,* ii, 3.

square itself with this Thing, the *res publica.* The gods have this advantage over their enemies, that they exist as instituted by our fathers. This institutional existence of the gods is the ground of their theoretical reality, and let every theory—says Cicero through Cotta—be squared with the fact that these gods, our own, live with us, and that if we carried the household deities from burning Troy, they in turn blessed the enterprise that is Rome.

Cicero, we repeat, truly gathers the positivist, historicist, and existentialist insights into his philosophy. But unlike the proponents of these theories, Cicero—as philosopher—cannot *really* reduce meaning either to utility, or to history, or to factuality. He is forced, as we have pointed out, to invent two truths, two orders of meaning that cross and clash and that therefore find themselves related one to another: the meaning of theoretical truth, of philosophy, is not that of society; but the former demands that the latter be upheld, no matter how false it may be theoretically. Centuries later Thomas Aquinas, a philosopher who had absorbed the experience of the Christian West, met a similar doctrine,[62] that of Siger de Brabant and the Parisian Averroeists, according to which one and the same thing can be true *theologically* and false *philosophically,* can be and ought to be believed on faith while rejected by reason, and pronounced it damnable. (We do not suggest that the Ciceronian and Brabantian positions coincide, but rather that the same theoretical principle is involved in the two cases.)

In order to live such a doctrine, a man needs an heroic cynicism that can face intellectual suicide in the name of the intelligence and the will at the service of society—an attitude that can be maintained only by a few, and by them not for long. Psychologically, man's drive towards unity pushes him to seek a third doctrine, a higher truth, that somehow reconciles the theoretical and existential contradiction. Cicero, writing in an age when ancient Roman patriotism was disintegrating but had not yet disintegrated under the impact of the Greek philosophical breakthrough to the truths of the soul, invented a strategy that soon collapsed in the tolerant theology of the late Empire, itself destined to give way soon enough to the Christian Empire of Constantine that incarnated a new orthodoxy (what we have since named "Orthodoxy"), a faith that could be and was believed by Western society at large.

[62] Saint Thomas Aquinas, *De unitate intellectu contra Aver.*

We have come close to fulfilling the purpose of this essay, the giving of a theoretical predicate to the subject: "public orthodoxy." The public orthodoxy, let us recall, involves propositions assent to which must be made not on political, but on ontological and religious grounds. It asserts something, let us recall, too, about the structure of things as they are, about man's relation to the divine and about the destiny of the human soul; and assent to that something on purely political grounds is not really assent at all, since—let us emphasize, even at the risk of laboring the point—the assent required is theoretical, ontological. Cicero teaches, let us recall finally, that the public orthodoxy is necessary for the preservation of the state: that although philosophical inquiry into the public orthodoxy might well support it, it also might well destroy it; and that the destruction of the public orthodoxy is the destruction of the state and therefore of justice, itself an imperative of nature. Now, as we confront this circle of meanings and this vicious contradiction we might well conclude that there is no way out. There may, however, be a way *in.* Should transcendence cross over into immanence, should God speak to man and thus reveal His Truth and His Will, the public orthodoxy—enshrining that Truth and Will—would have a guarantee beyond itself, beyond the immanent demands and requirements of society: the will of God. Were this so, man could reverently and intelligently probe the rationality of this orthodoxy, knowing in advance that whatsoever he might discover would conform itself with what has been taught, since what has been taught, has as its teacher God Himself, whose grace guarantees the faith with which we receive His Word. Such a man might well ask himself whether he has an immortal soul, whether justice is more than a word, and whether God exists. These questions would be the *videtur quod non* of the Middle Ages—not a doubt exercised on the origins of a civilized and Christian polity, but a weighing of possible objections to these origins, objections whose resolution man would confidently expect to discover by his own reason because God Himself had guaranteed their resolution.

Our conclusion, our predicate, belongs properly to political theory, but to a political theory dependent on a metaphysics open to Revelation. Where the public orthodoxy is not guaranteed by transcendence, it is always open to the charge that it is opposed to philosophical truth and is the enemy of the soul.

Conversely, the friend of the soul (a soul well-ordered in accord with the structure of reality as it is) might well find himself the enemy of the state, a state not necessarily completely evil in itself; he might find himself, therefore, the enemy of justice itself. His choice will be awful: the guaranteed well-being of society *versus* the demands that wisdom may lay upon him, even if these demands mean the end of society as he has known it. Should he choose to philosophize, and should society then silence him or even kill him for his pains, let him know that society is acting in its own self-defense, a self-defense demanded on philosophical grounds. Let him, therefore, rejoice at the moment of his execution that society has fulfilled *its* duty, a duty that he as philosopher is sworn to uphold in the name of philosophy itself.

But where the public orthodoxy is guaranteed by transcendence, by the Word of God, then the truths of the soul and of society, the first principles of the *politeia* and of metaphysics (that is, the very being of both), are theoretically guaranteed. Beyond this guarantee, which can be had only as a gift and as a blessing, there is no other for any human society born upon this earth.

9/Political Community and Civil Discourse

The Civilization of the Pluralist Society*

John Courtney Murray, S. J.

THE "FREE SOCIETY" SEEMS to be a phrase of American coinage. At least it has no comparable currency in any other language, ancient or modern. The same is true of the phrase "free government." This fact of itself suggests the assumption that American society and its form of government are a unique historical realization. The assumption is generally regarded among us as unquestionable.

However, we have tended of late to pronounce the phrase, "the free society," with a rising interrogatory inflection. The phrase itself, it seems, now formulates a problem. This is an interesting new development. It was once assumed that the American proposition, both social and political, was self-evident; that it authenticated itself on simple inspection; that it was, in consequence, intuitively grasped and generally understood by the American people. This assumption now stands under severe question.

What is the free society, in its "idea"? Is this "idea" being successfully realized in the institutions that presently determine the pattern of American life, social and personal? The web of American institutions has altered, rapidly and profoundly, even radically, over the past few generations. Has the "idea" of the

* From *We Hold These Truths: Catholic Reflections on the American Proposition* (New York: Sheed and Ward). Copyright © 1960 by Sheed and Ward, Inc. Reprinted by permission.

free society perhaps been strangled by the tightening intricacies of the newly formed institutional network? Has some new and alien "idea" subtly and unsuspectedly assumed the role of an organizing force in American society? Do we understand not only the superficial facts of change in American life but also the underlying factors of change—those "variable constants" that forever provide the dynamisms of change in all human life?

The very fact that these questions are being asked makes it sharply urgent that they be answered. What is at stake is America's understanding of itself. Self-understanding is the necessary condition of a sense of self-identity and self-confidence, whether in the case of an individual or in the case of a people. If the American people can no longer base this sense on naive assumptions of self-evidence, it is imperative that they find other more reasoned grounds for their essential affirmation that they are uniquely a people, uniquely a free society. Otherwise the peril is great. The complete loss of one's identity is, with all propriety of theological definition, hell. In diminished forms it is insanity. And it would not be well for the American giant to go lumbering about the world today, lost and mad.

The Civil Multitude

At this juncture I suggest that the immediate question is not whether the free society is really free. This question may be unanswerable; it may even be meaningless as a question, if only for the reason that the norms of freedom seem to have got lost in a welter of confused controversy. Therefore I suggest that the immediate question is whether American society is properly civil. This question is intelligible and answerable, because the basic standard of civility is not in doubt: "Civilization is formed by men locked together in argument. From this dialogue the community becomes a political community." This statement, made by Thomas Gilby, O.P., in *Between Community and Society,*[1] exactly expresses the mind of St. Thomas Aquinas, who was himself giving refined expression to the tradition of classic antiquity, which in its prior turn had given first elaboration to the concept of the "civil multitude," the multitude that is not a mass or a herd or a huddle, because it is characterized by civility.

The specifying note of political association is its rational de-

[1] New York: Longmans, Green & Co., 1953.

liberative quality, its dependence for its permanent cohesiveness on argument among men. In this it differs from all other forms of association found on earth. The animal kingdom is held together simply by the material homogeneity of the species; all its unities and antagonisms are of the organic and biological order. Wolves do not argue the merits of running in packs. The primal human community, the family, has its own distinctive bonds of union. Husband and wife are not drawn into the marital association simply by the forces of reason but by the forces of life itself, importantly including the mysterious dynamisms of sex. Their association is indeed founded on a contract, which must be a rational and free act. But the substance and finality of the contract is both infra- and supra-rational; it is an engagement to become "two in one flesh." The marital relationship may at times be quarrelsome, but it is not argumentative. Similarly, the union of parents and children is not based on reason, justice, or power; it is based on kinship, love, and *pietas*.

It is otherwise with the political community. I am not, of course, maintaining that civil society is a purely rational form of association. We no longer believe, with Locke or Hobbes, that man escapes from a mythical "state of nature" by an act of will, by a social contract. Civil society is a need of human nature before it becomes the object of human choice. Moreover, every particular society is a creature of the soil; it springs from the physical soil of earth and from the more formative soil of history. Its existence is sustained by loyalties that are not logical; its ideals are expressed in legends that go beyond the facts and are for that reason vehicles of truth; its cohesiveness depends in no small part on the materialisms of property and interest. Though all this is true, nevertheless the distinctive bond of the civil multitude is reason, or more exactly, that exercise of reason which is argument.

Hence the climate of the city is likewise distinctive. It is not feral or familial but forensic. It is not hot and humid, like the climate of the animal kingdom. It lacks the cordial warmth of love and unreasoning loyalty that pervades the family. It is cool and dry, with the coolness and dryness that characterize good argument among informed and responsible men. Civic amity gives to this climate its vital quality. This form of friendship is a special kind of moral virtue, a thing of reason and intelligence, laboriously cultivated by the discipline of passion, prejudice, and narrow self-interest. It is the sentiment proper to the city. It has nothing to do with the cleavage of a David to a Jonathan, or with the kinship of the clan, or with the charity, *fortis ut mors,* that makes the solidarity of the Church. It is in direct contrast with the passionate fanaticism of the Jacobin: "Be my brother or I'll kill you!" Ideally, I suppose, there should be only one passion in the city—the passion for justice. But the will to justice, though it engages the heart, finds its measure as it finds its origin in intelligence, in a clear understanding of what is due to the equal citizen from the city and to the city from the citizenry according to the mode of their equality. This commonly shared will to justice is the ground of civic amity as it is also the ground of that unity which is called peace. This unity, qualified by amity, is the highest good of the civil multitude and the perfection of its civility.

The Public Argument

If, then, society is civil when it is formed by men locked together in argument, the question rises, what is the argument about? There are three major themes.

First, the argument is about public affairs, the *res publica,* those matters which are for the advantage of the public (in the phrase as old as Plato) and which call for public decision and action by government. These affairs have their origin in matters of fact; but their rational discussion calls for the Socratic dialogue, the close and easy use of the habit of cross-examination, that transforms brute facts into arguable issues.

Second, the public argument concerns the affairs of the commonwealth. This is a wider concept. It denotes the affairs that fall, at least in decisive part, beyond the limited scope of government. These affairs are not to be settled by law, though law may be in some degree relevant to their settlement. They go beyond the necessities of the public order as such; they bear upon the quality of the common life. The great "affair" of the commonwealth is, of course, education. It includes three general areas of common interest: the school system, its mode of organization, its curricular content, and the level of learning among its teachers; the later education of the citizen in the liberal art of citizenship; and the more general enterprise of the advancement of knowledge by research.

The third theme of public argument is the most important and the most difficult. It concerns the constitutional consensus whereby the people acquires its identity as a people and the society is endowed with its vital form, its entelechy, its sense of purpose as a collectivity organized for action in history. The idea of consensus has been classic since the Stoics and Cicero; through St. Augustine it found its way into the liberal tradition of the West: *"Res publica, res populi; populus autem non omnis hominum coetus quoquo modo congregatus, sed coetus multitudinis iuris consensu et utilitatis communione sociatus"* (Scipio).

The state of civility supposes a consensus that is constitutional, *sc.*, its focus is the idea of law, as surrounded by the whole constellation of ideas that are related to the *ratio iuris* as its premises, its constituent elements, and its consequences. This consensus is come to by the people; they become a people by coming to it. They do not come to it accidentally, without quite knowing how, but deliberatively, by the methods of reason reflecting on experience. The consensus is not a structure of secondary rationalizations erected on psychological data (as the behaviorist would have it) or on economic data (as the Marxist would have it). It is not the residual minimum left after rigid application of the Cartesian axiom, *"de omnibus dubitandum."* It is not simply a set of working hypotheses whose value is pragmatic. It is an ensemble of substantive truths, a structure of basic knowledge, an order of elementary affirmations that reflect realities inherent in the order of existence. It occupies an established position in society and excludes opinions alien or contrary to itself. This consensus is the intuitional a priori of all the rationalities and technicalities of constitutional and statutory law. It furnishes the premises of the people's action in history and defines the larger aims which that action seeks in internal affairs and in external relations.

The whole premise of the public argument, if it is to be civilized and civilizing, is that the consensus is real, that among the people everything is not in doubt, but that there is a core of agreement, accord, concurrence, acquiescence. We hold certain truths; therefore we can argue about them. It seems to have been one of the corruptions of intelligence by positivism to assume that argument ends when agreement is reached. In a basic sense the reverse is true. There can be no argument except on the premise, and within a context, of agreement. *Mutatis mutandis,* this is true of scientific, philosophical, and theological argument. It is no less true of political argument.

On its most imperative level the public argument within the

city and about the city's affairs begins with the agreement that there is a reality called, in the phrase of Leo XIII, *patrimonium generis humani,* a heritage of an essential truth, a tradition of rational belief, that sustains the structure of the city and furnishes the substance of civil life. It was to this patrimony that the Declaration of Independence referred: "These are the truths we hold." This is the first utterance of a people. By it a people establishes its identity, and under decent respect to the opinions of mankind declares its purposes within the community of nations.

In later chapters an effort will be made to state the contents of the public consensus in America. Briefly, its principles and doctrines are those of Western constitutionalism, classic and Christian. This is our essential patrimony, laboriously wrought out by centuries of thought, further refined and developed in our own land to fit the needs of the new American experiment in government. In addition, as will later appear, the consensus has a growing end, as American society itself has a growing end. My point at the moment, however, is that there are two reasons why the consensus furnishes the basic theme of the public argument whereby American society hopes to achieve and maintain the mark of civility.

Initially, we hold these truths because they are a patrimony. They are a heritage from history, through whose dark and bloody pages there runs like a silver thread the tradition of civility. This is the first reason why the consensus continually calls for public argument. The consensus is an intellectual heritage; it may be lost to mind or deformed in the mind. Its final depository is the public mind. This is indeed a perilous place to deposit what ought to be kept safe; for the public mind is exposed to the corrosive rust of skepticism, to the predatory moths of deceitful *doxai* (in Plato's sense), and to the incessant thieveries of forgetfulness. Therefore the consensus can only be preserved in the public mind by argument. High argument alone will keep it alive, in the vital state of being "held."

Second, we hold these truths because they are true. They have been found in the structure of reality by that dialectic of observation and reflection which is called philosophy. But as the achievement of reason and experience the consensus again presents itself for argument. Its vitality depends on a constant scrutiny of political experience, as this experience widens with the developing—or possibly the decaying—life of man in society.

Only at the price of this continued contact with experience will a constitutional tradition continue to be "held," as real knowledge and not simply as a structure of prejudice. However, the tradition, or the consensus, is not a mere record of experience. It is experience illumined by principle, given a construction by a process of philosophical reflection. In the public argument there must consequently be a continued recurrence to first principles. Otherwise the consensus may come to seem simply a projection of ephemeral experience, a passing shadow on the vanishing backdrop of some given historical scene, without the permanence proper to truths that are "held."

On both of these titles, as a heritage and as a public philosophy, the American consensus needs to be constantly argued. If the public argument dies from disinterest, or subsides into the angry mutterings of polemic, or rises to the shrillness of hysteria, or trails off into positivistic triviality, or gets lost in a morass of semantics, you may be sure that the barbarian is at the gates of the city.

The barbarian need not appear in bearskins with a club in hand. He may wear a Brooks Brothers suit and carry a ballpoint pen with which to write his advertising copy. In fact, even beneath the academic gown there may lurk a child of the wilderness, untutored in the high tradition of civility, who goes busily and happily about his work, a domesticated and law-abiding man, engaged in the construction of a philosophy to put an end to all philosophy, and thus put an end to the possibility of a vital consensus and to civility itself. This is perennially the work of the barbarian, to undermine rational standards of judgment, to corrupt the inherited intuitive wisdom by which the people have always lived, and to do this not by spreading new beliefs but by creating a climate of doubt and bewilderment in which clarity about the larger aims of life is dimmed and the self-confidence of the people is destroyed, so that finally what you have is the impotent nihilism of the "generation of the third eye," now presently appearing on our university campuses. (One is, I take it, on the brink of impotence and nihilism when one begins to be aware of one's own awareness of what one is doing, saying, thinking. This is the paralysis of all serious thought; it is likewise the destruction of all the spontaneities of love.)

The barbarian may be the eighteenth-century philosopher, who neither anticipated nor desired the brutalities of the Revolution with its Committee on the Public Safety, but who prepared the ways for the Revolution by creating a vacuum which he was not able to fill. Today the barbarian is the man who makes open and explicit rejection of the traditional role of reason and logic in human affairs. He is the man who reduces all spiritual and moral questions to the test of practical results or to an analysis of language or to decision in terms of individual subjective feeling.

It is a Christian theological intuition, confirmed by all of historical experience, that man lives both his personal and his social life always more or less close to the brink of barbarism, threatened not only by the disintegrations of physical illness and by the disorganizations of mental imbalance, but also by the decadence of moral corruption and the political chaos of formlessness or the moral chaos of tyranny. Society is rescued from chaos only by a few men, not by the many. *Paucis humanum vivit genus.* It is only the few who understand the disciplines of civility and are able to sustain them in being and thus hold in check the forces of barbarism that are always threatening to force the gates of the city. To say this is not, of course, to endorse the concept of the fascist élite—a barbarous concept, if ever there was one. It is only to recall a lesson of history to which our own era of mass civilization may well attend. We have not been behind our forebears in devising both gross and subtle ways of massacring ancient civilities.

The Concept of Conversation

Barbarism is not, I repeat, the forest primeval with all its relatively simple savageries. Barbarism has long had its definition, resumed by St. Thomas after Aristotle. It is the lack of reasonable conversation according to reasonable laws. Here the word "conversation" has its twofold Latin sense. It means living together and talking together.

Barbarism threatens when men cease to live together according to reason, embodied in law and custom, and incorporated in a web of institutions that sufficiently reveal rational influences, even though they are not, and cannot be, wholly rational. Society becomes barbarian when men are huddled together under the rule of force and fear; when economic interests assume the primacy over higher values; when material standards of mass and quantity crush out the values of quality and excellence;

when technology assumes an autonomous existence and embarks on a course of unlimited self-exploitation without purposeful guidance from the higher disciplines of politics and morals (one thinks of Cape Canaveral); when the state reaches the paradoxical point of being everywhere intrusive and also impotent, possessed of immense power and powerless to achieve rational ends; when the ways of men come under the sway of the instinctual, the impulsive, the compulsive. When things like this happen, barbarism is abroad, whatever the surface impressions of urbanity. Men have ceased to live together according to reasonable laws.

Barbarism likewise threatens when men cease to talk together according to reasonable laws. There are laws of argument, the observance of which is imperative if discourse is to be civilized. Argument ceases to be civil when it is dominated by passion and prejudice; when its vocabulary becomes solipsist, premised on the theory that my insight is mine alone and cannot be shared; when dialogue gives way to a series of monologues; when the parties to the conversation cease to listen to one another, or hear only what they want to hear, or see the other's argument only through the screen of their own categories; when defiance is flung to the basic ontological principle of all ordered discourse, which asserts that reality is an analogical structure, within which there are variant modes of reality, to each of which there corresponds a distinctive method of thought that imposes on argument its own special rules. When things like this happen, men cannot be locked together in argument. Conversation becomes merely quarrelsome or querulous. Civility dies with the death of the dialogue.

On Debate and Existence*

Eric Voegelin

In our capacity as political scientists, historians, or philosophers we all have had occasion at one time or another to engage in debate with ideologists—whether Communists or intellectuals of a persuasion closer to home. And we all have discovered on such occasions that no agreement, or even an honest disagreement, could be reached, because the exchange of argument was disturbed by a profound difference of attitude with regard to all fundamental questions of human existence—with regard to the nature of man, to his place in the world, to his place in society and history, to his relation to God. Rational argument could not prevail because the partner to the discussion did not accept as binding for himself the matrix of reality in which all specific questions concerning our existence as human beings are ultimately rooted; he has overlaid the reality of existence with another mode of existence that Robert Musil has called the Second Reality. The argument could not achieve results; it had to falter and peter out, as it became increasingly clear that not argument was pitched against argument, but that behind the appearance of a rational debate there lurked the difference of two modes of existence, of existence in truth and existence in untruth. The universe of rational discourse collapses, we may say, when the common ground of existence in reality has disappeared.

Corollary: The difficulties of debate concern the fundamentals

* From the *Intercollegiate Review,* vol. 3, nos. 4–5 (March–April, 1967).

of existence. Debate with ideologists is quite possible in the areas of the natural sciences and of logic. The possibility of debate in these areas, which are peripheral to the sphere of the person, however, must not be taken as presaging the possibility in the future that areas central to the person (Max Scheler's distinction of *personperiphere* and *personzentrale* areas) will also move into the zone of debate. Among students of the Soviet Union there is a tendency to assume that the universe of discourse, at present restricted to peripheral subject-matters, will, by the irresistible power of reason, expand so as to include the fundamentals of existence. While such a possibility should not be flatly denied, it also should be realized that there is no empirical evidence on which such an expectation could be based. The matter is of some interest, because philosophers of the rank of Jaspers indulge in the assumption that there is a community of mankind in existence on the level of the natural sciences, and that scientists form a community. That raises the philosophical question whether community is something that can be established on the level of a common interest in science at all, a question which at present is far from being thought through.

The phenomenon of the breakdown as such is well known. Moreover, the various Second Realities, the so-called ideologies, have been the object of extensive studies. But the nature of the breakdown itself, its implications for the advancement of science, and above all the methods of coping with the fantastic situation, are by far not yet sufficiently explored. The time at our disposition will obviously not allow an exhaustive inquiry concerning so vast a topic; still, I propose in the present paper at least to circumscribe some of the relevant points of such an inquiry. And as a step toward establishing the relevant points, I shall place the phenomenon of the breakdown in historical perspective.

I.

The Second Realities which cause the breakdown of rational discourse are a comparatively recent phenomenon. They have grown during the modern centuries, roughly since 1500, until they have reached, in our own time, the proportions of a social and political force which in more gloomy moments may look strong enough to extinguish our civilization—unless, of course, you are an ideologist yourself and identify civilization with the victory of Second Reality. In order to distinguish the nature of the new growth, as well as to understand its consequences, we must go a little further back in time, to a period in which the universe of rational discourse was still intact because the first reality of existence was yet unquestioned. Only if we know, for the purpose of comparison, what the conditions of rational discourse are, shall we find our bearings in the contemporary clash with Second Realities. The best point of departure for the comparative analysis of the problem will be St. Thomas' *Summa Contra Gentiles.* The work was written as an exposition and defense of the truth of Christianity against the pagans, in particular against the Mohammedans. It was written in a period of intellectual turmoil through the contacts with Islam and Aristotelian philosophy, comparable in many respects to our own, with the important difference, however, that a rational debate with the opponent was still possible or—we should say more cautiously—seemed still possible to Aquinas. I shall reflect, therefore, on the opening chapters of the *Summa,* in which Aquinas sets forth the problem of debate, not simple even in his time.

Aquinas assumes the philosopher, as we have done, in the situation of debate with an opponent; he considers this the philosopher's situation of necessity. For "as it is incumbent on the *sapiens* to meditate on the truth of the first principle, and to communicate it to others, so it is incumbent on him to refute the opposing falsehood." Truth about the constitution of being, of which human existence is a part, is not achieved in an intellectual vacuum, but in the permanent struggle with pre-analytical notions of existence, as well as with erroneous analytical conceptions. The situation of debate thus is understood as an essential dimension of the existence that we recognize as ours; to one part, the quest for truth is the perpetual task of disengaging it from error, of refining its expression in contest with the inexhaustible ingenuity of error. Philosophy, as a consequence, is not a solitary but a social enterprise. Its results concern everyman; it is undertaken by the *sapiens* representatively for everyman. More specifically the represented have a right to receive answers not only to their own questions but also to hear answers to brilliant and well propagated errors which threaten to disintegrate the order of society by disintegrating the order of existence in everyman personally. It is a situation and an obligation that must be faced in our 20th century as much as

Thomas had to face it in his 13th. Hence, if the *sapiens* shuns the situation of debate, especially if he avoids the crucial intellectual issues threatening the beleaguered city, he becomes derelict in his duties to God and man, his attitude is spiritually, morally, and politically indefensible.

The philosopher's office thus is twofold: He must set forth the truth by elaborating it analytically, and he must guard the truth against error. But what is this truth the philosopher has to meditate and to set forth? I have called it the truth of existence, and by using this language I have terminologically modernized the problem that lies at the core of St. Thomas' endeavor, as well as of the earlier one of Aristotle to which Aquinas refers in the passages under consideration. The modernization is legitimate, as you will see presently, because it does not modify the problem but only its symbolic expression; and at the same time it is necessary, because without it we cannot understand that the scholastic and classic problem is indeed identical with our own. The source of the difficulties we moderns have with understanding Aristotle and Aquinas is the fact that the truth of existence, of the first reality as we called it, in their time was not yet questioned; hence, there was no need to distinguish it from an untrue existence; and consequently no concepts were developed for a problem that had not yet become topical. The truth of existence was taken so much for granted that, without further preparation, the analysis could proceed to develop the problems of metaphysics as they presented themselves to men who lived in the truth of existence. But let us now have a look at the manner in which Aquinas and Aristotle expressed their problem of truth.

II.

While the supporting argument is voluminous, the crucial formulations are succinct. Aquinas, following Aristotle, considers it the task of the philosopher to consider the highest causes of all being. "The end of each thing is that which is intended by its first author or mover. But the first author and mover of the universe is an intellect. The ultimate end of the universe must, therefore, be the good of an intellect. This good is truth. Truth must consequently be the ultimate end of the whole universe, and the consideration of the wise man aims principally at truth."

Aquinas then refers to the authority of Aristotle himself who established "that first philosophy is the science of truth, but of that truth which is the origin of all truth, namely, which belongs to the first principle whereby all things are. The truth belonging to such a principle is, clearly, the source of all truth; for things have the same disposition in truth as in being." So far the text (*SCG* I, 1. *Met.* alpha ellaton, 1,993b-20–30).

At first hearing, I presume, these formulations will sound as strange to you as they did to me. There is talk about a first mover of the universe—who must be assumed to be an intellect—from whom emanates somehow an order of being that is at the same time an order of truth. Why should we be concerned with a prime mover and his properties?—you will ask. And does the matter really improve when Aquinas identifies the prime mover with the God of revelation and uses the Aristotelian argument for the prime mover as a demonstration of the existence of God? At the risk of arousing the indignation of convinced Aristotelians and Thomists I must say that I consider such questions quite pertinent. The questions must be raised, for we no longer live, as did Aristotle and even Aquinas, at the center of a cosmos, surrounding us from all sides spherically, itself surrounded by the outer sphere of the fixed stars. We can no longer express the truth of existence in the language of men who believed in such a cosmos, moved with all its content by a prime mover, with a chain of *aitia,* of causes, extending from existent to existent down to the most lowly ones. The symbolism of the closed cosmos, which informs the fundamental concepts of classic and scholastic metaphysics, has been superseded by the universe of modern physics and astronomy.

Nevertheless, if we admit all this, does it follow that Aristotelian and Thomist metaphysics must be thrown on the scrap heap of symbolisms that once had their moment of truth but now have become useless?

You will have anticipated that the answer will be negative. To be sure, a large part of the symbolism has become obsolete, but there is a solid core of truth in it that can be, and must be, salvaged by means of some surgery. Two stages of such surgery seem to be indicated:

1) The first operation must extend to the demonstrations which depend for their validity on the imagery of a cosmos that is no longer ours. If, however, we survey the body of demonstrations in support of the formulations I have presented, and

if we remove from it everything that smacks of cosmological symbolism, there remains as a *pièce de résistance* the argument that a universe which contains intelligent beings cannot originate with a *prima causa* that is less than intelligent. Though the context of the argument is still the cosmos, at least the argument itself draws specifically on an experience of human existence which as such is independent of the experience of the cosmos.

2) The second operation must extend to the prime mover itself. We must distinguish between the symbolic construction and the reality to which it refers; and we must be aware of the curious relations between the firmness of conviction that such a reality exists and the credibility of the construct. If the motivating experiences are known to the reader and shared by him, the construct will appear satisfactory and credible; if the experiences are not shared, or not even too clearly known, the construct will become incredible and acquire the character of an hypostasis. Aristotle could indulge in his construction with assurance because the experiences which motivate the symbolism were taken for granted by everybody without close scrutiny; and Aquinas, in addition to living in the same uncritical safety of experience, could as a Christian theologian blend the truth of the prime mover into the truth of revelation. Today the validity of the symbol, and with its validity the reality to which it refers, is in doubt, because the experiences which motivated its creation for their adequate expression have slipped from public consciousness; and they could slip from public consciousness with comparative ease, because neither were they set forth with sufficient explicitness, nor did the problem of experience and symbolization come into clear focus at all, in classic and scholastic metaphysics. Hence, in order to reach the truth contained in the apparently hypostatic construct, we must make explicit the motivating experiences.

The immediate experiences presupposed in Aristotelian metaphysics are not difficult to find in the classic sources, if one looks for them; but after all this preparation, I am afraid, they will come as an anticlimax because of their apparent simplicity. For we find ourselves referred back to nothing more formidable than the experiences of finiteness and creatureliness in our existence, of being creatures of a day as the poets call man, of being born and bound to die, of dissatisfaction with a state experienced as imperfect, of apprehension of a perfection that is not of this world but is the privilege of the gods, of possible fulfillment in a state beyond this world, the Platonic *epekeina,* and so forth. I just have mentioned Plato; if we survey this list of experiences, we shall better understand why for Plato (who had a sharper sensitiveness for the problems of existence than either Aristotle or Thomas) philosophy could be, under one of its aspects, the practice of dying; under another aspect, the Eros of the transcendent Agathon; under still another aspect (that leads us back to the formulations of Aristotle and Aquinas), the love of the Wisdom that in its fullness is only God's. In these Platonic conceptions (the catalogue is not complete) we can see philosophy emerging from the immediate experiences as an attempt to illuminate existence. Moreover, we can understand how philosophy, once it had, thanks to Plato, developed its symbolism and become a going concern, could gain something like an autonomous life of construction and demonstration, apparently independent of the originally motivating experiences, how it could grow into an enterprise that would have to become unconvincing when, due to historical circumstances, the reader did no longer share the philosopher's understanding of existence.

III.

We have assembled the data of the problem of experience and symbolization as far as they were immediately connected with the formulations of Aquinas and Aristotle. We can now attempt the exegesis of existence that is implied, though not explicitly given, in classic and scholastic metaphysics. In the course of this attempt, however, further data of the problem will emerge that will compel us to revise the initial propositions. The reader should be warned, therefore, that after the first we have to make a second start.

Human existence, it appears, is not opaque to itself, but illuminated by intellect (Aquinas) or *nous* (Aristotle). This intellect is as much part of human existence as it is the instrument of its interpretation. In the exegesis of existence intellect discovers itself in the structure of existence; ontologically speaking, human existence has noetic structure. The intellect discovers itself, furthermore, as a force transcending its own existence; by virtue of the intellect, existence not only is not opaque, but actually reaches out beyond itself in various directions in search of knowledge. Aristotle opens his *Metaphysics* with the sentence:

"All men by nature desire to know." I shall not bother you with the detail of Aristotle's argument on the point, because I suspect that in his etiology of being, i.e., in the doctrine of the four causes and the organization of the demonstrations according to the four causes, we touch again one of the areas of symbols that is incompatible with the present state of science and, therefore, will have to be abandoned to a large part, if not entirely, in order to reach the core of truth. I shall rather use a shortcut and divide the objects to which the desire to know reaches out into the two classes of (1) things of the external world and (2) human actions.

With regard to things, the desire to know raises the questions of their origin, both with regard to their existence (I include under this title both the hyletic and kinetic arguments) and their essence (the eidetic argument). In both respects, Aristotle's etiological demonstration arrives ultimately at the eternal, immaterial *prima causa* as the origin of existent things. If now we shift the accent back from the construct of doubtful validity to the experiences that motivate its construction, and search for a modern terminology of great adequacy, we find it offering itself in the two great metaphysical questions formulated by Leibniz in his *Principes de la Nature et de la Grâce,* in the questions: (1) Why is there something, why not nothing? and (2) Why is something as it is, and not different? These two questions are, in my opinion, the core of true experience which motivates metaphysical constructions of the Aristotelian and Thomist type. However, since obviously no answer to these questions will be capable of verification or falsification, the philosopher will be less interested in this or that symbolism pretending to furnish the "true" answer than in the questions themselves. For the questions arise authentically when reason is applied to the experiential confrontation of man with existent things in this world; and it is the questions that the philosopher must keep alive in order to guard the truth of his own existence as well as that of his fellow-men against the construction of a Second Reality which disregards this fundamental structure of existence and pretends that the questions are illegitimate or illusionary.

Corollary I: Heidegger stresses very strongly the first of Leibniz' questions, but neglects the second one. Nor does he pay any attention to the Aristotelian argument of the final cause (to be treated presently). His fundamental ontology is based on an incomplete analysis of existence. Even at this initial stage our analysis of existence shows already its importance as an instrument for classifying Second Realities and their various techniques of construction, one of them being the omission of parts of the experience of existence.

Corollary II: The symbolism providing an answer to the questions is of secondary importance to the philosopher. That, however, is not to say that it does not have an important function in protecting the order of existence both in man and society. For the development of an answering construct, even if it should have to be revised in the light of a later, more penetrating analysis of existence, will at least guard for a time against error concerning the truth of existence. But only for a time. For the structure of existence is complicated; it is not known once for all. If it be forgotten that the answer of the construct depends for its truth on the understanding of existence that has motivated it; if it be erected into an idol valid for all time; its effect will be the very opposite of protection. For the sensed, if not clearly known, invalidity of the symbol at a later point in history will be extended by the critics of the symbol to the truth nevertheless contained in it. An obsolete symbol may have the effect of destroying the order of existence it was created to protect.

The second class of objects considered by Aristotle, more immediately our concern as political scientists, is human actions. With regard to this class the demonstration of Aristotle is more easily understood. To be sure, the analysis is cast in the form of an etiological demonstration like the others, this time concerning the final cause, but the etiological skeleton of the analysis can be more easily discounted because the generically human experience cast in the dubious form is immediately intelligible. Moreover, on occasion of the final cause the style of Aristotle changes noticeably; all of a sudden it becomes warm and incisive as if now we had reached the heart of the problem; and it becomes discursive enough to make it clear that here indeed we touch human existence at its center. The demonstration concerning the final cause, we may say, is the model demonstration; the three arguments concerning the *aitia* of things are derivative in the sense that their persuasiveness ultimately derives from the validity of the demonstration concerning the final cause. Hence, I shall quote the decisive passage: "The final cause is an end which is not for the sake of anything else, but for the sake of which everything else is. So if there is to be a last term of this kind, the process will not be infinite (*apeiron*); and if there is no such term there will be no final cause. Those who maintain an infinite series do not realize that they are destroying the very nature of the Good, although no one would try to do anything if he were not likely to reach some limit (*peras*); nor would there be reason (*nous*) in the world, for the reasonable man always acts for the sake of an end—which is a limit (*peras*)."

We must discount, as I said, the etiological language. If that is done, Aristotle insists that human action is rational, but that rationality hinges on the condition of an ultimate end. The indefinite regress from means to ends, which in their turn are means to further ends, must be cut short at some point by an ultimate end, by a *summum bonum.* The limit to the chain of means and ends is the condition of rationality in action. This in itself is true: To be sure, there would be pragmatic rationality, if a project of action adequately coordinates means toward an end, but there would be no substantive rationality in any action, if the whole network of a man's action could not be oriented toward a highest good from which such rationality radiates down to the single actions. Aristotle, however, goes farther on this occasion. Not only would the nature of the Good be destroyed without a limiting good that is no means to a further end, but there would be no reason (*nous*) in the world at large, because a man who has reason (*noun echon*) will only act for the sake of a limit-end. The limit seems to be something inherent in reason; and this qualification appears in the context of the analysis of action, betraying that here we have reached the experiential origin from which derives the argument concerning a limit also in the demonstrations concerning the knowledge of things. For the demonstrations culminating in the assumption of a prime mover do not rely ultimately on the proof that a thinker who denies the existence of a *prima causa* and assumes an infinite chain of causation will involve himself in contradictions (for there is no reason why the universe should not be unintelligible and on closer analysis should not involve the thinker in unsolvable contradictions), but on an experience that reason is indeed embedded in the order of being and it is the property of reason to have a limit. We have returned to the initial proposition concerning human existence (common to Aristotle and Aquinas) that intellect discovers itself as part of human existence. Here, in the exegesis of existence, seems to lie the critical area in which originate the propositions, advanced as self-evident, on the level of metaphysical doctrine. We must examine this problem of reason in existence once more.

Corollary: The modern reader, unless he is an expert in metaphysics, will have difficulties in understanding the Aristotelian etiology, as well as our present analysis, because the term *aition,* rendered in modern languages as *cause,* does not have the meaning of cause which the modern reader associates with it. The *aitia* have nothing to do with cause and effect in the natural sciences; they refer to a relation in the hierarchy of being that we can neutrally term "derivation." Aristotle can say for instance (*Met.* 994a3ff): "The hyletic generation of one thing from another cannot go on *ad infinitum* (e.g., flesh from earth, earth from air, air from fire, and so forth without end): nor can the kinetic causes form an endless series—man, for example, being moved by air, air by the sun, the sun by strife, and so on without limit." Obviously Aristotle's etiology is still deeply embedded in the Ionian speculation on the cosmos, which in his turn is still close to the realm of mythical symbolization. The etiology, therefore, must not be understood as having anything to do with the chain of cause and effect in time, in the modern sense. The problem of the limit belongs strictly to the analysis of existence; it has nothing to do with the infinity or createdness of the world. Aristotle himself held firmly that the world exists from infinity; his rejection of the infinite regress pertains exclusively to the hierarchy of being culminating in the prime mover. Moreover, Aquinas follows him in this issue: no philosopher, he concedes, has ever given a valid reason why the world should have a beginning in time; his conviction that the world is not infinite in time but created does not rest on philosophical argument but on faith in revelation. It should be noted that Aristotle was not emotionally upset, as far as we know, by the infinity of time; and we may wonder whether he would have been upset by the infinity of space that became acutely apparent with the development of physics and astronomy since the 16th century A.D. The question is of interest, because ever since Pascal it has become a fashion in the interpretation of modernity to acknowledge in the loss of man's position at the center of a closed cosmos one of the causes of psychic disturbance and unbalance. The interpretation of modernity would result in a quite different picture, if the infinity of time and space were experienced as disturbing because existence has lost its truth, and with its truth its balance.

In the light of the preceding analysis, which has introduced new factors into the problem of existence, we shall now make our second start, repeating first the propositions that will have to stand:

Man discovers his existence as illuminated from within by Intellect or *Nous.* Intellect is the instrument of self-interpretation as much as it is part of the structure interpreted. Existence, we said, has noetic structure. It furthermore turned out that Intellect can transcend existence in various directions in search of knowledge. These tentative formulations can now be given more precision. By virtue of the noetic structure of his existence, we may say, man discovers himself as being not a world unto himself, but an existent among others; he experiences a field of existents of which he is a part. Moreover, in discovering himself in his limitation as part in a field of existents, he discovers himself as not being the maker of this field of existents or of any part of it. Existence acquires its poignant meaning through the experience of not being self-generated but having its origin outside itself. Through illumination and transcendence, understood as properties of the Intellect or Nous, human existence thus finds itself in the situation from which the questions concerning origin and end of existence will arise.

Corollary: The preceding description seems to me more exact than Heidegger's descriptive term *Geworfenheit.* The passive *geworfen* requires a subject that does the throwing. Either the state of *Geworfenheit* must be made explicit by naming the subject, perhaps a daemonic creator in the gnostic sense; or the term must be considered methodologically defective inasmuch as it introduces an element of construction into the strictly noetic description of existence.

But where is the origin and end of existence to be found? As a preliminary to the answer we must interpret the phenomenon of questioning itself; and for this purpose we must add to illumination and transcendence two further properties of the Intellect, the properties of ideation and reasoning. Through illumination and transcendence existence has come into view as an existent thing in a field of existent things. Through the ideational property of the Intellect it is possible to generalize the discovered characteristics of existence into a nature of existence, to create an idea of existence, and to arrive at the proposition that origin and end of existence are to be found in one existent thing no more than in another. To be not the origin and end of itself is generically the nature of existent things. With this proposition we have reached the experiential basis for extensive demonstrations of both Aristotle and Aquinas that the infinite regress in search of origin can have no valid result; [the postulate of the *peras,* of the limit, is the symbolism by which both thinkers acknowledge the truth that the origin and end of existence is not to be found by ranging indefinitely over the field of existent things.] But if it is not to be found in the field of existent things, where is it to be found? To this question, Intellect, by virtue of its reasoning power, will answer that it is to be found in something beyond the field of existent things, in something to which the predicate of "existence" is applied by courtesy of analogy.

Corollary: The analysis of existence has to proceed step by step; and it has to use verbal expressions such as "illuminate," "become aware," "transcend," and so forth. The appearance of a process in time thus created, however, must not be taken for reality. The process is inherent to the analysis, not the existence. In reality all the moments of the structure, distended into analytical steps, are present at once and "known" at once in preanalytical experience. Prephilosophical wisdom has its compact expressions—such as "What comes into being must perish"—which at an intuitive glance size up the nature of existence. The analysis of existence can do no more than make explicit what everyman knows without it. That situation raises the question: to what purpose is the analysis undertaken at all—a question that will be dealt with presently in the text. And beyond this question arises the further one: to what purpose should an understanding of existence be expanded into the symbolic forms of metaphysics of the Aristotelian or Thomist type; what purpose could be served by the demonstrations of the prime mover, converted by Aquinas into proofs for the existence of God, especially since they prove nothing that is not known before the proof is undertaken? I have tried to show that the knowledge of the something that "exists" beyond existence is inherent to the noetic structure of existence. And this result is confirmed by Aristotelian and Thomist demonstrations in which the postulate of the *peras,* whenever it is formulated, is richly studded with the suspicious adverbial expressions "evidently," "obviously," "clearly," which indicate that the premise of the argument is not derived from any demonstration, but that the prime mover which emerges from the demonstration has in fact been smuggled in with the unproven premise. In search of the meaning of such demonstrations (setting aside the previously mentioned usefulness of symbols for protective and defensive functions) there seems to suggest itself the possibility that demonstrations of this type are a Myth of the Logos offered by the Intellect as a gift of veneration to the constitution of being.

At this point the analysis must stop. Any further elaboration would only obfuscate the basic structure just outlined. Hence, I shall not enter into such problems as the *via negativa,* or *via remotiva,* or *analogia entis,* which are rational instruments for arriving at clarity about the something; for all reasoning in such forms makes sense only if there is agreement on the structure of existence which requires the pursuit of its problems by such means. As in the case of the questions formulated by Leibniz, the philosopher is more interested today in the experiential structure which motivates speculation than in the answers themselves. The analysis has tried to show that the problems of transcendence, the questions of origin and end, and the postulate of the limit, are inherent to the noetic structure of existence; they are not doctrines or propositions of this or that metaphysical speculation, but precede all metaphysics; and these problems of existence cannot be abolished by discarding this or that speculation as unsatisfactory or obsolete. In an age that has good reasons to doubt the validity of large parts of classic and scholastic metaphysics, it is therefore of the first importance to disengage from the metaphysical efforts of the past the truth of existence that has motivated and informed them.

I have again used the expression "truth of existence." We can now define it as the awareness of the fundamental structure of existence together with the willingness to accept it as the *conditio humana.* Correspondingly we shall define untruth of existence as a revolt against the *conditio humana* and the attempt to overlay its reality by the construction of a Second Reality.

Corollary: The analysis of existence here offered pertains only to the structural elements that have informed the demonstrations of classic and scholastic metaphysics. It does by far not exhaust the structure of existence; large areas, as for instance historical existence, have not even been touched.

IV.

We have traced the problem of truth in reality as it appears in the strange-sounding formulations of Aquinas and Aristotle to its origin in the noetic structure of existence. We shall now resume the problem of debate as it presented itself to Aquinas.

The *Summa Contra Gentiles* defends the truth of faith against the pagans. But how can one do that, if the prospective partner to the debate will not accept argument from Scripture? Let us hear Aquinas himself on the question. It is difficult to argue the truth of faith against the Gentiles, he admits, because they do not agree with us in accepting the authority of any Scripture by which they may be convinced of their error. And then he continues: "Thus, against the Jews we are able to argue by means of the Old Testament, while against heretics we are able to argue by means of the New Testament. But the Mohammedans and Pagans accept neither the one nor the other. We must, therefore, have recourse to natural reason, to which all men are forced to give their assent."

The passage formulates succinctly the problem of debate in the 13th century and together with it, by implication the profound difference which characterizes the situation of debate in our own time. For every debate concerning the truth of specific propositions presupposes a background of unquestioned *topoi* held in common by the partners to the debate. In a debate with the Jews the unquestioned *topoi* are furnished by the Old Testament; in a debate with heretics, by the New Testament. But where do we find them in the debate with the Gentiles? It seems to me no accident when in the answer to this question Aquinas shifts from the earlier language of Intellect to the language of Reason, without further explaining the shift. We remember our analysis of existence: We had to distinguish between the various properties of Intellect, between Illumination, Transcendence, Ideation, and Reasoning. If Aquinas believes that he can rely on the power of Reason to force the assent of the Gentiles, he tacitly assumes that the reasoning of the Gentiles will operate within the same noetic structure of existence as his own—a quite justified assumption in view of the fact that the Mohammedan thinkers were the very transmitters of Aristotle to the Westerners. For obviously—that is, obviously to us—the logical operations of Intellect *qua* Reason will arrive at widely different results, if Reason has cut loose from the *conditio humana.* The unquestioned *topoi* which Thomas has in common with the Gentiles of his time, to whom he addresses his argument, so unquestioned that he does not even formulate them but can take them for granted, are the *topoi* of existence. He can justly assume that his opponents are just as much interested as he is himself in the Why and How of existence, in the questions of the nature of man, of divine nature, of the orientation of man towards his end, of just order in the actions of man and society, and so forth.

These, however, are precisely the assumptions that we can no longer make in the situation of debate in our time. Going over again the list of Aquinas, we must say that we cannot argue by the Old Testament, nor by the New Testament, nor by Reason. Not even by Reason, because rational argument presupposes the community of true existence; we are forced one step further down to cope with the opponent (even the word "debate" is difficult to apply) on the level of existential truth. The speculations of classic and scholastic metaphysics are edifices of reason erected on the experiential basis of existence in truth; they are useless in a meeting with edifices of reason erected on a different experiential basis. Nevertheless, we cannot withdraw into these edifices and let the world go by, for in that case we would be remiss in our duty of "debate." The "debate" has, therefore, to assume the forms of (1) a careful analysis of the noetic structure of existence and (2) an analysis of Second Realities, with regard to both their constructs and the motivating structure of existence in untruth. "Debate" in this form is hardly a matter of reasoning (though it remains one of the Intellect), but rather of the analysis of existence preceding rational constructions; it is medical in character in that it has to diagnose the syndromes of untrue existence and by their noetic structure to initiate, if possible, a healing process.

10/Public Opinion and the Public Interest

Public Opinion versus Popular Opinion*

Robert Nisbet

OF ALL THE HERESIES afloat in modern democracy, none is greater, more steeped in intellectual confusion, and potentially more destructive of proper governmental function than that which declares the legitimacy of government to be directly proportional to its roots in public opinion—or, more accurately, in what the daily polls and surveys assure us is public opinion. It is this heresy that accounts for the constantly augmenting propaganda that issues forth from all government agencies today—the inevitable effort to shape the very opinion that is being so assiduously courted—and for the frequent craven abdication of the responsibilities of office in the face of some real or imagined expression of opinion by the electorate.

Even worse is the manifest decline in confidence in elected government in the Western democracies, at all levels, and with this decline the erosion of governmental authority in areas where it is indispensable: foreign policy, the military, fiscal stability, and the preservation of law and order. For, as a moment's thought tells us, it is impossible for any government—consisting, after all, of those supposed to lead—to command respect and allegiance very long if it degrades its representative function through incessant inquiry into, and virtual abdication before, what is solemnly declared to be "the will of the people." But

* From *The Public Interest*, no. 41 (Fall 1975). Copyright © 1975 by National Affairs, Inc. Reprinted by permission.

what is thought or cynically announced to be the will of the people so often turns out to be no more than the opinion of special-interest advocates skilled in the techniques of contrived populism—a point I shall return to later.

The important point is that from the time representative government made its historic appearance in the 18th century, its success and possibility of survival have been seen by its principal philosophers and statesmen to depend upon a sharp distinction between representative government proper and the kind of government that becomes obedient to eruptions of popular opinion, real or false. This was of course the subject of one of Edmund Burke's greatest documents, his *Letter to the Sheriffs of Bristol*, in which he declared that those who govern, once elected, are responsible only to their own judgments, not those of the electors. Across the Atlantic an almost identical position was taken by the authors of *The Federalist* and by others arguing for acceptance of the Constitution. And in a long tradition down to the present, such minds as John Adams, John Randolph of Roanoke, Calhoun, Lincoln, Tocqueville, John Stuart Mill, Sir Henry Maine, and in our own century in this country, John Dewey, Brandeis, Cardozo, and Walter Lippmann have argued along the same line.

That a just government should rest upon the consent of the governed assuredly is as true today as it was when the Declaration of Independence was signed. Equally true is the principle that the people, when properly consulted, remain the most trustworthy source of that underlying and continuing wisdom needed when great choices have to be made—above all, choices of those representatives capable of providing leadership in political matters. But to move from these truths to the position that is now becoming so widely accepted, that opinion—of the kind that can be instantly ascertained by any poll or survey—must somehow govern, must therefore be incessantly studied, courted, flattered, and drawn upon in lieu of the judgment which true leadership alone is qualified to make in the operating details of government—this is the great heresy, and also the "fatal malady" (as Walter Lippmann called it) of modern democracies.

It is worse than heresy. It is fatuous. For always present is the assumption—nowhere propagated more assiduously than by the media which thrive on it—that there really *is* a genuine public opinion at any given moment on whatever issue may be ascendant on the national or the international scene, and that, beyond this, we know exactly how to discover this opinion. But in truth there isn't, and we don't. What the eminently wise Henry Maine wrote in *Popular Government* in 1885 still seems to be true: "*Vox Populi* may be *Vox Dei*, but very little attention shows that there never has been any agreement as to what *Vox* means or as to what *Populus* means." To these words Maine added: "The devotee of democracy is in much the same position with the Greeks and their oracles. All agreed that the voice of an oracle was the voice of a god; but everybody allowed that when he spoke he was not as intelligible as might be desired."

I do not question the fact that there is in fact public opinion and that, in the modern age at least, free, democratic government must be anchored in public opinion. There is, though, as a little reflection tells us, a substantial and crucial difference between *public* opinion, properly so called, and what, following ample precedent, I shall call *popular* opinion. The difference between the two types of opinion is directly related to the differences between the collective bodies involved. Fundamentally, this is the difference between organized community on the one hand and the mass or crowd on the other.

Communities and Transitory Majorities

A true public, as A. Lawrence Lowell stressed in his classic work on public opinion more than a half-century ago, is at bottom a community: built, like all forms of community, around certain ends held in common and also around acceptance of the means proper to achievement of these ends. Not the people in their numerical total, not a majority, nor any minority as such represents public opinion if the individuals involved do not form some kind of community, by virtue of possessing common ends, purposes, and rules of procedure. Public opinion is given its character by genuine consensus, by unifying tradition, and by what Edmund Burke called "constitutional spirit."

Popular opinion is by contrast shallow of root, a creature of the mere aggregate or crowd, rooted in fashion or fad and subject to caprice and whim, easily if tenuously formed around a single issue or personage, and lacking the kind of cement that time, tradition, and convention alone can provide. Popular opinion is an emanation of what is scarcely more than the crowd or mass, of a sandheap given quick and passing shape by whatever winds may be blowing through the marketplace at any given time. It would be incorrect to say that popular and public opinion are totally unconnected. What proves to be public opinion in a community is commonly generated by popular opinion, whether in majority or minority form; but it is only through a process of adaptation or assimilation—by the habits, values, conventions, and codes which form the fabric of the political community—that popular opinion ever becomes what we are entitled to call public opinion, the opinion that is in fact more than opinion, that is at bottom a very reflection of national character.

The distinction I am making may seem abstract to some, but it is a very real distinction and it has been so regarded by a long line of observers and students of government beginning in this country with the Founding Fathers, most profoundly with the authors of *The Federalist.* Few things seem to have mattered more to the architects of the American political community than that government should rest upon public opinion, upon public consent and affirmation. But in reading the key writings of that age, we are struck repeatedly by the seriousness of the thought that was given to the true nature of the public and the means proper to the eliciting from this public the will that would be most faithful to the actual character of the public, the character manifest in the people conceived as community—or rather as a community of smaller communities—rather than as mere mass or multitude brought into precarious and short-lived existence by some galvanizing issue or personality.

Hence the strong emphasis in the Constitution and in *The Federalist* upon the whole set of means whereby government, without being in any way severed from the will of the people, would respond to this will only as it had become refined through subjection to constitutional processes. Behind the pervasive emphasis in the Constitution upon principles of check and balance, division of power, and intermediate levels of government and administration ascending from local community through the states to the national government—principles which so many of the *philosophes* and then the Jacobins were to find unacceptable, even repugnant, in France when the Revolution burst there—lay a deep distrust of the human mind, of human nature, when it had become wrenched from the social contexts which alone can provide discipline and stability, which alone can put chains upon human appetites and make possible a liberty that does not degenerate into license.

There was, in short, no want of respect among the Founding Fathers for the wisdom of the people as the sole basis of legitimate, constitutional government. Neither, however, was there any want of recognition of the ease with which any community or society can become dissolved into, in Burke's words, "an unsocial, uncivil, unconnected chaos," with destructive passion dominant where restraint and principle ordinarily prevail. There were few if any illusions present in the minds of those responsible for the American Constitution concerning any native and incorruptible goodness of human nature or any instinctual enlightenment of the people considered abstractly. Steeped in the works of Thucydides, Aristotle, Cicero, and other classics of ancient civilization and profoundly respectful of the principles of society and government they were able to find in the writings of Locke, Montesquieu, and Burke, the Founding Fathers, and most particularly the authors of *The Federalist,* were well aware of the immense difference between the people conceived in terms of the social and moral attachments which precede political organization—which indeed must underlie it if either anarchy or despotism is to be avoided—and the people conceived in the romantic, metaphysical fashion of a Rousseau, for whom all such attachments were but so many chains upon human freedom.

From *The Federalist* through the works of such profound interpreters of the American political scene as Tocqueville, Bryce, and Lowell, down to the writings in our own time of such perceptive students of the political process as Lindsay Rogers and Walter Lippmann, there is a vivid and continuing awareness of the importance of the difference I have just described: the difference between public and mere aggregate, between the people as organized by convention and tradition into a community and the people as but a multitude, and between public opinion properly termed and opinion that is at best but a reflection of transitory majorities. It is this awareness, forming one of the most luminous intellectual traditions in American political thought, that I shall be concerned with in what follows.

Federalist Trust and Distrust

The Federalist, for the most part originally written in the form of individual letters to New York newspapers in 1787–88 by Hamilton, Madison, and Jay, is by common assent the single work in American political philosophy that can take its place among the very greatest classics in the West since the Greeks.

The unity and cogency of the work as a whole are astonishing, given the nature of its composition; so are the comprehensiveness of scope, the social and psychological insights united with political vision, and the sheer eloquence. Primarily concerned with constitutional structure and process, *The Federalist* is, among other things, a profound study of the relation of public opinion to republican government.

There is, I think, no better single insight into the *Federalist* view of the role of public opinion in government than that afforded by Number 49 of the papers. Here Madison addresses himself respectfully but negatively to the proposal, made by Jefferson, that "whenever any two of the three branches of government shall concur in opinion, each by the voices of two thirds of their whole number, that a convention is necessary for altering the constitution, or *correcting breaches of it*, a convention shall be called for the purpose."

Madison allows that there is great force in Jefferson's reasoning and that "a constitutional road to the decision of the people ought to be marked out and kept open, for certain great and extraordinary occasions." There are nevertheless, Madison writes, "insuperable objections" to Jefferson's proposal, and it is in the careful, restrained, but none the less powerful outlining of these that we acquire our clearest sense of *The Federalist* position concerning popular or public opinion.

In the first place, Madison writes, "every appeal to the people would carry an implication of some defect in the government" and "frequent appeals would deprive the government of that veneration which time bestows on everything, and without which perhaps the wisest and freest governments would not possess the requisite stability." What follows these words is central to Madison's argument and indeed to his entire political theory:

> If it be true that all governments rest on opinion, it is no less true that the strength of opinion in each individual, and its practical influence on his conduct, depend much on the number which he supposes to have entertained the same opinion. The reason of man, like man himself, is timid and cautious when left alone, and acquires firmness and confidence in proportion to the number with which it is associated. . . . In a nation of philosophers, this consider-

> ation ought to be disregarded. A reverence for the laws would be sufficiently inculcated by the voice of an enlightened reason. But a nation of philosophers is as little to be expected as the philosophical race of kings wished for by Plato.

There are two other objections Madison makes to Jefferson's proposal, both anchored in the same caution regarding the uses of public opinion. First is the serious danger of "disturbing the public tranquillity by interesting too strongly the public passions." Admittedly, we have had great success in the "revisions of our constitutions," all of which does "much honor to the virtue and intelligence" of the people. But it has to be remembered, Madison writes, that such constitution-making was at a time when manifest danger from the outside "repressed the passions most unfriendly to order and concord." Beyond this, he notes, there was the extraordinary confidence the people had then in their political leaders. We cannot, however, count on the future in this light: "The future situations in which we must expect to be usually placed, do not present any equivalent security against the danger which is apprehended."

But the greatest danger Madison foresees in any elevation of the popular will through frequent recourse to it on matters best left to the government is the unhealthy increase in legislative power, at the expense of executive and judiciary, that would inevitably follow habitual references to the people of matters of state. The legislators, Madison observes, have, by virtue of their number and their distribution in the country, as well as their "connections of blood, of friendship, and of acquaintance," a natural strength that neither the executive nor the judiciary can match: "We have seen that the tendency of republican governments is to an aggrandizement of the legislative at the expense of other departments. The appeals to the people, therefore, would usually be made by the executive and judiciary departments. But whether made by one side or the other, would each side enjoy equal advantages on the trial?"

Madison's answer is of course that they would not, that the legislators would, for the reasons just noted, tend always to outweigh the other two departments. But, he continues, even if on occasion this proved not to be the case—if, for example, the "executive power might be in the hands of a peculiar favorite of the people"—the upshot of any soliciting of popular opinion would undoubtedly be baneful. For, irrespective of where power might lie in the result, the matter would eventually turn upon not rational consideration but emotions and passions. "The *passions*, therefore, not the *reason*, of the public would sit in judgment."

How deeply Madison felt about this is attested by his repeating these arguments in *The Federalist* Number 50, where the subject is "periodical appeals to the people" rather than "occasional appeals," as in the preceding paper. Not even the institutionalization of such appeal, he thinks, would save the process from the kinds of consequences he has just described. Everything in the history of republican government suggests to Madison the ease with which issues become stripped of their rational substance and made into matters where prestige of opinion-leaders, factionalism among parties, and, not least, *passion* take command. He adduces the example of the Council of Censors which met in Pennsylvania in 1783 and 1784 to inquire into "whether the constitution had been violated." The results, Madison writes, were all that might have been expected: "Every unbiased observer may infer, without danger of mistake, and at the same time without meaning to reflect on either party, or any individuals of either party, that, unfortunately, *passion*, not *reason*, must have presided over their decisions."

Diversity and Representative Government

What shines through not merely Madison's thought but that of *The Federalist* generally is no simple, meretricious disdain for the people and its residual wisdom, no arrogation to some elite or natural aristocracy of the intelligence necessary to conduct government, but, instead, a solid conviction that *context* is vital in all situations where opinion and judgment are required. There are, as Madison and also Hamilton make plain, contexts in which reason and common sense will tend to come to the surface, but there are also contexts in which sheer emotions or, as Madison has it, passions dominate at the expense of rational thought. Everything possible, therefore, must be done to confine deliberations on government to the former contexts and to rely upon the vital principle of division of governmental power, of checks and balances, to maintain stability and freedom alike—hence *The Federalist* apprehensions concerning too easy, too frequent, and too regular submission of issues to the people.

It is impossible to catch the flavor of the political theory in *The Federalist*, and particularly its conception of the proper role of public opinion in government, without clearly understanding the view of human nature that was taken by Hamilton and his fellow authors. Here is no Rousseauan-romantic view of man born free and good, corrupted by institutions. On the contrary, what *The Federalist* offers us is a design of government for human beings who on occasion may be good, but who on occasion may also be evil, and for whom liberation from such institutions as family, local community, church, and government could only result in anarchy that must shortly lead to complete despotism. The essence of *The Federalist,* a notable scholar, Benjamin F. Wright, has written, "is that a government must be so constructed as to stand the strains that are inevitable. A government designed only for favorable circumstances would deserve to be rejected." And strains will exist, are bound to exist, so long as man remains what he is, invariably a compound of the good and the bad. One would look in vain for a spirit of pessimism or misanthropy in *The Federalist.* Its authors do not hate vices; they only recognize them. Edmund Burke, in his *Reflections on the Revolution in France*, would write of the French Revolutionists: "By hating vices too much, they come to love men too little." That can scarcely be said of the authors of *The Federalist.* The aim of government, free government, is simply that of providing institutions so strong, and also in such an equilibrial relationship, that neither calculated evil nor misspent goodness flowing from human nature could easily weaken or destroy them.

Where Rousseau, like so many of his impassioned fellow intellectuals in the salons of Paris, saw extermination of "factions" as the objective of government—and the extermination too, if possible, of all the smaller patriotisms in the social order in the interest of political legitimacy—*The Federalist* recognizes the inevitability of such factions and associations, with Madison declaring that "the latent causes of faction are . . . sown into the nature of man; and we see them everywhere brought into different degrees of activity, according to the different circumstances of civil society." There is to be expected a "landed interest," a "manufacturing interest," a "moneyed interest," and the like. Creditors and debtors, with their inevitably divergent interests, will always be with us. What Madison writes is: "The regulation of these various and interfering interests forms the principal task of modern legislation, and involves the spirit of party and faction in the necessary and ordinary operations of the government."

It is this recognition of the intrinsic and ineradicable diversity of the social and economic orders, of the pluralism of society, that leads the authors of *The Federalist* to their striking emphasis on *representative* institutions. Direct democracy is as foreign to the spirit of the *Federalist* as it is to the Constitution. In this, as in other respects, the philosophy of *The Federalist's* recommendations is utterly foreign to that philosophy of government inscribed in Rousseau's political writings and in the writings of most of the *philosophes*, which lay behind the greater part of the legislation of the French Revolution. For the French radicals (and the same is also true of Bentham and the English radicals), any thought of representation was repugnant. Representative institutions were (correctly) described by Rousseau, and castigated accordingly, as "feudal" in origin. It was, happily, Montesquieu, with his virtual reverence for "mixed" government, intermediate layers of authority, and representative bodies, who proved to be the greater influence upon the Americans.

The Intermediation of Political Authority

Montesquieu lies behind Madison's praise of political institutions as protecting society against the "diseases most incident to republican government," and behind what Madison calls "the delegation of government" to the small number of citizens elected by the rest. For pure democracy Madison has nothing but distrust: "From this view of the subject it may be concluded that a pure democracy, by which I mean a society consisting of a small number of citizens, who assemble and administer the government in person, can admit of no cure for the mischiefs of faction." Such democracies "have ever been spectacles of turbulence and contention; have ever been found incompatible with personal security or the rights of property; and have in general been as short in their lives as they have been violent in their deaths."

It is the *intermediation* of political authority, a principle that was the heart of medieval jurisprudence, as von Gierke and Maitland have told us, and that Montesquieu revived in his classic of 1748, that the authors of *The Federalist* see as vital to the proper relation of government and public opinion. Through the several ascending layers of government, local, regional, and national, it is possible "to refine and enlarge the public views, by passing them through the medium of a chosen body of citizens, whose wisdom may best discern the true interest of their country."

Accompanying *Federalist* distrust of pure democracy, and of majorities as such, is a distrust of equalitarianism. Human beings are no more equal in their opinions on governmental matters than they are in their strengths and talents: This is the evident view of the authors, particularly of Hamilton and Madison. In Number 10, written by Madison, we find explicit statement of this: "Theoretic politicians, who have patronized this species of government [i.e., equalitarian democracy], have erroneously supposed that by reducing mankind to a perfect equality in their political rights, they would, at the same time, be perfectly equalized and assimilated in their possessions, their opinions, and their passions."

Such an argument does not repudiate the Declaration of Independence. Not even Jefferson, in whom affection was probably greatest for the doctrine of natural rights, thought that any rigid deduction could be made from the phrase, "all men are created equal." Certainly Jefferson's notable plan for public education in Virginia reveals no hint of a dogmatic equalitarianism. That human beings are equal, in moral worth at least, and that they deserve equality before the law—this was no more objectionable to a Hamilton or a Madison than to a Jefferson. The respect in which Jefferson is held throughout *The Federalist* suggests that Madison and his fellow authors never thought that their rejection of equality as a social and economic dogma repudiated the spirit of the Declaration or the ideas of Jefferson—though it would be absurd to pretend that differences did not exist between Jefferson and the authors of *The Federalist.*

There is striking similarity between the fundamental ideas of *The Federalist* and those of Burke's *Reflections on the Revolution in France,* the latter published shortly after *The Federalist* letters had made their appearance in America. When Burke wrote that "those who attempt to level, never equalize" and that "the levellers . . . only change and pervert the natural order of things," he was but echoing the sentiments contained in the passage from Madison quoted above. But it is not only concerning equalitarianism that there is substantial agreement: There is common distrust of what Burke called "governmental simplicity," common recognition of the intricate nature of man and the complexity of society, common respect for public opinion but only when duly mediated by time and institution, common veneration for representative institutions and division of authority, and common apprehension concerning mere numerical majorities, so prone, as both Madison and Burke knew, to the rise of despotism.

Tocqueville and the Tyranny of the Majority

Similarly, there is affinity between *The Federalist* and Tocqueville's *Democracy in America*, especially the first part, which is concerned with political institutions. We know that Tocqueville admired *The Federalist,* particularly Madison's contributions. He read the book while on his nine-month visit to this country and later with studious concentration after he had returned to Paris, and most of his interviews in this country seem to have been with Americans of definitely Federalist persuasion. Tocqueville's book is in a great many respects the child of a union effected between his French-derived interest in the democratic revolution of the early 19th century and his American-derived respect for the kind of political structures and processes which *The Federalist* had advocated in its defense of the American Constitution. For Tocqueville, as for Madison, Hamilton, and Jay, the principles of decentralization of administration, of political pluralism, regionalism, and localism, and of division of power and institutional checks upon and balances of power are fundamental to and constituent of free republican government.

So is there fundamental likeness between *The Federalist* and *Democracy in America* on the role of public opinion and on the dangers which lie in direct, popular government unmediated by the representative, deliberative bodies prescribed by the Constitution. Nearly a half-century separates the America of *The Federalist* papers from the America Tocqueville and his friend Beaumont visited in 1831. Great changes had taken place. What had been prospect for the Founding Fathers was by now reality, and as Tocqueville's *Notebooks* make clear, there was not the slightest doubt among the Americans he talked with that America's future was a secure one. It would be hard to exaggerate the buoyancy of mind, the confidence, even at times the complacency, above all the spirit of manifest progress that existed in the Age of Jackson, so far as Tocqueville's observations are concerned. And yet, hovering over all of Tocqueville's impressions and reflections on the American scene, is his concern with, his apprehensions about, the power exerted by the majority in American society, the fetters which he thought were placed upon genuine individuality by public or majority opinion.[1]

Nowhere, he writes, does public opinion rule as in the United States. There is a revealing entry, under date of October 25, 1831, in the *Notebooks*: " 'The people is always right,' that is the dogma of the republic, just as 'the king can do no wrong' is the religion of monarchic states. It is a great question to decide whether the one is more important than the other; but what is sure is that neither the one nor the other is true."

As Bryce was to point out, correctly, I believe, Tocqueville exaggerated the degree of dominance by the majority in the United States that he visited, and he did not in any event ever distinguish between what he called "public opinion" and the ascendancy of the majority on a given matter. Beyond this, as political events and personages, and also literary and artistic productions within a decade or two after Tocqueville's visit, were to make incontestably clear, there was evidently not nearly the suffocating effect upon individuality in America that Tocqueville ascribes repeatedly to the majority, and (in the second part of his book) to equality. Nevertheless, Tocqueville's views on the majority are as important to us in our day as those on equality:

> When an individual or a party is wronged in the United States, to whom can he apply for redress? If to public opinion, public opinion constitutes the majority; if to the legislature, it represents the majority and implicitly obeys it; if to the executive power, it is appointed by the majority and serves as a passive tool

[1] It will always be a matter of debate among Tocqueville scholars as to the exact proportions of the influence exerted on his mind by preoccupation with France, especially with the circumstances under which Louis Philippe had been elevated to the throne in 1830, and the influence exerted by actual experience in the United States during his short visit. As many a reviewer noted at the time, so often when Tocqueville writes "America," his eye seems to be actually on France. Nevertheless, the book, especially the first part, is about American society, and I shall treat it here in that light.

in its hands. The public force consists of the majority under arms. . . . However iniquitous or absurd the measure of which you complain, you must submit to it as well as you can.

So impressed by and apprehensive of the majority is Tocqueville that he even compares its power to that of the Spanish Inquisition, noting that whereas the Inquisition had never been able to prevent large numbers of antireligious books from circulating in Spain, "the empire of the majority succeeds much better in the United States, since it actually removes any wish to publish them." In the United States no one is actually punished for reading this kind of book, "but no one is induced to write them; not because all the citizens are immaculate in conduct, but because the majority of the community is decent and orderly."

Individuality and American Society

It is in this context that Tocqueville utters one of his most frequently quoted observations: "I know of no country in which there is so little independence of mind and real freedom of discussion as in America." So great, he thought, was the influence of the majority's opinion upon the individual mind that the number of genuinely great or creative human beings was bound to diminish in the ages ahead. The first great generation of political leaders in the United States had, after all, been a product of different, even aristocratic, contexts. Moreover, "public opinion then served, not to tyrannize over, but to direct the exertions of individuals." Very different, Tocqueville thinks, are present circumstances. "In that immense crowd which throngs the avenues to power in the United States, I found very few men who displayed that manly candor and masculine independence of opinion which frequently distinguished the Americans of former times, and which constitutes the leading feature in distinguished characters wherever they may be found."

The effect of the majority is not merely to tyrannize the individual but also to diminish him. In the presence of the majority, Tocqueville observes, the individual "is overwhelmed by the feeling of his own insignificance and impotence." From the *Notebooks* it is evident that Tocqueville was genuinely distressed by his own observations, and by what was reported to him, of instances in which individual dissent, or, for that matter, even individual act, even though protected thoroughly by law, could be stifled by majority opinion. He refers to "the fury of the public" directed at a man in Baltimore who happened to oppose the War of 1812, and there is a long account of an interview with a white American (the gist of which went into a footnote in *Democracy in America*) on the failure of black freedmen in a Northern city to vote in a given election—the upshot of which, Tocqueville concludes, is that although the laws permit, majority opinion deprives. The majority thus claims the right of making the laws and of breaking them as well: "If ever the free institutions of America are destroyed, that event may be attributed to the omnipotence of the majority, which may at some future time urge the minorites to desperation and oblige them to have recourse to physical force. Anarchy will then be the result, but it will have been brought about by despotism."

Immediately after this passage comes a long, fully appreciative, and respectful quotation from Madison's Number 51 of *The Federalist,* in which the argument is that while it is of great importance to guard a society against the oppression of its rulers, it is equally important to "guard one part of the society against the injustice of the other part."

And yet, with all emphasis upon Tocqueville's apprehensions concerning individuality and freedom in American society as the result of majority opinion, we are also obliged to emphasize the sections of his work which deal with "the causes which mitigate the tyranny of the majority in the United States." He cites the absence of centralized administration, the presence of the frontier which made it possible for individuals to escape the conformities pressed upon them, the still vigorous regionalism and localism of American society, the checks which executive and judiciary exert upon the majority-dominated Congress, the ascendancy of the legal profession,[2] the institution of trial by

[2] " . . . Some of the tastes and the habits of the aristocracy may be . . . discovered in the characters of lawyers" and "in all free governments, of whatever form they may be, members of the legal profession will be found in the front ranks of all parties. The same remark is also applicable to the aristocracy."

jury, and, in many ways most important for Tocqueville, the unlimited freedom of association. The latter, both in its political form of party and its civil form of interest-group, can be counted upon. Tocqueville thinks, so long as the principle remains vital, to protect individuals from the majority and the kind of government majorities seek to create.

Tocqueville was not, in sum, wholly pessimistic about the United States. He refers to it in the final pages of the first volume as the freest and most prosperous people on earth, destined to achieve a commercial and military supremacy in the distant future that will be rivaled, he writes, only by Russia. How deeply this admiration for American political institutions lay in Tocqueville's mind is evidenced by the fact that in 1848—a tormenting year for him in French politics—when he wrote a new preface to the 12th edition of *Democracy in America,* he repeated and even added to the laudatory remarks earlier written in the final sections of the first volume. If Tocqueville himself was little read after about 1880 (the present Tocqueville revival did not begin until the late 1930s), the reason is in some part that the greatness he himself had been among the first to see in American political institutions was the subject of so many works written by Americans themselves that Tocqueville's own book tended to become lost, to seem dated, even inadequate.

Bryce and the Dominance of the Majority

There was another classic on American government that made its appearance in 1888, at the very height of American belief in American greatness. It is doubtful that Lord Bryce's *The American Commonwealth* will ever undergo the revival Tocqueville has known in our own age, but this is in considerable degree the consequence of the very virtues of Bryce's study. It is fair to say, taking both writers in their roles as analysts of the American political scene, that so far as our own attention to Bryce is concerned, he suffers from his virtues, just as Tocqueville prospers from his defects. Bryce's command of the details of American government and its surrounding society is far superior to Tocqueville's, but it is this very command that today makes him seem dated. Tocqueville's defects of observation are only too well known, but they are offset by abstract reflections, often at the level of genius, on democracy *sub specie aeternitatis.* Fewer such reflections are to be found in Bryce, and Woodrow

Wilson, then still a professor, was right in declaring them inferior to Tocqueville's. All the same, there is a significant amount of political theory or philosophy in Bryce, not least on the subject of public opinion.

Bryce's America is of course a vastly different one from that Tocqueville and Beaumont had travelled through 60 years before. The Civil War, the eruption of corporate capitalism, the unbroken expansion to the Pacific, the mushrooming of towns and cities, the development of the two large political parties and their machines, the whole public education movement, the establishment of colleges and universities everywhere in the country, the explosion of newspapers (some of great power), the spirit of nationalism, and, not least, the rise of America as a recognized world power—all of this made any treatment of American democracy in the 1880s necessarily different from anything possible in the Age of Jackson.

There are nevertheless interesting continuities to be seen in Bryce which reach back through Tocqueville to Hamilton and the other authors of *The Federalist,* a work that Bryce clearly admires as greatly as Tocqueville did. For Hamilton, Bryce reserved words of sheer eulogy, giving him status along with Burke, Fox, Pitt, Stein, von Humboldt, Napoleon, and Talleyraud as one among the greatest group of statesmen any single period of Western history has ever come up with. But his appreciation of the other authors of *The Federalist* is scarcely less, and the same holds for the principles which brought that volume into being.

What Bryce adds to *The Federalist* and to Tocqueville on the subject of public opinion is, first, a degree of systematic analysis in strictly scholarly style that public opinion as a concept had not had before, and second, a number of distinctions which we would not expect to find in the earlier works and which, so far as I can see, laid the essential ground on which all subsequent studies of American public opinion have been made. The section, 12 chapters in length, that Bryce gives us would have been worthy even then of separate publication, and I frankly don't think we have reached the point even yet in our knowledge of the subject that would make the reading of Bryce superfluous.

"In no country is public opinion so powerful as in the United States; in no country can it be so well studied." These opening words are followed by an inquiry into the nature of public opinion, its relation to government in earlier times and other countries, and then by a series of chapters on opinion, majority, processes of diffusion, and controlling influences upon opinion as these are to be found in the United States. In words which distinctly resemble those Walter Lippmann wrote a generation later on "stereotypes," Bryce tells us: "Everyone is of course predisposed to see things in some one particular light by his previous education, habits of mind, accepted dogmas, religious or social affinities, notions of his own personal interest. No event, no speech or article, ever falls upon a perfectly virgin soil: The reader or listener is always more or less biased already." Orthodox political theory, Bryce observes, assumes that every citizen has or ought to have "thought out for himself certain opinions. . . . But one need only try the experiment of talking to that representative of public opinion whom the Americans call the 'man in the cars' to realize how uniform opinion is among all classes of the people."

Yet Bryce, unlike Tocqueville, finds no tyranny of a majority. We may, he suggests, look for evidences of this tyranny in three places: Congress, the statutes of the states, and in the sentiments and actions of public opinion outside the law. But in none, he concludes, is there in fact manifestation of the dominance of the majority. Too many checks exist upon this majority in all three spheres. Bryce is skeptical indeed that such majority tyranny existed in America even in Tocqueville's day, noting dryly the great efflorescence of individuality in so many sectors of American life shortly after Tocqueville's visit.

But, Bryce continues, even if we assume that such majority tyranny did in fact exist in Tocqueville's America, a great many things have happened to check or disperse it. When Tocqueville visited the United States, the nation "was in the heyday of its youthful strength, flushed with self-confidence, intoxicated with the exuberance of its own freedom. . . . The anarchic teachings of Jefferson had borne fruit. Administration and legislation, hitherto left to the educated classes, had been seized by the rude hands of men of low social position and scanty knowledge."

Very different, Bryce writes, is the America of the 1880s. The dark and agonizing issue of slavery has been removed through the Civil War—an event, Bryce believes, that purged the American nation of many issues on which ruthless majorities were willing to ride roughshod over the rights of individuals and minorities during the years leading up to the war: "The years which have passed since the war have been years of immensely extended and popularized culture and enlightenment. Bigotry in religion and everything else has broken down." He continues: "If social persecution exists in the America of today, it is only in a few dark corners. One may travel all over the North and the West, mingling with all classes . . . without hearing of it."

In no respect, Bryce observes, is there to be found in America the kinds of violence or repression against unpopular opinions which one still finds in Ireland, France, and Great Britain. On balance, Bryce believes in the first place that Tocqueville had misperceived the nature of majority, and had greatly underestimated the authentic willingness of minorities to submerge themselves and their views in a national consensus, and in the second place that a signal change had taken place in America and, with this, in the whole structure of public opinion.

The "Fatalism of the Multitude"

In one respect, however, Bryce can be seen as almost a pure reflection of Tocqueville, and that is in his notable chapter on "the fatalism of the multitude." It is this fatalism—one found, Bryce argues, in all large populations characterized by "complete political and social equality"—that Tocqueville and others have confused with "tyranny of the majority." As the result of such fatalism (we would today describe it in the language of mass conformity), individuals and groups are led to acquiesce in numbers, to abandon personal and sectarian beliefs for the sheer relief of participating in the special kind of community and of power that great, undifferentiated masses represent: "This tendency to acquiescence and submission, this sense of the insignificance of individual effort, this belief that the affairs of men are swayed by large forces whose movement may be studied but cannot be turned, I have ventured to call the Fatalism of the Multitude."

Anyone who knows Tocqueville will recognize instantly that Bryce's "Fatalism of the Multitude" is indeed different from what Tocqueville had called "tyranny of the majority" in the first part of *Democracy in America.* But it is not different from, it is almost pure reflection of, the social mass—undifferentiated, monotonous, enveloping, and uniform—that Tocqueville describes in such detail in the second part of his work, the part that is devoted to equality rather than the majority. If it had been the majority in the first part that had, for Tocqueville, extinguished individuality, it is equality in the second. And in this he and Bryce are in close accord. But like Tocqueville, Bryce finds in America a large number of forces—among others, localism, regionalism, voluntary association, faith in institutions and also in the future of the country, and persisting freedom of discussion, all factors that Tocqueville had cited—which moderate this fatalism of the multitude, this inclination of mass populations to favor uniformity and the resultant sterilization of individuality.

These are the forces too which, in Bryce's judgment, give some degree of security to bona fide public opinion and its necessarily slow and deliberate spread through American society—security against the effects of suddenly formed movements and crusades. Bryce was deeply impressed by the still regnant localism and regionalism of opinion in the America of his day—the existence of, say, a profound antipathy in California toward Orientals that most of the rest of the country could only regard as bizarre, to say the least. But he was also struck by the long-run tendency of localisms and regionalisms of opinion to become fused, the elements in common to become the real stuff of American public opinion, which he did not doubt could become powerful:

> So tremendous a force would be dangerous if it moved rashly. Acting over and gathered from an enormous area, in which there exist many local differences, it needs time, often a long time, to become conscious of the preponderance of one set of tendencies over another. The elements of both local difference and of class difference must (so to speak) be well shaken up together and each part brought into contact with the rest, before the mixed liquid can produce a precipitate in the form of a practical conclusion.

Lowell and the Political Community

It was left to A. Lawrence Lowell, writing 20 years later at Harvard, to develop a crucial point that neither Tocqueville nor Bryce had given emphasis or focus to: the necessity of a genuine *political community,* and with this of a clearly perceived *public interest,* as the context of public opinion worthy of the name.

Lowell's *Public Opinion and Popular Government,* published in 1913, is somewhat neglected these days—which is a pity, for its essential themes remain highly pertinent. The book is, so far as I am aware, the first systematic treatise on public opinion, the first to lift the subject from the ancillary if important position it has in the works of Tocqueville, Bryce, and A. V. Dicey's slightly earlier work on law and opinion in 19th-century England, and to give it a virtually prior role in the study of the governmental process. Written more or less as a textbook, Lowell's work is actually a scholarly, ground-breaking inquiry fully the equal in intellectual substance of his more famous, earlier study of English political institutions. It is this work that makes explicit the distinction I have used in this essay between public and popular, or merely majority, opinion.

It is not strange, taking the historical context into consideration, that Lowell should have made the political community a paramount consideration, for the American of his day had become increasingly torn by economic, class, regional, and ethnic interests which were being translated into political expression. Many of the voices generated by the passage of America from a predominantly agricultural to an industrial society, and by an economic system that could seem to a great many participants and observers to be in the hands of the great trusts and monopolies, were by Lowell's time becoming clamant. Populism, Progressivism, an increasingly active labor movement, socialism—at least in tractarian form, and here and there in organizational shape—and an increasingly reform-oriented Democratic Party were among the realities of Lowell's day. Woodrow Wilson, after all, had been elected on a platform of "The New Freedom" the year before Lowell's book appeared. That period of Good Feeling which Bryce had been so struck by in the period from the 1870s to the 1890s seemed suddenly to be ending, its place taken by one in which strife between parties, classes, and sections of the country over such matters as control of wealth and property, tariffs, workmen's wage and hour and safety laws, direct tax on income, and a host of others, could appear almost endemic. This was also the period in which a variety of proposals for direct, popular democracy were becoming law in many parts of the United States: the initiative, the referendum, and the recall among other such innovations.

It is impossible to miss in Lowell's book, its scholarship and objectivity notwithstanding, an undercurrent of deep concern that *public opinion,* rooted in the people as genuine national community, generated by deeply held convictions and sentiments, and forming the necessary substratum of any free, representative government, would become confused with and blurred by mere *popular opinion,* the kind of so-called collective opinion that can be had from any person on any subject, however complex or remote, merely by the asking. The following passage from Lowell might well have been written by one of the authors of *The Federalist:*

> A body of men are politically capable of public opinion only so far as they are agreed upon the ends and aims of government and upon the principles by which those ends shall be attained. They must be united, also, about the means whereby the action of the government is to be determined, in a conviction, for example, that the views of a majority—or it may be some other portion of their numbers—ought to prevail; and a political community as a whole is capable of public opinion only when this is true of the great bulk of the citizens.

Communities and Legitimate Majorities

Lowell is the first to define specifically the public, properly so called, as a community, one consisting—as does any form of community—of common values, ends, and acceptance of means, and endowed with the capacity to create a sense of membership and to generate belief in the reality of common or public interest. Such opinion is rooted, Lowell stresses, not simply in political motivations alone but in the lives of individuals as revealed in the full gamut of social, economic, and moral existence. Whatever may be the origin of a given expression of public opinion—in the ideology of a minority, a single party or even sect, or in even the presence of a signal personage—its reality and ultimate power as public opinion take shape only through assimilative processes whereby belief or conviction becomes bred into family, neighborhood, religion, job, and the other contexts of individual life and thought. At any given moment there may be dozens, hundreds, of popular impressions or sentiments, all capable of being voiced by one or another interest or ideology. But few of these ever become transposed into the substance of genuine public opinion. For that, time and also historical circumstance are required.

Lowell is particularly concerned with stressing the difference between a public and a mere majority. "When two highwaymen meet a belated traveller on a dark road and propose to relieve him of his watch and wallet, it would clearly be an abuse of terms to say that in the assemblage on that lonely spot there was a public opinion in favor of a redistribution of property." Lowell's example is a homely one, but it is given enlarged and pertinent significance just afterward in some words aimed at the political state: "May this not be equally true under organized government, among people that are for certain purposes a community?" In sum, a majority of voters is easily imaginable in support of redistribution of property in society or of any of a large number of proposals affecting the very social and economic base of human life. It does not follow, however, from Lowell's point of view, that such a majority necessarily reflects public opinion. For him public opinion is limited, as it was indeed for *The Federalist,* to expressions of views relating to a community and to the purposes for which the community is founded. There are legitimate and illegitimate majorities so far as the state is concerned. And a great deal that passes for "public opinion" in the judgments of interested individuals may be, and often is, no more than "popular opinion," something, as we have seen, inherently more superficial, ephemeral, and transitory.

True public opinion, Lowell adds, in words taken from his contemporary, Arthur Hadley, is composed of beliefs a man is prepared "to maintain at his own cost," not simply "at another's cost." For any of us there is a wide range of matters on which, if pressed, we are willing to vouchsafe a "yes," "no," or "maybe": matters often extending into the most recondite and specialized realms of knowledge or experience. But the only judgments which really count, so far as genuine belief—individual or public—is concerned, are those which are, in Justice Holmes's words, "out of experience and under the spur of responsibility." These are, in the aggregate, public opinion, and—alas, for analytical purposes—are not commonly worn on the sleeve, not easily given verbal expression on the spur of the moment, least of all in simple affirmatives and negatives. "Habits of the heart," Tocqueville had called them; and they are precisely what Burke earlier had epitomized in the word "prejudice," with what Burke called its "latent wisdom," which engages the mind "in a steady course of wisdom and virtue, and does not leave the man hesitating in a moment of decision, skeptical, puzzled, and unresolved."

Lowell was clearly troubled by the problem of ascertaining public opinion in advance of its expression through regular, legitimate political processes. There are, as he notes, individual leaders in politics with superior gifts in this respect; they are the stuff of which the Washingtons and Lincolns are made. But Lowell is no more confident than either Bryce or Dicey, or Maine in his *Popular Government* had been that there exists, or even can exist, any quick and certain means of finding one's way to public—in contrast to ordinary popular—opinion. Polls and surveys did not exist in Lowell's day, but I think it evident, reading him carefully at the present time, that he would have been at least as skeptical of these as a few later students, notably Lindsay Rogers in his classic *The Pollsters,* published in 1949, have been. I do not doubt that Lowell would have approved of Rogers words: "So far as the pollers of public opinion are concerned, the light they have been following is a will-o'-the-wisp. They have been taking in each other's washing, and have been using statistics in terms of the Frenchman's definition: a means of being precise about matters of which you will remain ignorant."

Lowell knew, as had Hamilton and Madison, as had Tocqueville and Bryce, that language as often conceals as it communicates. Hence the untrustworthiness, or at least the precariousness, of verbalized responses to verbalized questions concerning matters of profoundest moral, social, and political significance. We have all been struck by the shifting character of response to persisting issues as revealed in polls. But without trying to consecrate *public* opinion, I think it fair to say that this shifting, kaleidoscopic character is in fact one aspect of *popular* opinion, as mercurial in nature as the fashions, fads, and foibles which compose it. By the very virtue of its superficiality, its topical and *ad hoc* character, popular opinion lends itself to facile expression, in the polls as well as in drawing rooms and taverns, and hence, as is the case with all fashions, to quick and often contradictory change. Very different is public opinion: It changes, to be sure, as the history of the great moral and political issues in America and other nations makes evident. But change in public opinion tends to be slow, often agonizing, and—in the deepest realms of conviction—rare. The greatest political leaders in history have known this; hence their success in enterprises which, on the basis of soundings of merely popular opinion, might have seemed suicidal.

"Public Interest Populism"

It is the ease with which popular opinion can be confused with public opinion that accounts in substantial degree for not only the polls in American public life but also the great power of the media. The impact, the frequently determining influence of television commentators, newspaper editors, reporters, and columnists upon individual opinions is not to be doubted. In the scores of topics and issues dealt with by the media daily, the shaping, or at least conditioning, effect of the media is apparent, certainly so far as popular opinion is concerned. In this fact lies, however, a consequence that would not, a couple of decades ago, have been anticipated by very many makers of opinion in America: the rising disaffection with, even hatred of, the media in public quarters where, though the matter may not be given verbal articulation, it is believed that the media are flouting, not reflecting, *public* opinion. There should be for a long time an instructive lesson in the overnight conversion of Spiro Agnew (before the fall) from nonentity to near-hero as the result of sudden and repeated attacks upon the media, particularly television. How do we explain the fact that a medium to which tens of millions of people are drawn magnetically night after night, one that manifestly has a conditioning effect upon national thought and behavior, should face wells of potential hostility in the public, a hostility only too easily drawn upon by the right kind of political presence? Only, I suggest, through distinction between popular opinion and public opinion, difficult as this distinction may be to identify in concrete cases.

There is also what Irving Kristol has admirably described as "public interest populism," a phenomenon also, I suggest, to be accounted for in terms of popular opinion. Such populism can, as we have learned, be utterly at odds with the sentiments of large majorities, and yet, through the always available channels of popular opinion—newspapers and television, preeminently—take on striking force in the shaping of public policy. In only the remotest and most tenuous fashion, it indeed at all, does the uproar about the C.I.A., or Congress' acceptance of the H.E.W. ban on single-sex physical education classes accord with the fundamental values of American public opinion. Given, however, the variety and ingenuity of means whereby a popular opinion can be created overnight, given credence by editorial writers, columnists, and television commentators, and acquire the position of a kind of superstructure over genuine public opinion, it has not proved very difficult for a point of view to assume a degree of political strength that scarcely would have been possible before the advent of the media in their present enormous power.

A great deal of the recent turning of literally thousands of college students to law schools can be explained precisely in terms of this "public interest populism." The Warren Court first, then the judiciary as a whole, have proved to be often fertile contexts for the achievement of ends, some of them revolutionary in implication, which almost certainly would not have been achieved had they been obliged to wait for changes in American public opinion expressed through constitutional legislative and executive bodies. Mandated busing for ethnic quotas will serve for a long time as the archetype of this peculiar kind of populism. The Founding Fathers thought, and accordingly feared, legislatures in this light. We have learned, though, that the executive and the judiciary can only too easily become settings of actions which run against the grain of public opinion.

Walter Lippmann and "The Public Philosophy"

It is useful to conclude this essay by reference to a work that deserved better than its fate in the hands of most of its reviewers when it was published in 1955: Lippmann's *The Public Philosophy.* The author's interest in the subject of public opinion was doubtless generated while a student in Lowell's Harvard. His epochal *Public Opinion,* which came out in 1922, has many points of similarity with Lowell's own views and also those of Bryce. To this day, Lippmann's *Public Opinion* remains the best known and most widely read single book on the subject. Whatever may be its roots in earlier thinking, it possesses a striking originality and cogency. Even with all that has mushroomed since the 1930s in the field of the study of public opinion, Lippmann's work of half a century ago continues to offer a valuable insight into the nature and sources of public opinion in the democracies.

Even so, I prefer to deal here with Lippmann's later work, *The Public Philosophy,* for it is here, to a degree not present in the more analytical and discursive *Public Opinion,* that we find this eminent journalist-philosopher reviving and giving pertinence to the tradition that began with *The Federalist,* and that has such exemplary statements in the other works I have mentioned. I would not argue that the book is without flaw, chiefly in the difficult enterprise of trying to describe precisely and concretely the public and its genuine manifestations. But such flaws apart, it is a profound and also courageous restatement of a point of view regarding representative government that began with such minds as Burke and Madison.

"The people," Lippmann writes in words reminiscent of the apprehensions of *The Federalist,* "have acquired power which they are incapable of exercising, and the governments they elect have lost powers which they must recover if they are to govern." What, we ask, are the legitimate boundaries of the people's power? Again it could be Hamilton or Madison rather than Lippmann responding: "The answer cannot be simple. But for a rough beginning let us say that the people are able to give, and to withhold, their consent to being governed—their consent to what the government asks of them, proposes to them, and has done in the conduct of their affairs. They can elect the government. They can remove it. They can approve or disapprove of its performance. But they cannot administer the government. They cannot themselves perform."

Lippmann draws a distinction respecting the public, or people, that has been present in Western thought since the very beginning of the tradition I have been concerned with. It is the distinction between the people as mere multitude or mass, a sandheap of electoral particles, and, to use Lippmann's phrasing, "*The People* as a historic community":

> It is often assumed, but without warrant, that the opinions of The People as voters can be treated as the expression of *The People* as a historic community. The crucial problem of modern democracy arises from the fact that this assumption is false. The voters cannot be relied upon to represent *The People*. . . . Because of the discrepancy between The People as voters and *The People* as the corporate nation, the voters have no title to consider themselves as the pro-

> prietors of the commonwealth and to claim that their interests are identical with the public interest. A prevailing plurality of the voters are not *The People.*

It is easy enough to caricature that statement and to draw from it a variety of uses, some without doubt immoral and despotic in character. In politics as in religion and elsewhere, many a leader has at times justified arbitrary and harsh rule by recourse to something along the line of what Lippmann calls "*The People,*" the people, that is, as an historic, tradition-anchored, and "corporate" nation rather than as the whole or a majority of actual, living voters. None of this is to be doubted. And yet, however difficult to phrase, however ambiguous in concrete circumstance, the distinction may be—it is, I would argue—a vital one if, on the one hand, liberty is to be made secure and, on the other hand, the just authority of government is to be made equally secure.

In truth, Lippmann's distinction is but a restatement of the core of an intellectual tradition going back at very least to Burke's famous description of political society as a contract between the dead, the living, and the unborn. That description too was capable, as Tom Paine made evident, of being pilloried and mocked, of being declared a mere verbal mask for opposition to all change or a rationalization of government policy flouting the interests of the governed. And yet it is, as is Lippmann's, a valid, even vital, distinction, one that lies at the heart of a philosophy—so often termed "conservative," though it is in fact liberal—which in the 20th century, under whatever name, we have discovered to be the only real alternative to the kinds of awful power which are contained in "people's governments" or are, in our own country, hinted at in declared programs of "common cause" populism. The distinction which Burke and Lippmann make between the two conceptions of "the people" is fundamental in a line of 19th and 20th century thought that includes Coleridge, Southey, John Stuart Mill, Maine, Tocqueville, Burckhardt, Weber, and, in our own day, Hannah Arendt, Bertrand de Jouvenel, and Jacques Ellul. Basically, it is a distinction between constituted society and the kind of aggregate that, history tells us, threatens to break through the interstices of the social bond in all times of crisis, the aggregate we call the mass or crowd, always oscillating between anarchic and military forms of despotism.

Paralleling this distinction between the two conceptions of the people is the distinction, as I have tried to show here, between public opinion and what I have called popular opinion. The one distinction is as pertinent to present reality as the other. We live, plainly, in a kind of twilight age of government, one in which the loss of confidence in political institutions is matched by the erosion of traditional authority in kinship, locality, culture, language, school, and other elements of the social fabric. The kind of mass populism, tinctured by an incessant search for the redeeming political personage, where militarism and humanitarianism become but two faces of the same coin, and where the quest for centralized power is unremitting, is very much with us. More and more it becomes difficult to determine what is genuinely public opinion, the opinion of the people organized into a constitutional political community, and what is only popular opinion, the kind that is so easily exploited by self-appointed tribunes of the people, by populist demagogues, and by all too many agencies of the media. The recovery of true public opinion in our age will not be easy, but along with the recovery of social and cultural authority and of the proper authority of political government in the cities and the nation, it is without question among the sovereign necessities of the rest of this century.

The Public Interest*

Walter Lippmann

What Is the Public Interest?

We are examining the question of how, and by whom, the interest of an invisible community over a long span of time is represented in the practical work of governing a modern state.

In ordinary circumstances voters cannot be expected to transcend their particular, localized and self-regarding opinions. As well expect men laboring in the valley to see the land as from a mountain top. In their circumstances, which as private persons they cannot readily surmount, the voters are most likely to suppose that whatever seems obviously good to them must be good for the country, and good in the sight of God.

I am far from implying that the voters are not entitled to the representation of their particular opinions and interests. But their opinions and interests should be taken for what they are and for no more. They are not—as such—propositions in the public interest. Beyond their being, if they are genuine, a true report of what various groups of voters are thinking, they have no intrinsic authority. The Gallup polls are reports of what people are thinking. But that a plurality of the people sampled in the poll think one way has no bearing upon whether it is sound public policy. For their opportunities of judging great issues are in the very nature of things limited, and the statistical sum of their opinions is not the final verdict on an issue. It is, rather, the beginning of the argument. In that argument their opinions need to be confronted by the views of the executive, defending

* From *Essays in The Public Philosophy* (Boston and Toronto: Little, Brown and Co.). Copyright © 1955 by Walter Lippmann. Reprinted by permission.

and promoting the public interest. In the accommodation reached between the two views lies practical public policy.

Let us ask ourselves, How is the public interest discerned and judged? From what we have been saying we know that we cannot answer the question by attempting to forecast what the invisible community, with all its unborn constituents, will, would, or might say if and when it ever had a chance to vote. There is no point in toying with any notion of an imaginary plebiscite to discover the public interest. We cannot know what we ourselves will be thinking five years hence, much less what infants now in the cradle will be thinking when they go into the polling booth.

Yet their interests, as we observe them today, are within the public interest. Living adults share, we must believe, the same public interest. For them, however, the public interest is mixed with, and is often at odds with, their private and special interests. Put this way, we can say, I suggest, that the public interest may be presumed to be what men would choose if they saw clearly, thought rationally, acted disinterestedly and benevolently.

The Equations of Reality

A rational man acting in the real world may be defined as one who decides where he will strike a balance between what he desires and what can be done. It is only in imaginary worlds that we can do whatever we wish. In the real world there are always equations which have to be adjusted between the possible and the desired. Within limits, a man can make a free choice as to where he will strike the balance. If he makes his living by doing piecework, he can choose to work harder and to spend more. He can also choose to work less and to spend less. But he cannot spend more and work less.

Reality confronts us in practical affairs as a long and intricate series of equations. What we are likely to call "facts of life" are the accounts, the budgets, the orders of battle, the election returns. Sometimes, but not always, the two sides of the equations can be expressed quantitatively in terms of money, as supply and demand, as income and outgo, assets and liabilities, as exports and imports. Valid choices are limited to the question of where, not whether, the opposing terms of the equation are to be brought into equilibrium. For there is always a reckoning.

In public life, for example, the budget may be balanced by reducing expenditures to the revenue from taxes; by raising taxes to meet the expenditures, or by a combination of the two, by borrowing, or by grants in aid from other governments, or by fiat credit, or by a combination of them. In one way or another the budget is in fact always balanced. The true nature of the reckoning would be clearer if, instead of talking about "an unbalanced budget," we spoke of a budget balanced not by taxes but by borrowing, of a budget balanced by inflation, or of a budget balanced by subsidy. A government which cannot raise enough money by taxes, loans, foreign grants, or by getting its fiat money accepted, will be unable to meet its bills and to pay the salaries of its employees. In bankruptcy an involuntary balance is struck for the bankrupt. He is forced to balance his accounts by reducing his expenditures to the level of his income.

Within limits, which public men have to bear in mind, the choices as to where to balance the budget are open. In making these choices, new equations confront them. Granted that it is possible to bring the budget into balance by raising taxes, how far can taxes be raised? Somewhat but not ad infinitum. There are no fixed criteria. But though we are unable to express all the equations quantitatively, this does not relieve us of the necessity of balancing the equations. There will be a reckoning. Practical judgment requires an informed guess: what will the taxpayers accept readily, what will they accept with grumbling but with no worse, what will arouse them to resistance and to evasion? How will the taxpayers react to the different levels of taxes if it is a time of peace, a time of war, a time of cold war, a time of social and economic disturbance, and so on? Although the various propositions cannot be reduced to precise figures, prudent men make estimates as to where the equations balance.

Their decisions as to where to balance the accounts must reflect other judgments—as to what, for example, are the military requirements in relation to foreign affairs; what is the phase of the business cycle in relation to the needs for increased or decreased demand; what is the condition of the international monetary accounts; which are the necessary public works and welfare measures, and which are those that are desirable but not indispensable. Each of these judgments is itself the peak of a pyramid of equations: whether, for example, to enlarge or to reduce the national commitments at this or that point in the world—given the effect of the decision at other points in the world.

We may say, then, that public policy is made in a field of

equations. The issues are the choices as to where the balance is to be struck. In the reality of things X will exact an equivalence of Y. Within the limits which the specific nature of the case permits—limits which have to be estimated—a balance has to be reached by adding to or subtracting from the terms of the equation.

Oftener than not, the two sides of the equation differ in that the one is, as compared with the other, the pleasanter, the more agreeable, the more popular. In general the softer and easier side reflects what we desire and the harder reflects what is needed in order to satisfy the desire. Now the momentous equations of war and peace, of solvency, of security and of order, always have a harder or a softer, a pleasanter or a more painful, a popular or an unpopular option. It is easier to obtain votes for appropriations than it is for taxes, to facilitate consumption than to stimulate production, to protect a market than to open it, to inflate than to deflate, to borrow than to save, to demand than to compromise, to be intransigent than to negotiate, to threaten war than to prepare for it.

Faced with these choices between the hard and the soft, the normal propensity of democratic governments is to please the largest number of voters. The pressure of the electorate is normally for the soft side of the equations. That is why governments are unable to cope with reality when elected assemblies and mass opinions become decisive in the state, when there are no statesmen to resist the inclination of the voters and there are only politicians to excite and to exploit them.

There is then a general tendency to be drawn downward, as by the force of gravity, towards insolvency, towards the insecurity of factionalism, towards the erosion of liberty, and towards hyperbolic wars.

11/History and Political Existence

The Loss and Recovery of History*

Gerhart Niemeyer

PHILOSOPHY OF HISTORY IS a concept coined by Voltaire, who can be said to have originated this form of consciousness in the middle of the eighteenth century. From the beginning, philosophy of history had an antitheistic character. The tableau of world-immanent developments and evolutions which Voltaire constructed was meant as a substitute for the concept of Providence that still had dominated Bossuet's *Histoire Universelle.* We have Voltaire's word for it: "Let us respectfully leave the divine to those who are its keepers, and attach ourselves solely to history."[1]

After Voltaire created the first model of what he called history *en philosophe,* his successors, with Hegel and Marx at their head, went even further in deliberately making of philosophical history an alternative to religious faith. They relied on history to provide man with a destiny and a goal, and the goal, both of time and in time, served as a replacement for all moral values. The philosophy of history, therefore, cannot be understood properly except in terms of its negative relation to Christianity. That is not the same as a negative relation to religion. Philosophy of history is not in itself hostile to religion.

[1] François Voltaire. "Essai sur les moeurs et l'esprit," *Oeuvres complètes,* vol. 2, ed. E. de la Bédolière and Georges Avenal (Paris: Bureau du Siècle, 1867), p. 65.

First, among the great systems of philosophy of history constructed between 1750 and 1850 there are a few in which a deist god figures as the absentee landlord of Nature. Second, at least two of these systems of history, those of Saint-Simon and Auguste Comte, supplemented the scheme of successive ages of history with a newly invented civil religion expressly designed to displace Christianity. Third, in Hegel's system, history figures as a kind of biography of the Absolute Mind, which is Hegel's formula for god, no longer "the maker of heaven and earth" but rather a god coming to be himself through the development of human consciousness. Philosophy of history, then, far from being antireligious, pretends to the status of an "ersatz religion," a new religion proposed to take the place of faith in God, the Father of Jesus Christ.

Philosophy of history is a form of the loss of reality. "Loss of reality," a concept coined by Eric Voegelin, has a profound meaning in the context of Voegelin's philosophy of consciousness, a meaning which it would take too long to explain fully at this point. As I am going to steer this paper in the direction of empirical evidence, I hope that the phenomena will speak for themselves and illustrate the concept.

At this point I should like to remark only that the sentence "philosophy of history is a form of the loss of reality" can be taken in two meanings. First, it can mean that philosophy of history is a symbolic form giving expression to the experience of having lost consciousness of reality. In other words, human beings, feeling themselves threatened by a sense of sliding into nothingness, grab hold of history in a desperate effort to construct some meaning of human existence and to save themselves from dying by boredom, or melancholy. Second, the sentence could mean that the construction of a philosophy of history in itself entails a deliberate contraction or reduction of reality, so that the reality that goes into the image is less than the full reality. Let us, for the time being, dwell on this second meaning.

Let me describe a few varieties of the "loss of reality" as a function of the partial destruction of reality by the philosopher of history. The construction of history *en philosophe,* as Voltaire named it, relies on a more or less arbitrary selection of facts. Voltaire expressly stated that he obtained something like a unified picture of history only as he chose from the record "what is worthy to be known" and "what is useful,"[2] and that only by

[2] *Ibid.,* p. 4.

so choosing could he make "out of this chaos a general and well-articulated tableau."[3]

Likewise Friedrich Schiller, who in 1789 gave a lecture on universal history at the University of Jena, remarked that the record of past events showed wide and obvious gaps, but rejoiced in this as an advantage to his enterprise, since it allowed him to fill the space between the fragments using materials of his own imagination. Only in this way, he said, would he be able to arrive at a totality of universal history that had the quality of "concealing the narrow boundaries of birth and death," in other words, "expanding his brief and oppressive existence into an infinite space, and to merge the individual into the species,"[4] i.e., into a man-made ersatz immortality. Voltaire and Schiller thus knew that their constructions contained no more than fragments of reality, combined with products of their own fabulation. The result, part fact and part fiction, nevertheless claimed to be the whole of reality, so that the reduction of reality was undertaken deliberately by the authors.

A reduction of a different kind stems from the selection of one causal factor as a key to the entire course of history. After Voltaire, philosophical constructions of history confined themselves to efficient causation as the propellant of change and progress, rejecting the other three of Aristotle's causes, above all, final causes. This, in itself, is a reductive idea, claiming exclusive reality only for what can be explained as the effect of efficient causation. Besides, the selection of one causal factor as containing the key to the knowledge of history reduces other causal factors or aspects of existence to an inferior grade of reality or to unreality.

We refer, by way of example, to Marx's *German Ideology*. The single and permanent cause of history, Marx says there, is the change from one mode of economic production to another. "Morality, metaphysics, all the rest of ideology and their corresponding forms of consciousness, thus no longer retain their semblance of independence. They have no history, no development. . . ."[5] This, of course, is Marx's vaunted correction of

[3] *Ibid.*, p. 48.

[4] Friedrich Schiller, "Was heisst und zu welchem Ende studiert man Universalgeschichte?" *Sämtliche Werke,* vol. 4 (Munich: Carl Hanser Verlag, 1962), p. 765.

[5] Karl Marx, *The German Ideology* (New York: International Publishers, 1947), p. 14.

Hegel, who had attributed history exclusively to the developments of human consciousness. Marx, then, reduces consciousness to a derivative of economic factors which alone have the character of historical reality. Hegel's selection of consciousness as the sole factor of history, however, is no less a reduction than Marx's selection of economic structures, for Hegel reduced God to his incarnation in human affairs and to the evolution of human consciousness.

Incidentally, the fallacy of Marx's reduction shows up only a few pages after he had proclaimed it, when Marx, having said that there was only the history of modes of economic production, introduces the history of the class struggle, which obviously presupposes some degree of an autonomous consciousness, the proletariat's consciousness "of its historic mission," as mentioned later in *The Communist Manifesto*.

The problems stemming from Marx's approach to history are immediately evident: the reduction of history to the succession of modes of economic production resulted not only in the neglect of political order by the socialists, but in their demonstrated inability to construct anything like a political theory, as becomes clear when one looks at the frantic but unsuccessful efforts of Engels, Lenin, Stalin, and Khrushchev to arrive at principles of political order, on the basis of Marxian premises. It just could not be done.

A third variety of reduction stems from the concept of a goal, in the form of a future society in space and time, a society that would constitute a full, harmonious, and perfect human existence. Incidentally, this idea of a goal is what distinguishes philosophy of history from a philosophy of process. The latter, a doctrine about change as such, requires no goal concept. To refer again to Marx, his teaching on revolution as "the locomotive of history" does not require the idea of a culmination, a final goal. Revolutionary change could be expected to go on indefinitely. That would be a philosophy of process.

Marx, however, postulated an end to this process, by introducing into his series of revolutions one revolution that differs from all the others. The proletariat, unlike all other revolutionary classes, has no property of its own, so that its victory will mean the end of all class societies and the end of the class struggle. This means, of course, that Marx attributes to that socialist society a quality of being which he denied to all previous societies. To use the language of Parmenides, only in the socialist future can Marx find being (or "is-ing"), so that by comparison all previous ages must be seen as nothing but "coming-to-be," provisional and instrumental existence.

This differentiation of societies corresponds to a similar image of man, in the Marxian mind. Marx believes that the reality of man is wholly dependent on the social conditions. In any one of the societies prior to the final socialist society, then, man is not man. Marx sees man as separated from his own essence, separated from his fellow beings, and from himself, a mere fragment of a man, a being wholly determined in its existence, like an animal. That means, among other things, that all of man's attempts to know himself cannot be anything else but speculations on the utopian future, that neither the present nor the past can give us any clues about our own humanity.

An interesting confirmation of the loss of reality can be found in the concept of a spark of reality having persisted through all the past dark ages. Auguste Comte, who divided history into the theological, the metaphysical, and the positivist age, the latter being his concept for the society of the imminent future, attributes to the past a weak trace of inchoate positivism mixed both with the theology of the first and the metaphysics of the second age, and accounting for the forward momentum.

A similar concept is that of the so-called forerunners of Communism, such men as Spartakus, John Ball, Thomas Muentzer, Jean Meslier, and Morelly. If we look at these concepts we find that the past is not depicted as either society, or man, in an embryonic or inchoate stage of early development. Rather, it is only a tiny little spark, a segment of the whole, that is considered real because it prefigures the future, meaning that all the rest of the past does not have the character of even inchoate reality.

It will have become clear that philosophy of history, far from philosophical in character, is an enterprise of modern mythmaking. The totality of history, made imaginatively out of fragments of facts, and assertion of causes has the character of a myth. Certainly the alleged goal of history, to occur in space and time, as the fulfillment of human destiny, is a myth. The human agency or enterprise through which this denouement is to be brought about, has likewise mythical character. The philosophy of history transgresses the bounds of genuine classical philosophy both in front and in back, expressing its meaning through images of speculation which pretend to historical reality. This brings up the problem of the difference between ideological myths serving as the "cause" of movements and the myths that have ordered civilizations.

Sacred myths of all cultures acknowledge the givenness and mystery of the reality in which humans participate. By the naming of the gods and the telling of mythical stories they seek to grasp the relatedness or unity as well as the fittingness of the parts in the whole. Whatever is experienced is thus accounted for. There are the life processes of generation, decay and renewal, the returning cycles of growth, seasons, days, and nights. There is man with his powers of speech, arts, and actions, the mysterious terminals of his birth and death, the struggle of good and evil in his life. There are human societies with their hierarchical order, the ups and downs of their existence, their endurance through changing generations of individual members. The cosmos is full of wonders, and thus full of gods, as Thales put it.

The myth-making mind neither denies nor destroys the experienced reality and man's participation. His myths subtract nothing that is experienced, and they contribute the communicability of meaning, through stories, and rites. They fully acknowledge the facts of reality, its tangibilities, visibilities, usabilities, terribilities, together with the partly hidden wherefores and uncertain wheretos, the uncanny powers and unstable frailties of reality.

This kind of mythical fabulation does not have the character of willful fantasy, and thus can provide for a rational being a basis of operation in a cosmos which man acknowledges not to have made himself. It furnishes the human mind with a hypothetical order of the cosmos and existence which makes sense and thus supports thought, and also serves man's practical needs as effectively as did the explanation of the pump through the notion of *horror vacui*. Sacred myth, then, is fabulation in the attitude of deference to, and full awareness of, the reality that is not man-made and in which man experiences himself as participating.

We have already seen that the myths created by the philosophy of history imply a loss of reality, to a large extent through a willful intellectual destruction of reality, a contraction of its scope and character. At the beginning of this lecture, I allowed for the possibility of an original experience of lost reality to which these myths might seek to give expression. Such experiences were indeed recorded in the 17th and 18th centuries. One thinks of Pascal's horror of "the infinite immensity of spaces . . . which know me not."[6]

Undoubtedly there must have been countless cases of a loss of faith, of the resulting disorientation and confusion, during the Enlightenment. One might look on philosophy of history as possibly the expression either of such lamentable and lamented experiences of a reality lost, or maybe of the jubilant experience of a new reality having been found. There is some evidence of the latter, as when Feuerbach's assertion that gods were the projections of man's own noble attributes to some phantasmal set of beings, touched off a wave of enthusiasm among young Hegelians. One also recalls the atmosphere of religious awe gripping the audience at Hegel's lectures, or the lectures of Hegel's successor, Professor Gans.

Precisely this evidence, however, tells us that what we have here are secondary experiences, i.e., experiences touched off by the contrivance of ideas rather than primary experiences of reality. In other words, if we look for evidence of a newly discovered reality—symbolization of both experiences in and through ideologies, we find that actually the series is reversed.

Pascal, who did have an experience of cosmic loneliness, reacted by regaining his Christian faith. Voltaire, who rejected Christianity, never seems to have had an experience similar to Pascal's. In Voltaire's case his formula "the human mind, left to itself,"[7] is an axiom of his philosophy of history and, as such, a deliberate and aggressive choice rather than a primary experience. It suggests that philosophy of history does not have the character of a remedial system to comfort man as he feels left to himself. Rather, it begins by creating the position of "the human mind, left to itself," and then begins the enterprise of drawing philosophical and historiographical results from its own creation.

The replacement of Providence by efficient causation, of a self-enclosed human mind for a participating soul, of human self-salvation for divine salvation, all bear the stamp of grim and combative eristic rather than of jubilant discovery. In other

[6] Blaise Pascal, *Pensées* (New York: E. P. Dulton, 1958), nr, 205, p. 81.

[7] Voltaire, "Essai," p. 9.

words, a new reality was not discovered in the soul's experience but rather defiantly made up of deficient parts and, with full knowledge of the deficiency, passed on as if it were the whole. The experience followed from the astonishing success of the trick, rather than from meditation preceding it. Or, to put it in other words, the experience was a response to the artifice of a system, rather than to a manifestation of reality.

Philosophy of history, as a system, is a whole consisting of three parts: the fixed element in it is a permanent causal factor alleged to bring forth the succession of history's phases; the variable element is the utter plasticity of man seen as a function of progressively higher social arrangements; the third element is neither variable nor fixed but rather an anticipated product of human making: the future utopia.

Once this kind of thinking is around and accepted as if it were reality, it touches off its own experiences. The experiences are roughly two: the jubilant lust of apparently limitless power, and the complaint of abysmal alienation. The lust of power manifests itself in the intellectual postulate of "certain knowledge" replacing the former uncertainty of faith and the fuzziness of moral philosophy. Hegel triumphantly proclaimed "certainty of knowledge" as the attribute of his speculation, replacing Plato's "love of truth." Feuerbach's bid to "take back" from a nonexisting deity the noble attributes which in truth are man's own implies the same character of certain possession. "Certainty:" Marion Montgomery muses, "the death of love, and so of poetry, since it is the death of the possible or probable. Certainty destroys wonder, desire, joy, sorrow—those inclinations swayed from love to love."[8]

The resulting lust of power, or lust of certain possession, eventually found its supreme expression in the phrase "God is dead." One should note that in Nietzsche's *fröhliche Wissenschaft* this formula is embedded in philosophy of history, as manifested by the following sentences: "We have killed him—you and I! We all are his murderers!"[9] The murder is an historical event, dividing a before from an after. Thus philosophy of his-

[8] Marion Montgomery, *Fugitive* (New York: Harper and Row, 1974), p. 5.

[9] Friedrich Nietzsche, *Die fröhliche Wissenschaft,* 1881/2, Aphorism nr. 125.

tory shifted the order of human action from the truth of goodness to the goal of history, or, as Camus put it, "from vertical to horizontal transcendence."[10]

The "horizontal transcendence," history's utopia, appearing as the highest product of human salvific enterprise, entailed the corresponding depreciation of the past and the present. Man's sense of uncertainty made a roundabout turn. It used to be that from the past there came a sense of solidity and direction. The commonsense man is "a boatman," who "moves intelligently forward as he looks backward,"[11] to use the words of John A. Mackay.

The lust of power and certainty, however, now flamed up over the prospect of a salvific future, to be built by human forces and efforts. Consequently, the future was invested with certainty, while past and present were subordinated to that future not only as prolegomena, but also as antitheses. It is instructive to find Marx praising his "forerunner," Fourier, not for any of Fourier's constructive ideas, but rather for Fourier's scathing and, indeed, total criticism of the present, which implies a similar disdain for the past.

The curious result of this reversal of certainty is the loss of that history which philosophy of history sought to construct. The future, which has not yet occurred, governs the ideas of the present and the past. So the past, no longer providing a solidity of background, becomes infinitely malleable, subject to rewritings, deletions, additions, whatever is needed to justify the movement toward the utopian future. Similarly, the present is described as nothing but darkness inhabited by monstrous human types.

However, the future, which alone is supposed to shed light, actually recedes further and further as the years go by in unmitigated bleakness.

Something similar happens to the concept of man. The concept of human nature does play, or is meant to play, a central role in the philosophy of history, depicted as the movement toward the ultimate realization of human nature. First of all,

[10] Albert Camus, *The Rebel* (New York: Vintage Books, 1956), pp. 142, 233.

[11] John A. Mackay, *Heritage and Destiny* (New York: Macmillan, 1943), p. 12.

however, man's coming-to-be in the course of historical ages requires the concept of man's infinite malleability, through changing social arrangements. Second, since the present, as Ernst Bloch put it, is darkness wholly unintelligible, and the past is utterly lost, no experience is available to tell us about human nature. To put it in other words, a concept of human nature could only be drawn from the future utopia. That utopia, however, has not yet occurred, and, what is more, such ranking Marxists as Lenin and Ernst Bloch consider the real possibility that it may be missed. Thus the entire tripartite system fails to fit reality, to explain reality, to draw meaning from reality. On the contrary, it finds itself in open conflict with reality on three of four fronts.

Its myths neither support nor are supported by man's existence, man's experience of the limits of birth and death, man's experienced transcending of his natural existence, man's depth of memory, man's sense of being. Instead, the myths of philosophy of history go together only with the human will to power in its Promethean defiance of the divine.

It is because of their perennial conflict with human experience and reality that these myths have been surrounded with intellectual and physical means of enforcement. They have been converted into dogmas, in open contradiction to their own claim to constitute a "science." Dogmas do have their place in human affairs, but are wholly out of place when the matter supposedly is science, empirically founded and based on strict logic. The rigid dogmatism of an ideology presenting itself in the language of science thus insults the critical sense of even the man in the street, whose day-by-day experiences give the lie to those dogmatized myths. The myths, however, the less tenable they are, are all the more tenaciously enforced, imposed, and inflicted as the monopoly of truth. For by their own destruction of past and present, and of the concept of man, they have opened up behind and around them the abyss of nothingness and the corresponding anxiety of alienation.

These myths are deliberately accepted only by a minority. To the others who still continue to be guided, more or less, by common sense, the dogma of history that is no history constitutes a web of lies. Russia has become a country deprived of its history. On this condition, Solzhenitsyn remarks as follows:

> One cannot help fearing that the abnormality of the conditions which underlie the study of Russian history, similar to a general displacement of geological strata, creates . . . a common *systematic* error, as mathematicians would say. The error displaces and distorts all the results of research. The abnormality I speak of lies, first of all, in a paradox: the fact that the country studied is your contemporary—it leads a real and stormy existence—and yet, at the same time, it behaves like the archeologist's prehistory: the spine of its history has been fractured, its memory has failed, it has lost the power of speech. It has been denied the possibility of writing the truth about itself, to tell honestly how things are, to discover itself.[12]

Solzhenitsyn points here to a condition affecting scholarship, which he has tried to counteract by his own scholarly novels on Russia's history, as well as by his *Gulag Archipelago.*

In the life of the ordinary citizen, however, this same "displacement" manifests itself as the necessity of lying in order to live:

> The permanent lie becomes the only safe form of existence, in the same way as betrayal. Every wag of the tongue can be heard by someone, every facial expression observed by someone. Therefore, every word if it does not have to be a direct lie, is nonetheless obliged not to contradict the general, common lie. . . . But that was not all: Your children were growing up! . . . And if the children were little, then you had to decide what was the best way to bring them up; whether to start them off on lies instead of the truth (so that it would be *easier* for them to live) and then to lie forevermore in front of them too; or to tell them the truth, with the risk that they might make a slip, that they might let it out, which meant that you had to instill in them from the start that the truth was

[12] Aleksandr Solzhenitsyn, *Solzhenitsyn Speaks at the Hoover Institution on War, Revolution, and Peace,* May–June 1976, Stanford, Calif.

murderous, that beyond the threshold of the house you had to lie, only lie, just like papa and mama.[13]

Summing it all up, Solzhenitsyn adds: "And the lie has, in fact, led us so far away from a normal society that you cannot even orient yourself any longer; in its dense, gray fog not even one pillar can be seen."[14]

"Russia is a country that has officially been deprived of its history." This sentence is not a metaphorical statement but a fact of life in Russia. One piece of evidence is the list of official textbooks that have been issued for use in schools at the university level. The first is a book on political economy: that, according to Marx, is the essential though truncated reality of man. A second textbook is called *Marxism-Leninism*; it contains the communist ideology and the ideological version of society. Its companion is a textbook on Marxist philosophy, presenting dialectical materialism, the only philosophy taught in Soviet Russia. Then there is the history of the CPSU, in other words, a history of the Party in lieu of a history of Russia: Russia had history only until 1917, then its place was taken by the history of the Communist Party numbering less than five percent of the Russian people. The last textbook is called *Scientific Communism*; it surveys on the one hand, the forerunners of the Communist Party in the past of Western civilization, and, on the other hand, the problems of the transition from capitalism to communism, especially the transition of the present phase of socialism to the final phase of communism, in the Soviet Union. This last book, then, puts the CPSU, the Communist Party of Russia, in the framework of a wider past and a universal future, attributing all dimensions of history exclusively to the communist enterprise.

Russia as an agglomeration of people without history. What does that mean in day-by-day reality? Solzhenitsyn tells us:

> In half a century we have not succeeded in calling anything by its right name or thinking anything

[13] Aleksandr Solzhenitsyn, *The Gulag Archipelago 1918–1956,* vols. III–IV (New York: Harper and Row, 1975), p. 646f.

[14] *Ibid.,* p. 649.

> through. . . . For decades, while we were silent, our thoughts straggled in all possible and impossible directions, lost touch with each other, never learned to know each other, ceased to check and correct each other.[15]

It is in Russia, however, that a movement has begun to which we must attribute the quintessential character of a recovery of history in our time. It is a movement composed of intellectuals to whom the Western world refers by the belittling name of "dissidents."

The movement owes its cohesion to the catalytic effect of Solzhenitsyn's publications. Solzhenitsyn has also coined the appropriate descriptive title of the movement, the name of his lead article in *From Under the Rubble*: "As Breathing and Consciousness Return." In what way is consciousness returning to this increasingly articulate group of Russian writers and thinkers? Solzhenitsyn again is the one who provides the answer, through the whole of his work and life. Neither his life nor his work are governed by a note of dissidence, which has a chiefly negative connotation. Solzhenitsyn's achievement is, above all, to have regained, in experience, thought, and word, the reality of man, God, and history.

The experience came as he began to accept the hardly imaginable degradation of his existence in prison camp and, simultaneously, to rediscover his own humanity in the surrounding humanity of all others, his own torturers included. Under conditions of near-annihilation he learned to be grateful for the tiniest manifestation of life, so that, years later, he could sincerely write: "*Bless you, prison,* for having been in my life."[16] The experience revealed to him, all at once, both man and God, the rediscovery of God occurring in the same motion of his soul as the rediscovery of human reality.

What followed upon that experience was hard intellectual work: "As breathing returns after our swoon, as a glimmer of consciousness breaks through the unrelieved darkness, it is difficult for us at first to regain clarity of vision, to pick our way

[15] Aleksandr Solzhenitsyn, *From Under the Rubble* (Boston: Little, Brown & Co., 1975), pp. 3, 4.

[16] Solzhenitsyn, *Gulag III–IV,* p. 617.

among the clutter of hurdles, among the idols planted in our path."[17] The "rubble" is ideology, the willed falsehood of consciousness, which to remove is tantamount to the recovery of history. "Our present system," writes Solzhenitsyn of Russia, "is unique in world history, because over and above its physical and economic constraints, it demands total surrender of our souls, continuous and active participation in the general, conscious *lie.*"[18] Hence, he concludes, "the absolutely essential task is not political liberation, but the liberation of our souls from participation in the lie forced upon us."[19] This lead article in *From Under the Rubble* is a profound criticism of Sakharov, who, far more than Solzhenitsyn, deserves to be called a "dissident," a man who differs with the Soviet rulers on policy but is not deeply concerned with what his soul participates in. Solzhenitsyn's critique is hard and inexorable: "No one who voluntarily runs with the hounds of falsehood, or props it up, will ever be able to justify himself to the living, or to posterity, or to his friends, or to his children."[20]

The problem, as Solzhenitsyn sees and describes it, emerges with life-and-death urgency in Russia, but is a concern of the entire modern world. In the West, it is no less the burden of foreign policy than it is in Russia the burden of false participation. The political dimension of the problem turns out to be secondary to the religious aspect, and the latter turns out to be a revelation to those who have lived in the man-made hell of *Gulag Archipelago.* Thus the Russians have the advantage over us of having suffered more deeply, and having reaped from their suffering the experienced ripening of their souls.

The movement began, in Russia, in the personal experience of sundry prisoners. It took on the shape of a group movement with the publication of Solzhenitsyn's *One Day in the Life of Ivan Denisovitch,* which appeared as a bright light in the darkness of Soviet life. Solzhenitsyn has neither in Russia nor abroad tried to form anything like a political conspiracy. His endeavor is to induce others to join in "the return of consciousness." Hence the publication of the volume *From Under the Rubble,* a book that relates itself to the 1909 publication called *Vekhi* (*Landmarks*),

[17] Solzhenitsyn, *Rubble,* p. 12.

[18] *Ibid.,* p. 24.

[19] *Ibid.,* p. 25.

[20] *Ibid.,* p. 25.

and, like *Landmarks,* is a joint publication of a group of authors. Solzhenitsyn also is a contributor to *Kontinent,* a periodical publication edited by Vladimir Maximov. All these, and other works, address primarily Russians but at the same time also the non-Communist world. Among these writers, Solzhenitsyn is the one person fully aware of that and how his breathing and consciousness have returned, and that that return to reality is the recovery of history. Without any trace of vanity, but in deep seriousness, he can state: "History is us—and there is no alternative but to shoulder the burden of what we so passionately desire and bear it out of the depths."[21]

[21] *Ibid.,* p. x.

12/Authority

On Authority*

Thomas Molnar

Our ordinary experience in today's family, school, court, church, and nation is that authority—of father, teacher, judge, priest, and president—is hard to maintain, if, indeed, it has not actually broken down. Whose fault is this? Is authority undermined by identifiable people and forces—or is it simply not exercised? Some would point to the popular pedagogic theories of John Dewey—"democracy in the classroom," for example—as the culprit. Others, like the late Jean Cardinal Daniélou speaking about the causes of the church's turmoil, would say that authority does exist, it is there, but those who ought to exercise it hesitate doing so.

Almost two decades ago, sociologist David Riesman called our attention in his book *The Lonely Crowd* to a new type of man that he labeled "other-directed." Such a man, nurtured by our civilization at this point, has no strong convictions and beliefs; he receives anonymous orders from his social environment and social peers, conforms to them, obeys them mechanically. According to Riesman, this type is a changeover from the earlier American "inner-directed" man who knew what he wanted, made individual choices, and had the courage to defend them. Now a superficial observer may conclude from Riesman's study that the "other-directed" man is more conscious, rather than less, of the existence of authority, which he recognizes and to which he conforms. The truth is different. The "inner-directed" man is aware of authority because he, too, exercises it. He knows his

* From *Authority and Its Enemies* (New Rochelle N.Y.: Arlington House Publishers). Copyright © 1976 by Thomas Molnar. Reprinted by permission.

place in the hierarchy of society, his personality has clear contours, he makes decisions and receives decisions. All around him there are "inner-directed" men, exercising authority: father, teacher, pastor, family physician. When he accepts their authority, he copies firm attitudes which he learns to value and admire. He wants to be like they are. This shows that by its nature authority is *personal,* or, at least, it has personal ingredients even though it is not necessarily visible. We obey God not because we see him; great moral and political leaders do not have to be present—in fact they may be long dead—in order to be respected; tradition has authority over us because our forebears had set down its meaning and its structure. However, when the social situation is more restricted and its manifestations are more frequent, as in the family, the school, and in the maintenance of order in the street, authority must be concretely present in visible form. It is exercised regularly, perhaps even uninterruptedly, by parent, teacher, and policeman.

Is authority really needed in these smaller social spheres? The question is legitimate since we often hear and read statements that, except for very small children, every individual ought to be allowed freedom of expression and the right to decide what is best for him on all matters. This, at any rate, is the prevailing view; contradicting it may bring social penalties. A few years ago over the waves of a New York radio station I debated a lawyer who insisted that no authority (law) ought to curb dealers in pornographic literature in the display of their wares in shop windows. Also, recently, the ACLU proposed that primary school children should have the right to take their parents to court. A number of court cases ensued when long-haired pupils were ordered by principals or teachers to cut their hair.

These are samples taken from a vast number of situations where many of us feel that while freedom to act as we wish is a good thing, nevertheless *someone* ought to have the right to enforce a certain norm. Reflecting upon it, we soon find that this norm cannot in all cases be the outcome of a consensus or of a majority choice. Majorities are shifting, and what gives a norm its value (its *normative* character) is precisely that it is durable, not subject to popular whim or majority pressure. A norm is then a way of believing, speaking, or acting, which is consecrated by both reason and custom, one strengthening the other. And authority, if we base it on this formulation, appears as speech and action from the secure base of a norm. Otherwise, speech and action may be incidental, not binding beyond an immediate effect, or outright arbitrary, enforced but unreasonably.

After these somewhat abstract considerations, let us turn to the problem of the presence and absence of authority in situations where we experience the problem. Experience and reflection will tell us that there are natural groups and others which, while also natural, are better described as consequences of complex interactions between individuals and groups. I call the family a natural group—it is the basic social cell—and I call, for example, an art movement or a censorship bureau a complex social group. There are no societies without some form of the family—extended or simple—but many societies do not have artists associated according to devotion to a style, or censorship which deals with complicated matters of value and moral or political critique of existing norms.

The mere fact of speaking of families indicates that certain functions—permanent ones—are fulfilled by a group of people called father, mother (eventually grandparents), and children (eventually uncles, aunts, and cousins). The functions are relatively easy to list: protection, the creation of an intimate and warm environment, the regularity of habits, the acquisition of a language, a frame of reference supplying and reenforcing the identity of the members. These functions, which are so "natural" that we hardly perceive them, follow from biological and psychological necessities, and also from an added element which we can only call *love.* It is often argued that this latter is merely our awareness that the biological functions are performed in a manner that satisfies us. To argue thus is, however, a willed depreciation, a conscious impoverishment of an experience we all have and which cannot be, without violence done to it, reduced to anything else. Family love is as much *given* as its external, functional manifestations. The child and the parent do not dissociate, when giving or receiving the act of protection, care, respect, obedience, and authority, from the love which permeates those acts and is one with them.

Now my contention is that *authority* is analogous to love. Every act within the family is either a manifestation of authority (and corresponding obedience or refusal) or a manifestation of its absence. At first sight, love could be represented by a larger circle, authority by a smaller one inscribed in the first. Love is always present in the form of care, consideration, gifts, gestures, and so on, whereas authority needs a precise external sign, a regular reaffirmation, a direction. I once heard a father say how he envied his brother who merely had to signal to his teenage sons in order to silence them when he was talking with other adults. "My son would continue talking," he lamented in a resigned tone. The case of the two brothers displays similar situations and similar sentiments of parental love, but they are made dissimilar by the presence or absence of authority. It is not difficult to conclude that love is more effective (and mutually more satisfying) when accompanied by authority. The latter is indeed a way of channeling love; instead of a general and ubiquitous emotionalism, love becomes structured, apportioned, is made directive, I would even say "educational" if the term had not been devalued as a part of the bureaucratic jargon. Anyway, love is formative and humanizing when coupled with authority; in combination, the two are the cement of the family structure.

A popular writer on family life and teenage psychology insists that authority ought not to be obvious because then it provokes rather than soothes the child's temper. One of his illustrations is a 14-year-old boy playing ball in the family living room and being reprimanded by his mother. The boy not only continues, he becomes impertinent and exasperates his mother, who, in turn, begins to shriek, then breaks down in a fit of sobs. The writer's advice is that the mother ought to have explained why she would not tolerate ball-playing in the apartment. If a family situation were a formula of physics or mechanical engineering, the adviser would be right: the best way to save energy and unnecessary expenditure (in this case, of tears and anger) would be a rational planning of each participant's place and movement, a set of preexisting formulas for dos and don'ts. The living family is, however, not a mechanism with wound-up parts; there authority must be exercised and accepted in many instances without prior discussion, not mechanically but on the grounds of the function that each member has as a result of age, status, experience, and consciousness of the general welfare (common good).

With the last expression we have made an important step toward understanding the nature and role of authority. Society consists of individuals and groups, the one as important and fundamental as the other. Rousseau was dangerously wrong with the first statement of his work on "social contract," that "man is born free, yet we see him everywhere in chains." Man is born free as God's child, but neither as a member of nature nor of society, if freedom means self-creation, self-sustenance, and unlimited license to do as one pleases. Man's (rather already the child's) freedom, and with it his individuality, is circumscribed by the freedom and reality of the social group. Philosophers will forever debate which comes first, man or society, but we can safely assert that the problem is falsely formulated. Man cannot function outside society, and the latter does not exist without the individuals who compose it. Yes, one may object, but the individual can at least survive alone. Even this is questionable. We have never seen an *individual alone.* There are, to be sure, sporadic instances: Tarzan, the hermits, or a few Japanese soldiers who, after World War II, disappeared in the jungle of the Pacific islands rather than surrender to American troops. But if we take a more careful look, we realize that not even these individuals were ever alone and that it is impossible to say whether they sustained themselves by their own efforts, outside the physical (animal) act of feeding and finding shelter. Tarzan, or whoever his prototype had been, was not a complete human being until he learned to speak; besides, prior to his encounter with other men, he had been nurtured by animals and was a member of *their* tribe; hermits carry their memories and skills, even their motivation to become hermits, from society to the solitude of the forest; and the Japanese soldier chose his lonely life on the grounds of a prior loyalty—to the Emperor—which continued to sustain him morally. The Thoreaus of the world owe to society the very formulation of their wish for utter privacy.

Authority, at its elementary level, is then the natural price that the individual pays for membership in society, without which he would not be an individual, let alone a protected and integrated one. By these terms I do not mean exclusively "defense against aggression," which is practically the only grounds on which social philosophers of a certain school justify the existence of society and state; I mean by integration and protection the fact that we learn society's language, mores, and traditions, without which we would be individuals physiologically, but not in the human sense, that is, infinitely rich in thought, modes of expression and articulation, with a sense of identity and belonging, with rather clear reflective choices, preferences, refusals, and aspirations. Thus if nature shapes our immediately given body, society fashions our reflective life, our ethical being, our tastes, our personality. And by "society," let us remember, we mean family, school, church, state—all the social articulations that one calls institutions.

None of them could exist without *authority*. Just as individual man is unimaginable without the social group membership which helps him become a fully conscious, challenged, and challenging person—in the same way each social group can only hold together if it is differentiated according to objectives, functions, and persistence in survival. We have seen that, in the last analysis, there can exist individuals not belonging to society, but that it is questionable whether (1) they are men and women in the full sense of these words, and whether (2) they can survive. Similarly, there can be societies not held together by authority. In such a case, however, they are (1) temporary and fragile groups, threatened by the canceling of the coexistence contract at any moment, and (2) unable to survive due to the permanent inner defiance of decision-making. One may argue here, too, that some families grant complete freedom to their members, that children are brought up permissively, and that husband and wife give each other sexual freedom to gratify their desires with any outsider of their choice. Or one may cite the latest examples of hippy communes and others, similarly modeled. Nevertheless, such families are held together by outside pressure, that is, by a degree of conformity to social mores where defiance of it would meet ostracism and even the intervention of the law. In the last analysis, they, too, submit to society's authority—if not in regard to behavior inside the family, at least in regard to what society considers as its own minimum requirement of external adjustment. The same is the case with hippy communes: they last as long as the inner tensions do not disrupt them, or, simply, until a secessionist subgroup decides to set up its own commune.

In short, groups not structured, or only loosely structured, by internal authority, may survive if they are few in number in proportion to the groups within that society. They pose no threat to the concept of authority because the authority exercised all around them creates a network by which they, too, benefit. (Similarly, conscientious objectors and pacifists can act according to their convictions only because theirs is an infrequent occurrence. Society around them provides for its own, and for their protection. Should their number increase beyond a certain percentage, the whole society, now defenseless, would succumb to a determined enemy.)

Authority, then, does not define a social group—what defines it are its objectives, tradition, the quality and loyalty of its members—but it is the chief instrument in all these respects and directions. Authority formulates, and when there is need for it, modifies the objectives, articulates and keeps alive tradition, and reminds the members of the loyalty they owe to the social group. For these reasons, we may distinguish between two types of authority: *charismatic* and *institutional*. The first is an unplanned exception, and in spite of its rareness, it strengthens the human material over which it is exercised; the second is the rule, the normal, the routine. Thus it is understandable that we are awed by the first and are tempted to regard the second as unjustified, saying that only such authority should be respected which "deserves" it, which is outstandingly good, just, spontaneously exercised, and accepted. Yet those who crave charismatic authority and scorn or would disobey institutional authority make a grievous mistake: an institution might be defined as the place where all members benefit by the authority that the best among them would have naturally. Let us take an illustration. The majority of teachers in a school, like people in any community situation, are average persons in terms of talent and inspiration to their students. We assume their pedagogic and cultural background as well as their goodwill to be more or less the same. One or a few of them excel and they are loved and obeyed: they have *charismatic,* or let us only say, natural authority. Should the majority of teachers not be obeyed on the grounds that they lack natural authority? The answer obviously is that obedience on the students' part ought to be equal to every teacher so that the institution's objectives, teaching and learning, might be carried out as regularly as possible. The average teacher with no commanding personality thus benefits by the institutionalization of authority. The exceptional teacher does not need it; the average teacher does. And in this forever imperfect world the average will always be far more numerous than the exceptional. The institution as such equalizes, and makes possible, a certain function—in a situation where a noninstitution, based on a few exceptional persons' ability to attract pupils, would have to remain a perhaps exhilarating but rare and precarious thing.

The same example could be shown to be valid in the family,

too. A father and a mother are not always admirable figures, and a child may often envy a friend for the outstanding personal or acquired qualities of his parents. Should this inequality invalidate the less admirable parent's authority, even though in terms of sheer "performance" of his parental function he does not live up to the high standard set by the other? In consequence, even when authority operates at less than the ideal, less than the desirable level, its essence must remain firmly implanted in the given social group by its institutionalization. And institutionalization, in turn, is a signal to the members that the human condition is such that majorities are mediocre, in need of protection in their functions, thus benefiting by a standard established for less mediocre minorities. Again, take an example: a subway car in a big city and an aggressive person riding it among more silent and peaceable travelers. The ideal situation would be that all occupants of the car are equally robust, muscular, able to defend themselves against the eventual aggressor. This is obviously not the case; some are weak, and one actually has the beaten "victim" look on his face. Why does the aggressive man not attack him? There may be, of course, several reasons, but one is certainly the authority of the law, even if not represented by a policeman. One might say, again, that the strong—as in the previous example, the teacher with a personal authority—do not need the presence of authority, they possess sufficient strength to protect themselves. But most people *are* weak; their only protection is an authority watching over situations in which they are at a disadvantage. And, understandably, the strong, too, are often in situations of weakness; they, too are protected by authority.

Consequently, the nature of authority is that it extends beyond the person who could or would directly exercise it. In this sense, authority resembles the law. The law, however, is promulgated in the name of all people of a given society, so that by definition it covers a wide and distinctly circumscribed social area. Authority, as distinct from the law, is exercised on bases different from sheer enforcement. Its essential nature is that it is *exercised* in what would otherwise be a social vacuum, and that it is *accepted* voluntarily. By "voluntary" I do not mean that those who obey authority give the bearer of authority their explicit consent each time after a consultation; I mean, rather, that authority appeals to a number of motives in us, as varied as are the personal and social responses in general: loyalty, fear, prudence, regard for others, desire to imitate, corporate feeling, and so on. Thus while law coerces, authority addresses itself to a preexisting consent of heart, mind, habit, and respect; while we *behave* before the law even if our intentions (literally: "inner directions") contradict or oppose it, we *consent* to authority (we are of one sentiment with it), we agree with its demands upon us. Ultimately we do so because respect for authority is as natural a response of our whole person as are love, contentment, pity, or pride of achievement.

13/Education and Political Community

Education and the Individual*

Richard Weaver

THE GREATEST SCHOOL THAT ever existed, it has been said, consisted of Socrates standing on a street corner with one or two interlocutors. If this remark strikes the average American as merely a bit of fancy, that is because education here today suffers from an unprecedented amount of aimlessness and confusion. This is not to suggest that education in the United States, as compared with other countries, fails to command attention and support. In our laws we have endorsed it without qualification, and our provision for it, despite some claims to the contrary, has been on a lavish scale. But we behold a situation in which, as the educational plants become larger and more finely appointed, what goes on in them becomes more diluted, less serious, less effective in training mind and character; and correspondingly what comes out of them becomes less equipped for the rigorous tasks of carrying forward an advanced civilization.

Recently I attended a conference addressed by a retired general who had some knowledge of this country's ballistics program. He pointed out that of the 25 top men concerned with our progress in this now vital branch of science, not more than two or three were Americans. The others were Europeans, who had received in their *European* educations the kind of theoretical discipline essential to the work of getting the great missiles aloft.

* From *The Intercollegiate Review,* vol. 2, no. 1 (September 1965).

It was a sad commentary on a nation which has prided itself on giving its best to the schools.

It is an educational breakdown which has occurred. Our failure in these matters traces back to a failure to think hard about the real province of education. Most Americans take a certain satisfaction in regarding themselves as tough-minded when it comes to successful ways of doing things and positive achievements. But in deciding what is and is not pertinent to educating the individual, far too many of them have been softheads.

An alarming percentage of our citizens, it is to be feared, stop with the word "education" itself. It is for them a kind of conjuror's word, which is expected to work miracles by the very utterance. If politics become selfish and shortsighted, the cure that comes to mind is "education." If juvenile delinquency is rampant, "education" is expected to provide the remedy. If the cultural level of popular entertainment declines, "education" is thought of hopefully as the means of arresting the downward trend. People expect to be saved by a word when they cannot even give content to the word.

Somewhat better off, but far from sufficiently informed and critical, are those who recognize that education must, after all, take some kind of form, that it must be thought of as a process that does something one can recognize. Most of these people, however, see education only as the means by which a person is transported from one economic plane to a higher one, or in some cases from one cultural level to another that is more highly esteemed. They are not wholly wrong in these assumptions, for it is true that persons with a good education do receive, over the period of their lifetime, larger earnings than those without, and it is true that almost any education brings with it a certain amount of cultivation. But again, these people are looking at the outward aspects and are judging education by what it does for one in the general economic and social ordering. In both of these respects education is valued as a means of getting ahead in life, a perfectly proper and legitimate goal, of course, but hardly one which sums up the whole virtue and purpose of an undertaking, which, in a modern society, may require as much as one quarter of the life span. Education as a conjuror's word and education viewed as a means of insuring one's progress in relation to his fellows both divert attention from what needs to be done for the individual as a person.

Education is a process by which the individual is developed

into something better than he would have been without it. Now when one views this idea from a certain perspective, it appears almost terrifying. How does one go about taking human beings and making them better? The very thought seems in a way the height of presumption. For one thing, it involves the premise that some human beings can be better than others, a supposition that is resisted in some quarters. Yet nothing can be plainer, when we consider it, than this fact that education is discriminative. It takes what is less good physically, mentally, and morally and transforms that by various methods and techniques into something that more nearly approaches our ideal of the good. Every educator who presumes to speak about his profession has in mind some aim, goal, or purpose that he views as beneficial. As various as are the schemes proposed, they all share this general concept of betterment. The teacher who did not believe that his efforts contributed to some kind of improvement would certainly have lost the reason for his calling. A surface unanimity about purpose, however, is not enough to prevent confusion and chaos where there is radical disagreement about the nature of the creature who is to be educated.

If man were merely an animal, his "education" would consist only of scientific feeding and proper exercise. If he were merely a tool or an instrument, it would consist of training him in certain response and behavior patterns. If he were a mere pawn of the political state, it would consist of indoctrinating him so completely that he could not see beyond what his masters wanted him to believe. Strange as it may seem, adherents to each of these views can be found in the modern world. But our great tradition of liberal education supported by our intuitive feeling about the nature of man, rejects them all as partial descriptions.

The vast majority of people conscious of this tradition agree that the purpose of education is to make the human being more human. Every generation is born ignorant and unformed; it is the task of those whom society employs as educators to bring the new arrivals up to a certain level of humanity. But even with this simple statement, we find trickiness in the terms. The word "human" is one of varying implications. In estimating what constitutes a complete human being some persons today are willing to settle for a pretty low figure. To some of them, as previously noted, he is nothing more than an animal in an advanced state of evolution. His brain is only a highly developed muscle, useful to him in the same way that the prehensile tail is to the monkey;

his needs are a set of skills which will enable him to get his sustenance from nature, and his purpose is to enjoy himself with the minimum amount of anxiety and the maximum amount of physical satisfaction. Others go somewhat beyond this and insist that in addition to his requirements as an animal, man has certain needs which can be described as social, intellectual, and aesthetic, and that these in turn require a kind of education which is not limited to practical self-survival. Others go beyond this and say that man is an incurably spiritual being—that he is this even when he says he is not—and that he cannot live a satisfying sort of life until certain ends which might be called psychic are met. Man has an irresistible desire to relate himself somehow to the totality, to ask what is the meaning of his presence here amid the great empirical fact of the universe. Many feel that until this question receives some sort of answer, none of the facts of life can be put in any kind of perspective.

We will not pause to weigh the opinion of those who consider man merely an animal. This view has always been both incredible and repugnant to the majority of mankind, and is accepted only by the few who have bound themselves to a theoretical materialism.

All others agree that the human being has a distinguishing attribute in *mind.* Now mind is something more than brain. Many anatomists and surgeons have seen a brain, but nobody has ever seen a mind. This is because we believe that the mind is not merely a central exchange of the body's system, where nerve impulses are brought together and relayed; it is a still mysterious entity in which man associates together the various cognitive, aesthetic, moral, and spiritual impulses which come to him from the outer and inner worlds. It is the seat of his rational faculty, but it is also the place where his inclinations are reduced to order and are directed. Most importantly for the concerns of education, mind is the place where symbols are understood and are acted upon.

Man has, in fact, been defined as the symbol-using animal. This definition makes symbol-using the distinguishing characteristic which separates him from all the other creatures with which he shares animal attributes. Even though the definition may be a partial one, it points to the faculty which has enabled man to create cultures and civilizations. The significance of the symbol is that it enables us to express knowledge and to communicate in an intellectual and not in a sensate way. Even in the matter of economy, this gain is an enormous one. If a man wishes to indicate six, he uses the symbol "6"; he does not have to lay out six pieces of wood or other objects to make his meaning clear to another. If he wishes to indicate water, he does not have to go through the motions of drinking or some other pantomime. If he wishes to express his insight into a wide complex of physical phenomena, he can do this by means of a mathematical formula, like the now famous $E = mc^2$. This is a highly symbolic form of expression, in the absence of which, it is hardly needful to point out, man's power to deal with nature would be very much smaller than it is at present. But symbolism is not used only to convey information about the physical world. Through the use of symbols man expresses those feelings and states of being which are none the less real for being subjective. His feelings of love, of delight, of aversion have been put in forms transmissible from generation to generation through the use of symbols—letters in literature, notation in music, symbolic articles in dress and in ceremonials, and so on. It is impossible to realize how poor our lives would be without the intellectual and emotional creations which depend upon this symbolic activity.

It might seem that all of this is too obvious to need a case made for it. But there exists a crisis in education today which forces all who believe in the higher nature of man to come to the defense of those subjects which discipline the mind through the language of sign and symbol.

For some while now there has been a movement among certain people styling themselves educators to disparage and even do away with the very things that were once considered the reason for and the purpose of all education. There has been a bold and open attempt to deny that man has a nature which is fulfilled only when these higher faculties are brought into play, educated, and used to make life more human in the distinctive sense. Oddly enough, the movement has arrogated to itself the name "progressive." That seems a curious term to apply to something that is retrogressive in effect, since it would drag men back toward the presymbolic era. In preempting the adjective "progressive" for their brand of education, these innovators were trying a rhetorical maneuver. They were trying to give the impression that their theory of education is the only forward-looking one, and that the traditional ones were inherited from times and places that sat in darkness. Now it is quite true that "progressive" education represents a departure from an ideal that has prevailed ever since the ancient Hebrews, the people of the Bible, thought about religion, and the Greeks envisioned the life of reason. This new education is not designed for man as an immortal soul, nor is it designed to help him measure up to any ideal standard. The only goal which it professes to have in view is "adjustment to life." If we examine this phrase carefully, we will see that it, like a number of others that these educational imposters have been wont to use, is rather cleverly contrived to win a rhetorical advantage. "Adjustment" has an immediate kind of appeal, because no one likes to think of himself as being "maladjusted"; that suggests failure, discomfort, and other unpleasant experiences. And furthermore, "adjustment to life" may be taken by the unwary as suggesting a kind of victory over life—success and pleasure and all that sort of thing. But as soon as we begin to examine the phrase both carefully and critically, we find that it contains booby traps. It is far from likely that the greatest men of the past, including not only famous ones but also great benefactors of humanity, have been "adjusted" in this sense. When we begin to study their actual lives, we find that these were filled with toil, strenuousness, anxiety, self-sacrifice, and sometimes a good bit of friction with their environment. In fact, it would be much nearer the truth to say that the great creative spirits of the past have been maladjusted to life in one or more important ways. Some kind of productive tension between them and their worlds was essential to their creative accomplishment. This indeed seems to be a necessity for all evolutionary progress, not merely on the organic level but on the cultural level as well. This must not be taken to mean that such persons never achieve happiness. "Happiness" as employed by today's journalism is a pretty flabby and misleading word. Certain distinctions must be made before it can be safely used. The moments of happiness of creative people, though perhaps comparatively rare, are very elevated and very intense. This is characteristic of the life of genius. And when a culture ceases to produce vital creative spirits, it must cease to endure, for these are necessary even to sustain it.

Now let us look carefully at the second term of this formula. The prophets of the new education say that they are going to teach the young to adjust to *life.* But when we begin to elicit what they have in mind, we begin to wonder what kind of thing they imagine life to be. They seem to have in mind some simulacrum of life, or some travesty, or some abstracted part. They do not contemplate adjusting students to life in its fullness and mystery, but to life lived in some kind of projected socialist commonwealth, where everybody has so conformed to a political pattern that there really are no problems any more. Adjustment to real life must take into account pain, evil, passion, tragedy, the limits of human power, heroism, the attraction of ideals, and so on. The education of the "progressives" does not do this. It educates for a world conceived as without serious conflicts. And this is the propaganda of ignorance.

Furthermore, nearly all of the great lives have involved some form of sacrifice for an ideal; nearly all great individuals have felt the call for that kind of sacrifice. But sacrifice does not exist in the vocabulary of "progressive" education, since for them everything must take the form of "adjustment" or self-realization. Were Buddha, Socrates, and Jesus "adjusted to life"? The way in which one answers that question will reveal whether he stands with those who believe that man has a higher self and a higher destiny or whether he is willing to stop with an essentially barbaric ideal of happiness. The adjustment which the progressive educators prate of is, just because of its lack of any spiritual ideal, nothing more than the adjustment of a worm to the surface it is crawling on.

When we turn to the practical influence of their theorizing, we find that it has worked to undermine the discipline which has been used through the centuries to make the human being a more aware, resourceful, and responsible person. As would be expected, the brunt of their attack has been against those studies which, because they make the greatest use of symbols, are the most intellectual—against mathematics and language study, with history and philosophy catching a large share also of their disapproval. (There are excellent reasons for terming certain subjects "disciplines" and for insisting that the term be preserved. For "discipline" denotes something that has the power to shape and to control in accordance with objective standards. It connotes the power to repress and discourage those impulses which interfere with the proper development of the person. A disciplined body is one that is developed and trained to do what its owner needs it to do; a disciplined mind is one that is developed and trained to think in accordance with the necessary laws of thought, and which therefore can provide its owner with true casual reasoning about the world. A person with a disciplined will is trained to want the right thing and to reject the bad out of his own free volition. Discipline involves the idea of the negative, and this is another proof that man does not unfold merely naturally, like a flower. He unfolds when he is being developed by a sound educational philosophy according to known lines of truth and error, of right and wrong.)

Mathematics lies at the basis of our thinking about number, magnitude, and position. Number is the very language of science. So pervasive is it in the work of the intellect that Plato would have allowed no one to study philosophy who had not studied mathematics. But these are the very reasons that mathematics is calculated to arouse the suspicion of the "progressives"; it works entirely through symbols and it makes real demands upon the intellect.

Language has been called "the supreme organon of the mind's self-ordering growth." It is the means by which we not only communicate our thoughts to others but interpret our thoughts to ourselves. The very fact that language has the public aspect of intelligibility imposes a discipline upon the mind; it forces us to be critical of our own thoughts so that they will be comprehensible to others. But at the same time it affords us practically infinite possibilities of expressing our particular inclinations through its variety of combinations and its nuances. Most authorities agree that we even *think* in language, that without language thought would actually be impossible. Those who attack the study of language (whether in the form of grammar, logic, and rhetoric or in the form of a foreign language) because it is "aristocratic" are attacking the basic instrumentality of the mind.

History has always been a sobering discipline because it presents the story not only of man's achievements but also of his failures. History contains many vivid lessons of what can happen to man if he lets go his grip upon reality and becomes self-indulgent; it is the record of the race, which can be laid alongside the dreams of visionaries, with many profitable lessons. Yet the modern tendency is to drop the old-fashioned history course and to substitute something called "social science" or "social studies," which one student has aptly dubbed "social stew." What this often turns out to be is a large amount of speculation based on a small amount of history, and the speculation is more or less subtly slanted to show that we should move in the direction of socialism or some other collectivism. Often this kind of study is simply frivolous; the student is invited to give his thought to the "dating patterns" of teen agers instead of to those facts which explain the rise and fall of nations. There is more to be learned about the nature of man as an individual and as a member of society from a firm grounding in ancient and modern history than from all the "social studies" ever put together by dreamy "progressive" educators.

Philosophy too is an essential part of liberal education because it alone can provide a structure for organizing our experience and a ground for the hierarchical ordering of our values. But under "progressive" education that is but one kind of philosophy, that of experimental inquiry in adapting to an environment. This has no power to yield insight and no means of indicating whether one kind of life is higher than another if both show an adjustment to the externals around them.

Thus with amazing audacity the "progressive" educators have turned their backs upon those subjects which throughout civilized history have provided the foundations of culture and of intellectual distinction.

If this has been stressed at some length, it is in order to deny the claim that "progressive" education fosters individualism. It may have the specious look of doing so because it advocates personal experience as a teacher and the release of the natural tendencies of the person. Yet it does this on a level which does not make for true individualism. Individualism in the true sense is a matter of the mind and the spirit; it means the development of the person, not the well-adjusted automaton. What the progressivists really desire to produce is the "smooth" individual adapted to some favorite scheme of collectivized living, not the person of strong convictions, of refined sensibility, and of deep personal feeling of direction in life. Any doubt of this may be removed by noting how many "progressive" educators are in favor of more state activity in education. Under the cloak of devotion to the public schools, they urge an ever greater state control, the final form of which would be, in our country, a federal educational system directed out of Washington and used to instill the collectivist political notions which are the primary motives of this group.

No true believer in freedom can contemplate this prospect with anything but aversion. If there is one single condition necessary to the survival of truth and of values in our civilization, it is that the educational system be left independent enough to espouse these truths and values regardless of the political winds of doctrine of the moment. The fairest promises of a hands-off policy on the part of federal educational authorities would come to nothing once they were assured of their power and control. If education were allowed to become a completely statist affair, there is no assurance that the content of even science courses would be kept free from the injection of political ideas. The latter might seem a fantastic impossibility, yet it has actually occurred in the Soviet Union. This is a case well worth relating as a warning to all who would put faith in centralized education under a paternalistic state.

Some years ago the leading Soviet geneticist was one T. D. Lysenko, who occupied the post of President of the All-Union Lenin Academy of Agricultural Science. Lysenko claimed that he had disposed of the genetic theories of Mendel and Morgan, his motive being that these were "reactionary" and counter to the theories of socialism. Western scientists exposed the fallacies in his work and denounced him as an ignorant quack. But Lysenko, working through a stooge named Michurin, established what he called "Michurin science" in genetics, to which Soviet geneticists still have to bow because it is in accord with the Marxist political line. How far the Communists are willing to go in perverting science to the uses of politics may be seen in the following excerpts from an article in the *USSR Information Bulletin* written by Lysenko himself.

> It was the great Lenin who discovered Michurin and the great Stalin who launched Michurin's materialistic biological theories on the highroad of creative work.
>
> Not only has the great Stalin rescued the Michurin teaching from the attempts of reactionaries in science to destroy it; he has also helped to rear large forces of Michurinist scientists and practical workers. His guiding ideas have played and are playing a decisive role in the triumph of the materialistic Michurin teaching over the reactionary, idealistic Weissmannism-Morganism in the Soviet land.
>
> The works of Joseph Stalin are an invaluable and inexhaustible fount for the development of theoretical Michurinist biology. His classic work, *Dialectical and Historical Materialism,* is an indispensable general

> theoretical aid to all agrobiologists, which helps them to gain a correct understanding of biological facts. Only when examined in the light of dialectical and historical materialism, the principles of which have been further developed by Stalin, does the Michurinist biological teaching gradually reveal its full depth and truth to us.

Where education is under the control of collectivist fanatics, not only is the individual's loyalty to truth despised, but the objective findings of science may be thus perverted to serve the ends of a political ideology.

Even though this may be regarded as an extreme case, we are living in a world where extreme aberrations occur suddenly, so that "It can't happen here" may be followed rather abruptly by "Now it has happened here." Dangers are always best met at the frontier, and the frontier in this instance is just where the state proposes to move in on education. Education's first loyalty is to the truth, and the educator must be left free to assert, as sometimes he needs to do, unpopular or unappreciated points of view.

Education thus has a major responsibility to what we think of as objectively true. But it also has a major responsibility to the person. We may press this even further and say that education must regard two things as sacred: the truth, and the personality that is to be brought into contact with it. No education can be civilizing and humane unless it is a respecter of persons. It may be that up to a certain utilitarian point, everyone's training can be more or less alike. But in a most important area, no educational institution is doing its duty if it treats the individual "just like everybody else." Education has to take into account the differing aptitudes produced by nature and individual character, and these differing aptitudes are extremely various. Physiologists are just beginning to understand how widely men differ in their capacities to see, to taste, to bear pain, to assimilate food, to tolerate toxic substances, and in many other physical respects. On top of this are the multifarious ways in which individuals differ psychologically through their nervous systems, reflexes, habits, and patterns of coordination. And above this are the various ways in which individuals differ physically in their ways of intuiting reality, their awareness of ideals, their desires for this or that supersensible satisfaction, and so on. When all of these factors are brought into view, it is seen that every individual is a unique creation, something "fearfully and wonderfully made," and that the educator who does not allow for special development within the discipline which he imposes is a represser and a violator.

Now the educator who is aware of all the facts and values involved in his difficult calling will recognize in the individual a certain realm of privacy. Much of present-day education and many of the pressures of modern life treat the person as if he were a one-, or at best two-dimensional being. They tend to simplify and indeed even to brutalize their treatment of the person by insisting that certain ways are "good for everybody." Yet it is a truth of the greatest importance that our original ideas and our intuitions of value form in certain recesses of the being which must be preserved if these processes are to take place. The kind of self-mastery which is the most valuable of all possessions is not something imposed from without; it is a gestation within us, a growth in several dimensions, an integration which brings into a whole one's private thoughts and feelings and one's private acts and utterances. A private world alone is indeed dangerous, but a personality whose orientation is entirely public is apt to be flat, uncreative, and uninteresting. The individual who does not develop within himself certain psychic depths cannot, when the crises of life have to be faced meet them with any real staying power. His fate is to be moved along by circumstances, which in themselves cannot bring one to an intelligent solution.

Most people have marveled how Abraham Lincoln was able to develop such a mastery of logic and such a sense of the meaning of words while growing up in a society which set little store by these accomplishments. Yet the answer seems easy enough; Lincoln had a very real private life, in which he reflected deeply upon these matters until he made them a kind of personal possession. He was an individual—keeping up a train of personal reflection, even while mingling in a friendly and humorous way with the people of his frontier community. Lincoln paid a price for this achievement, of course, the rule of this world being "nothing for nothing." But no one who believes in greatness will say that the price was out of proportion to what was gained. If it is true that Lincoln "belongs to the ages," it is so because he learned to think about things in a way that enabled him to transcend time and place. This what is meant by developing a personality.

How far modern theorists have drifted from these truths may be seen in the strange remarks of the "progressive" educator John Dewey.

> . . . the idea of perfecting an "inner" personality is a sure sign of social divisions. What is called inner is simply that which does not connect with others—which is not capable of full and free communication. What is termed spiritual culture has usually been futile, with something rotten about it, just because it has been conceived as a thing which a man might have internally—and therefore exclusively.

For Dewey an inner consciousness is exclusive, aristocratic, separative. What Dewey denies, what his spurious system forces him to deny, is that by achieving a depth of personality, one does develop a power and a means of influencing the community in the best sense of the term "influence." To speak personally is to speak universally. Humanity is not a community in the sense of a number of atoms or monads, knocking together; it is a spiritual community, in which to feel deeply is to feel widely, or to make oneself accessible to more of one's fellow members. In consequence, it cannot be too forcefully argued that the education which regards only development with reference to externals is not education for a higher plane of living, for the individual and for the society of which he is a part, but for a lower—for an artificially depressed level of living which, were it to be realized, would put an end to human development.

Although it may at first seem paradoxical to insist both upon discipline and the development of private and inner resources, the cooperative working of the two is a proved fact of education. Nothing today more needs recovering than the truth that interest develops *under pressure.* Man is not spontaneously interested in anything with an interest that lasts or that carried him beyond attention to superficial aspects. Natural interest which is left to itself nearly always proves impermanent, disconnected, and frivolous. It is only when we are made to take an interest in something that we become exposed to its real possibility of interesting us. It is only then that we see far enough into its complications and potentialities to say to ourselves, here is a real problem, or a real opportunity. We need not suppose that institutions are the only source of this kind of pressure. The situation a person finds himself in when he must earn a living or achieve some coveted goal may exert the necessary compulsion. But here we are talking about what formal education can do for the individual, and one of the invaluable things it can do is face him with the necessity of mastering something, so that he can find the real richness that lies beyond his threshold indifference to it. An interest in mathematics, in music, in poetry has often resulted from an individual's being confronted with one of these as a "discipline"; that is, as something he had to become acquainted with on pain of penalties. The subject then by its own powers begins to evoke him, and before long he is wondering how he could ever have been oblivious to such a fascinating world of knowledge and experience. From this point on his appreciation of it becomes individual, personal, and creative.

As individuality begins to assert itself in the man or woman, we realize that its movement is toward a final ethical tie-up of the personality. Individuality should not be equated with a mere set of idiosyncrasies. Idiosyncracy is casual, fortuitous, essentially meaningless. No enlightened believer in individualism rests his case on anything as peripheral as this. To be an individual does not mean to be "peculiar" or somehow curious in one's outlook. It does, however, mean to be distinctive.

Individuality as a goal must be explained by men's inclinations toward the good. All of us aspire toward something higher, even though there are varying ways in which that something higher can be visualized or represented. Whether one is prone to accept an ethical humanism, a tradition of religious principles, or a creed having its authority in revelation, the truth cannot be ignored that man is looking for something better both in himself and in others. But because different persons have, through their inheritance, nurture, and education different faculties, they have different insights into the good. One man is deeply and constantly aware of certain appearances of it; another of others; and sometimes these differences are so great that they lead to actual misunderstanding. Nevertheless, the wisest have realized that such differences express finally different orientations toward values, and that the proper aim of society is not to iron them out but to provide opportunity for their expression. Variations appearing in these forms do not mean simply that one man is right and another wrong; they mean that the persons in question are responding according to their different powers to apprehend an order of reality. In this kind of perception, some persons are fast movers; others are slow but deep; some have to see things concretely; others are more successful in working out ideas and principles; some people are profoundly sensitive to place; others would do about the same kind of thinking anywhere; some do their best work while feeling a sense of security; others require the excitement and stimulus of uncertainty to draw forth their best efforts. Such a list of differences could be extended almost endlessly. But what it comes down to is this: the reason for not only permitting but encouraging individualism is that each person is individually related toward the source of ethical impulse and should be allowed to express his special capacity for that relation. This is at the same time the real validation of democracy. Democracy cannot rest upon a belief in the magic of numbers. It rests upon a belief that every individual has some special angle of vision, some particular insight into a situation which ought to be taken into account before a policy is decided on. Voting is perhaps only a rough way of effecting this, but the essential theory is clear: every person is deemed to have something worthy to contribute to decision-making, and the very diversity and variety of these responses are what makes democracy not indeed a more efficient, but a fairer form of government than those in which one, or a few men at the top assume that their particular angle upon matters contains all the perception of the good that is needed.

Yet there is a very true sense in which one does not become such an individual until he becomes aware of his possession of freedom. One cannot act as a being until one is a being; one can not *be* a being unless he feels within himself the grounds of his action. The people in this world who impress us as nonentities are, in the true analysis, people whose speech and actions are only reflections of what they see and hear about them, who have no means of evaluating themselves except through what other people think of them. These are the "other directed men," the hollow men, the men who have to be filled with stuffing from the outside, of which our civilization is increasingly productive. The real person is, in contrast, the individual who senses in himself an internal principle of control, to which his thoughts and actions are related. Ever aware of this, he makes his choices, and this choosing is the most real thing he ever does because it asserts his character in the midst of circumstances. Then the feeling of freedom comes with a great upsurging sense of triumph: to be free is to be victorious; it is to count, whereas the nonentity by his very nature does not count.

A liberal education specifically prepares for the achievement of freedom. Of this there is interesting corroboration in the word itself. "Liberal" comes from a Latin term signifying "free," and historically speaking, liberal education has been designed for the freemen of a state. Its content and method have been designed to develop the mind and the character in making choices between truth and error, between right and wrong. For liberal education introduces one to the principles of things, and it is only with reference to the principles of things, that such judgments are at all possible. The mere facts about a subject, which may come marching in monotonous array, do not speak for themselves. They speak only through an interpreter, as it were, and the interpreter has to be those general ideas derived from an understanding of the nature of language, of logic, and of mathematics, and of ethics and politics. The individual who is trained in these basic disciplines is able to confront any fact with the reality of his freedom to choose. This is the way in which liberal education liberates.

Finally, therefore, we are brought to see that education for individualism is education for goodness. How could it be otherwise? The liberally educated individual is the man who is at home in the world of ideas. And because he has achieved a true selfhood by realizing that he is a creature of free choice, he can select among ideas in the light of the relations he has found to obtain among them. Just as he is not the slave of another man, with his freedom of choice of work taken from him, so he is not the slave of a political state, shielded by his "superiors" from contact with error and evil. The idea of virtue is assimilated and grows into character through exercise, which means freedom of action in a world in which not all things are good. This truth has never been put more eloquently than by the poet Milton.

> I cannot praise a fugitive and cloistered virtue unexercised and unbreathed, that never sallies out and sees her adversary, but slinks out of the race, where that immortal garland is to be run for, not without

> dust and heat. Assuredly we bring not innocence into the world; we bring impurity much rather; that which purifies us is trial, and trial is by what is contrary.

Freedom and goodness finally merge in this conception; the unfreeman cannot be good because virtue is a state of character concerned with choice, and if this latter is taken away, there is simply no way for goodness to assert itself. The moment we judge the smallest action in terms of right and wrong, we are stepping up to a plane where the good is felt as an imperative, even though it can be disobeyed. When education is seen as culminating in this, we can cease troubling about its failure to accomplish this or that incidental objective. An awareness of the order of the goods will take care of many things which are now felt as unresolvable difficulties, and we will have advanced once more as far as Socrates when he made the young Athenians aware that the unexamined life is not worth living.

The Commitments of Political Education*

Gerhart Niemeyer

A 14-YEAR-OLD ABORIGINE Australian undergoes his tribe's initiation ceremonies. He passes through a number of symbolic acts signifying death and regeneration, the beginning of a new life, but they also include instruction. The boy learns the names of the gods, the stories of creation, the ceremonies proper to an ordered life. "From initiation one learns the true theophany, the myth of tribal genealogy, the corpus of laws, moral and social, in a word, man's place in the cosmos." (M. Eliade, *Patterns of Comparative Religion,* 1963, p. 56.) Here we have a prime example of political education, consisting in ritual and also the communication of "knowledge, the global understanding of the world, the interpretation of the unity of nature, the revelation of the final causes underlying existence," all this aimed not so much at "satisfying the neophyte's thirst for knowledge, but primarily at consolidating his existence as a whole, promoting continuity of life and prosperity and assuring a happier life after death."

Let us now imagine an Athenian youth in the late fifth century B.C. His father, being able to afford the not inconsiderable tuition, has sent him to school with the famous Sophist Hippias. The boy is being instructed in mathematics, astronomy, music, as well as in grammar, rhetoric, and dialectic. Hippias makes him memorize copious facts and subjects him to severe drills in useful skills. There is no question here of "consolidating the

* From *Modern Age,* vol. 15, no. 1 (Winter 1971).

neophyte's existence as a whole," since such questions as the order of being and the moral quality of man's entire life are slighted. Hippias has undertaken to sharpen the young man's wit and tongue, to furnish him with intellectual tools that would enable him, step by step, to climb the ladder of prestige, public office, power, and wealth, all the while making shrewd use of Athens' political institutions.

One day, however, the youth encounters Socrates who has come to Hippias' house to involve the famous Sophist in profound argument. The depths which Socrates' discourse opens to the boy's trembling wonder induce him from that day to "turn around," away from his self-seeking passions, toward the quest for truth and the love of the good. Socrates brings the young man to rational examination of the movements that he can experience in the depth of his soul, and thereby to an awareness of a public order congruous with the order of being itself. Not only Hippias' shallow instructions but also the boy's traditional lessons in Homer drop away from him like last year's skin from a snake. Not only his own life but also Athens as a whole become to him a problem of a "serious play." The truth which the young man is learning to discern in the depth of his own soul thus also turns into an ever-present critique of society. But Socrates' civil loyalty in life and death remind him at all times that a critique of society rooting in love of the divine ground never amounts to sedition and rebellion.

Skipping many centuries, let us now look over the shoulder of a young Russian intellectual of about a hundred years ago. At the university and in the rooms of his companion students, his feverish brain gulps down large doses of Helvétius, Holbach, Fourier, Hegel, Feuerbach, and Comte. Through this reading, his mind acquires the habit of dismissing the realities of his historical situation: Russia, Christianity, Europe. He begins by rejecting the past, then condemns all of the present civilization, and spins out shiny models of other realities which he deems possible, which according to his reading might have been or, given the appropriate effort, could be made to supersede all that now exists. As for the realities around him, they seem to him to amount to no more than a series of obstacles that still frustrate—but not for long, now!—the Promethean desire to create a new, wholly different world, one so much better than the one which men have so far inhabited, a world without evil, limitations, or distortions. The key to that world is, of course, political revolution. One could say that this young man's education moulds in him a political will not for, but against society.

A hundred years later, this same man's great-grandson emerges from a Soviet institution of higher learning. His training has prepared him to assume a carefully defined role in the Soviet's planned economy. Both before and during his university years, he has gone through years of indoctrination in such subjects as the history of the working class and the Communist Party, the Communist ideology, or the requirements of the "phase of transition" from capitalism to Communism. When still in grade school, his imagination was properly oriented by stories of Soviet heroes, men and women who, disregarding injuries, handicaps, and every pain, gave their all to Soviet production. These heroes were prefigurations of the coming "new Soviet man," a novel creature for whom there is no good except the Party and its interests, who has wholly subordinated his person and his own good to the utility of the totalitarian movement that manages the country.

These five instances might be looked upon as universal types, even though we have found them in diverse historical situations. Accordingly, we could then classify educational patterns as either instruction in the order-sustaining myths, or training for the clever pursuit of private utility, or attunement to the experienceable truth of being, or social critique in the name of a utopian "possible reality," or conditioning for a ruling sect's public utility. Should we call all five examples of "political education?" Suppose we were to deny that attribute to some of these types and vindicate it to others, would it follow that we should prefer the latter over the former? We are now talking about political education as our subject, and one could begin by defining political education as the moulding of man to the requirements of a particular society. Such a definition might tell us something about what we should seek were we committed to political education, but it cannot commit us to political education as such. After all, we are familiar with societies in which the best find politics beneath their dignity and unworthy of their attention, who would say with Goethe:

> *Ein garstig Lied. Pfui, ein politisch Lied, Ein leidig Lied . . .*
> (A nasty song! Fie! a political song—a most offensive song! . . .)

On this view of human life, education should begin where politics leave off. It was this educational ideal that Wilhelm von Humboldt preached to 19th-century Germany, replacing political education with *Bildung,* "the highest and proportional unfolding of an individual's personal energies to a whole" (cf. Eric Voegelin, "Universität und Öffentlichkeit," *Wort und Wahrheit,* Vol. XXI, pp. 497–518). Such education is emphatically uncommitted to the form of political existence and substitutes a commitment to the idea of "science" conceived as something "not yet wholly attained and never to be wholly attained," instruction in which "science" is to constitute "the moral culture of the nation." Humboldt's idea of education that is indifferent to society and instead geared to an asocial person and an unpolitical "science," is characteristic of much of modern Western civilization, resulting in widespread political apathy. If we call this pattern unpolitical, we should attribute the same predicate to education that produces an attitude of alientation from society, even though that same education may aim at some kind of political action. Revolutionary action means the dissolution or destruction of political form and is the opposite of commitment to the form of political existence. Hans Buchheim (*Totalitarian Rule, its Nature and Characteristics,* Wesleyan Univ. Press, 1968, p. 89 ff.) argues that even the public rule of a totalitarian-minded group is apolitical since it is subversive of social norms and of the state, and hostile to the society's traditions, and considers itself "the germ cell of a new element within the old whole that has already lost its historic right to exist." On this showing we would have to call unpolitical the education through which a totalitarian movement conditions people to support it rather than the form and norms of their society.—Among the universal types, then, we find two that are political (instruction in the myth, and attunement to the order of being) and three unpolitical (education for private utility, revolutionary education, and education for the utility of a totalitarian movement).

Such taxonomic distinctions as such say nothing about whether it is good to have political education. That question usually is answered in terms of man's need for society and authority. One wonders, though, whether such an answer fits the problem. Let us look at our own political education, to the extent to which we still have one. In essence it does not differ from that of the Australian aborigines. In both cases teachers, in the name of the whole society, pass on to youngsters the assumptions on which the going social concern is predicated. In Australia, this teaching comes in the form of stories about gods, creation, and ceremonies. Our teachers, too, communicate myths, albeit in different form, by conveying assumptions about man, nature, morals, this country, its past and heroes, and other civilizations. They inculcate attitudes not only by words and music but also by ceremonies: the invocation, the pledge of allegiance, the respect shown to the flag and the country's military uniforms, reverence for the Constitution, the ritual forms of democracy (Robert's Rules), deference to instituted authority, obligation to the laws. This teaching, and the corresponding pressures from a person's peers, result in Americans who are so committed to their country and its ways that they cannot do without its external paraphernalia when living abroad, even in another highly civilized country like, let us say, Italy. Thus one cannot answer the question whether man should have political education by answering in terms of a general need of man for society. There are some, of course, who deny even this general proposition. But should we agree on the abstract statement as such, we still would not have answered our question. For that question, surely, must be whether man is to be educated to the form of a particular society, to that society's "character," as Aristotle used the term. For there is no society other that the particular ones. We cannot make our approval of political education hinge on an abstract image of social perfection that has no historical actuality. If there is to be political education, we must expect it to have a content shaped by the underlying myths of the given historical society in which we live, and to be committed to sustain its character, institutional system, and practical limitations.

A statesman might possibly leave it at this point. Political scientists, however, cannot stop here, for they are committed to the truth of human order. The quest for truth must take us beyond the given historical society, beyond its constitution, beyond even such concepts as democracy. Beyond all contingencies we "are forced" (the term Plato used in the allegory of the Cave) to ascend to the unconditioned, the timeless, to probe for the ground of being. Plato's quest fastened on "the good," Aristotle's on "the best," Augustine's on the creator and redeemer God and the "tranquillity of order" of all created things. Political science emerged in history as a disciplined inquiry into the unconditioned truth beyond public order, and apart from such an inquiry there could be no political science. For a mere description of the various parts of an institutional pattern and their way of fitting together surely does not rank the name and dignity of a science. Political scientists, therefore, could not settle for a political education that treated the contingent as if it were all there is and thereby perverted a historical particularity into an absolute, clothing society with the illegitimate mantle of divinity.

At this point, then, we move beyond the kind of political education that limits itself to the myth sustaining a particular society. By insisting that political education must also commit itself to absolute truth beyond and above historical givenness, we furnish each citizen with a yardstick of the source of order, available to him as a man rather than a citizen, knowledge rather than myth, accessible to the autonomous mind that experiences directly the participation of man in the divine ground of reality. Aristotle has taught us that political science must be double-pronged, concerning itself "with (1) what is best in the abstract but also with (2) that which is best relatively to circumstances." In the same way political education, ever since Plato, must embrace both the contingent and the absolute. That means that it has two commitments: to the character and the sustenance of a particular historical society as well as to the critique of that society in the light of transcendent truth.

We seem to have arrived at the primafacie assumption underlying reflective contemporary political education which, more than anything else, is education for social criticism. What gives us pause at this point, however, is that the above mentioned three types of apolitical education all are rooted exclusively in social criticism. We must infer, not necessarily that all social criticism is incompatible with political education, but at least that there seems to be a kind of criticism which results in the loss of political substance and political education. Thus the nature of criticism itself becomes a problem, and we need critical standards by which to examine and judge criticism itself. Modern social criticism can be traced to Hobbes (according to Marx, he was "the father of us all") who introduced into political thought his method of "analysis," i.e. the taking asunder of a body into its component particles. The atomic particles which Hobbes obtained when he thus dissected the body social appeared to him as self-centered, self-seeking, asocial, and apolitical individuals. Referring to them as the yardstick for political criteria he based his social critique on the requirements of separate and insular human atoms rather than on the *zoon politikon*. Education embracing the apolitical basic assumptions of Hobbes, or the subsequent ones of Locke, Adam Smith, Wilhelm von Humboldt, or John Stuart Mill would tend to bring up men who consider themselves above all private men rather than citizens. Thus a critique derived from asocial assumption cannot be compatible with political education. A different buy yet similar effect results when criticism of society stems from the image of an order that never was, either the *ordre naturel* of the 18th century, or the future millennium of contemporary ideologies. One should emphatically include in this latter category Hegel, whose yardstick of absolute rationality in history belongs to the utopian possible realities rather than to real historical possibilities. The influences of both Hobbes and Hegel on education lead to nonhistorical thinking, because they envisage behind historical societies a transcending reality which is both world-immanent, human, contingent, and yet apolitical and transhistorical. Hegel's absolute rationality is revealed in its nonpolitical character by Marx whose absolute yardstick is the stateless society of the future. An education that takes its clues from this type of social critique will tend to dwell on apparently practical goods which are yet conceived without regard to the possibilities and limitations of given historical realities. One might call this an emphasis on the moral practical good inordinately excluding attention to existence, the kind of emphasis that characterizes Kant's *Perpetual Peace.*

The good, or "the best," however is only one of two prongs, the other one being actual historical existence, human organization for action in a particular place, at a particular time, and in a particular historical setting. The human situation is in the midst of historical contingencies, facing limited practical possibilities, an open future without certainty of the outcome, in the framework of a given set of people and institutions. No education can be political unless it takes the historicity of human existence seriously. It fails to take it seriously whenever it pretends to a knowledge of history as a whole, as if there were available to men a point above history from which a human mind could survey past, present, and future. Even when it avoids the pitfalls of totalitarian ideologies, education embracing history as a whole implicitly claims some certainty above the future and will try to prepare men for this alleged outcome of things. That, however, amounts to ignoring the entire problem of human action in history. I incline to be suspicious of all textbooks that indulge in sweeping generalizations on history, either by arranging it in a series of ages (the age "of faith," "of reason," "of machines") or in terms of process (evolution, progress, dialectic), or by attributing value to time ("advanced" or "progressive" = good; "backward" or "reactionary" = bad) to all of which I would oppose Ranke's dictum that every moment in history is immediately toward eternity. What I understand Ranke to say is that man's dwelling place is neither the past nor the future but the historical present, which is a dwelling place because in it and through it man, having to take contingent action, makes his decisions facing eternity, in the perspective of death.

As we have seen, the contingent and historical can never be the last word, in a situation in which philosophy has come to shape our consciousness and the Prophets of Israel our conscience. Historical decisions are taken not merely by the standards of traditions and existence, but also *sub specie aeternitatis.* The eagle eye that probes the depth of the soul or gauges the reach of divine purpose must always look beyond a historical position to the source of order in which any human actualization appears peace-meal. A critique of society in the light of transcendent truth is compatible with an education that takes seriously the human condition in the midst of historical contingencies. Nobody could be more realistic about historical givens than Augustine who also at times was "making the movements of infinity." This phrase occurs in Kierkegaard's portrait of the "knight of faith" (*Fear and Trembling*) the man who lives in the here and now with unusual intensity because at every moment he also resigns from it all and turns to the Eternal. The concrete world of history and the transcendent absolute are fully compatible as long as man is aware of his standing "in between," the contingencies of change below and the eternal Absolute above. The only critique of society that will not destroy historicity is one that looks, from the point of given historical reality accepted as one's undeniable situation, to the timeless divine ground of being.

Most of today's political thought also measures society by transcendencies, but transcendencies explicitly conceived as denials of and substitutes for, the divine ground of being: Progress, History's Dialectic, the Class Struggle, the Economic Order, Race, Revolution, the Subconscious, the Autonomous Self. In one sense or another, such concepts seem to stand for something that transcends particular societies, and in this way they serve as absolutes to today's ideological thought. But as far as history is concerned, they are not above and beyond but within history, contingencies which some perverted thinker lifted from the stream of change and treated as if it were the source of order. We are told that the contingencies immediately surrounding us are to be judged and measured by contingencies somewhat more remote. Hence these are pseudo-transcendencies, falsely divinized moments of history or possibly even pseudo-history. History, however, cannot stand this divinization of any of its moments or aspects, and neither can nature. A social criticism based on pseudo-transcendencies results in the destruction of past and present, leaving only the dream of a future and the false cause of "liberation" by which the divinized contingency would be freed from all the other impediments of history. If we desire political education, we must realize that we can have it only as a combination of a commitment to the historically extant society combined with the openness to the transcendent absolute, and we must guard not only against the absolutization of the first commitment but also against the perversion of the second.

What about the tasks of the present moment? It is obvious that we are not called upon to face the problem of political education *ab ovo* but rather to look at our actual practices in this regard and decide where to move from here. With much simplification, one may describe our situation in the following terms.

Much, indeed most of present-day political education still flows from our tradition and customs. It comes in the form of an unreflective patriotism and common sense value judgments of people whose world is still intact, whose sense of priorities remains untroubled, whose loyalties are unquestioning. Most of this type of education occurs in public schools where we can witness again and again the spectacle of sons and daughters of immigrants being turned into Americans in less than one generation. Some political education of this type is performed by the media, some by public leaders. The entire process is nothing but America handing down its sustaining myths to the young.

Over against this, we have a type of education governed by articulate premises and principles representing the critical mind, mostly nurtured on modern political ideologies. One may distinguish three varieties:

1. *Atomistic liberalism,* focusing on individualistic self-sufficiency and serving chiefly an apolitical notion of human life. As far as

On Classical Studies*

Eric Voegelin

A REFLECTION ON CLASSICAL studies, their purpose and prospects, will properly start from Wolf's definition of classic philology as the study of man's nature as it has become manifest in the Greeks.[1]

The conception sounds strangely anachronistic today, because it has been overtaken by the two closely related processes of the fragmentation of science through specialization and the deculturation of Western society. Philology has become linguistics; and the man who manifested his nature in the Greek language has become the subject matter of specialized histories of politics, literature, art, political ideas, economics, myth, religion, philosophy, and science. Classical studies are reduced to enclaves in vast institutions of higher learning in which the study of man's nature does not rank high in the concerns of man. This fragmentation, as well as the institutional reduction, however, are not sensed as a catastrophe, because the "climate of opinion" has changed in the two hundred years since Wolf's definition. The public interest has shifted from the nature of man to the nature of nature and to the prospects of domination its exploration opened; and the loss of interest even turned to hatred when the nature of man proved to be resistant to the changes dreamed up by intellectuals who want to add the lordship of society and history to the mastery of nature. The alliance of indifference and hatred, both inspired by *libido dominandi*, has

* From *Modern Age*, vol. 17, no. 1 (Winter 1973).

[1] Friedrich August Wolf (1759–1824) created the science of "philology." The work on which his fame still rests is the *Prolegomena ad Homerum* (1795).

created the climate that is not favorable to an institutionalized study of the nature of man, whether in its Greek or any other manifestation. The protagonists of the Western deculturation process are firmly established in our universities.

Still, the end of the world has not come. For "climates of opinion," though they last longer than anyone but their libidinous profiteers would care, do not last forever. The phrase was coined by Joseph Glanvill (1638–1680); it received new currency when Alfred N. Whitehead resumed it in his *Science and the Modern World* (1925); and, following the initiative of Whitehead, the changes of this modern climate ever since the 17th century have become the subject of Basil Willey's perceptive and extensive *Background* studies, beginning in 1934. Through Whitehead's, as well as through other initiatives, we know by now what the problem is; Whitehead has stated it flatly: "Modern philosophy has been ruined." More explicitly I would say: The Life of Reason, the ineluctable condition of personal and social order, has been destroyed. However, though these statements are true, one must distinguish between the climate of opinion and the nature of man. The climate of our universities certainly is hostile to the Life of Reason, but not every man is agreeable to have his nature deformed by the "climate" or, as it is sometimes called, the "age." There are always young men with enough spiritual instinct to resist the efforts of "educators" who pressure for "adjustment." Hence, the climate is not static; through the emotionally determined constellation of opinions of the moment there is always at work the resistance of man's nature to the climate. The insight into this dynamics underlies the studies of Willey. As a matter of fact, neither the changes in the climate from indifference to hostility, nor the concomitant waning of institutional support for the Life of Reason, nor the fanatically accelerated destruction of the universities since the Second World War, could prevent the problem of the climate from being recognized, articulated, and explored in the light of our consciousness of human nature. The reflections in which we are engaged here and now are as much a fact in the contemporary situation as the notorious "climate." The freedom of thought is coming to life again, when the "climate of opinion" is no longer a massive social reality imposing participation in its partisan struggles, but is forced into the position of a pathological deformation of existence, to be explored by the criteria of reason.

This is the setting in which the question of classical studies must be placed. On the one hand, there is a powerful climate of opinion in our universities opposed to accord them any function at all, because classical studies inevitably represent the nature of man as it has become manifest in the Greeks. On the other hand, there are undeniable symptoms of the climate cracking up and the nature of man undeformed reasserting itself. If this movement toward a restoration of reason should gain sufficient momentum to affect the institutional level, classical studies would become an important factor in the process of education. I shall reflect on the two points in this order—though some disorder may creep in as we are dealing not with alternatives belonging to the past but with an ongoing process.

The effort of the Greeks to arrive at an understanding of their humanity has culminated in the Platonic-Aristotelian creation of philosophy as the science of the nature of man. Even more than with the Sophistic of their times the results are in conflict with the contemporary climate of opinion. I shall enumerate some principal points of disagreement:

1. *Classic:* There is a nature of man, a definite structure of existence that puts limits on perfectibility.
   Modern: The nature of man can be changed, either through historical evolution or through revolutionary action, so that a perfect realm of freedom can be established in history.

2. *Classic*: Philosophy is the endeavor to advance from opinion (*doxa*) about the order of man and society to science (*episteme*); the philosopher is not a philodoxer.
   Modern: No science in such matters is possible, only opinion; everybody is entitled to his opinions; we have a pluralist society.

3. *Classic*: Society is man written large.
   Modern: Man is society written small.

4. *Classic*: Man exists in erotic tension toward the divine ground of his existence.
   Modern: He doesn't, for I don't; and I'm the measure of man.

5. *Classic*: Man is disturbed by the question of the ground; by nature he is a questioner (*aporein*) and seeker (*zetein*) for the whence, the where to, and the why of his existence; he will raise the question: Why is there something, why not nothing?

Modern: Such questions are otiose (Comte); don't ask them, be a socialist man (Marx); questions to which the sciences of world-immanent things can give no answer are senseless, they are *Scheinprobleme* (neopositivism).

6. *Classic*: The feeling of existential unrest, the desire to know, the feeling of being moved to question, the questioning and seeking itself, the direction of the questioning toward the ground that moves to be sought, the recognition of the divine ground as the mover, are the experiential complex, the *pathos,* in which the reality of divine-human participation (*metalepsis*) becomes luminous. The exploration of the metaleptic reality, of the Platonic *metaxy,* as well as the articulation of the exploratory action through language symbols, in Plato's case of his Myths, are the central concern of the philosopher's efforts.

   Modern: The modern responses to this central issue change with the "climate of opinion."

   In Locke the metaleptic reality and its noetic analysis is transformed into the acceptance of certain "common opinions" which still bear an intelligible relation to the experience from which they derive. The reduction of reality to opinion, however, is not deliberate; Locke is already so deeply involved in the climate of opinion that his awareness of the destruction of philosophy through the transition from *episteme* to *doxa* is dulled. Cf. Willey's presentation of the Lockean case.

   Hegel, on the contrary, is acutely aware of what he is doing when he replaces the metaleptic reality of Plato and Aristotle by his state of alienation as the experiential basis for the construction of his speculative system. He makes it explicitly his program to overcome philosophy by the dialectics of a self-reflective alienated consciousness.

   In the 20th century, the "climate of opinion" has advanced to the tactics of the "silent treatment." In a case like Sartre's, metaleptic reality is simply ignored. Existence has the character of meaningless *facticité*; its endowment with meaning is left to the free choice of man. The choice of a meaning for existence falls with preference on the opinion of totalitarian regimes who engage in mass murder, like the Stalinist; the preference has been elaborated with particular care by Merleau-Ponty. The tactics of the "silent treatment," especially employed after the Second World War by the "liberation rabble," however, make it difficult to decide in individual cases, whether the counterposition to metaleptic reality is deliberate, or whether the *libido dominandi* is running amok in a climate of opinion that is taken for granted, without questioning, as ultimate reality. On the whole, I have the impression, that the consciousness of a counterposition is distinctly less alive than it still was at the time of Hegel. Philosophical illiteracy has progressed so far that the experiential core of philosophizing has disappeared below the horizon and is not even recognized as such when it appears in philosophers like Bergson. The deculturation process has eclipsed it so thoroughly by opinion that sometimes one hesitates to speak even of an indifference toward it.

7. *Classic*: Education is the art of *periagoge,* of turning around (Plato).
   Modern: Education is the art of adjusting people so solidly to the climate of opinion prevalent at the time that they feel no "desire to know." Education is the art of preventing people from acquiring the knowledge that would enable them to articulate the questions of existence. Education is the art of pressuring young people into a state of alienation that will result in either quiet despair or aggressive militancy.

8. *Classic*: The process in which metaleptic reality becomes conscious and noetically articulate is the process in which the nature of man becomes luminous to itself as the life of reason. Man is the *zoon noun echon.*
   Modern: Reason is instrumental reason. There is no such thing as a noetic rationality of man.

9. *Classic*: Through the life of reason (*bios theoretikos*) man realizes his freedom.
   Modern: Plato and Aristotle were fascists. The life of reason is a fascist enterprise.

The enumeration is not even remotely exhaustive. Everybody can supplement it with juicy items gleaned from opinion literature and the mass media, from conversations with colleagues and students. Still, they make it clear what Whitehead meant when he stated that modern philosophy has been ruined. Moreover, the conflicts have been formulated in such a manner that the character of the grotesque attaching to the deformation of humanity through the climate of opinion becomes visible. The grotesque, however, must not be confused with the comic or the humorous. The seriousness of the matter will be best understood, if one envisions the concentration camps of totalitarian regimes and the gas chambers of Auschwitz in which the grotesqueness of opinion becomes the murderous reality of action.

The climate of opinion is unfavorable to classical studies; and the institutional power of its representatives in the universities, the mass media, and the foundations must not be underrated. Nevertheless, cracks in the establishment become noticeable. In particular, the international student revolt has been an eye-opener. Even the spiritually and intellectually underprivileged who live by the bread of opinion alone have become aware that something is wrong with our instituions of higher learning, though they do not quite know what. Could it be perhaps the professors and not the war in Vietnam? With grim amusement have I watched the discomfiture of assorted leftist professors in Frankfurt and Berlin when their students turned against them, because the professors did not go along when their "critical theory" (a euphemism for irrational, nihilistic opining) was translated by the students into uncritical violence; and the same spectacle is provided in America by the liberal professors who suddenly become conservative, when a lifetime of strenuous effort to ruin the minds of one generation of students after another has at last borne fruit and the minds are really ruined. An incident from my own teaching practice will illuminate the critical point. In the mid-60s I gave a course in classical politics at a major university. All went well as long as the students believed they were offered the customary fare of information on Plato's "opinions." An uproar ensued when they found out that philosophy of politics was to be taken seriously as a science. The idea that some propositions concerning the order of man and society were to be accepted as true, others to be rejected as false, came as a shock; they had never heard of such a thing before. A few actually walked out of the course; but the majority, I am glad to report, stayed on; they became enchanted by Plato, and at the end they profusely expressed their gratitude to have at last learned of an alternative to the drivel of opinions they were routinely fed. But I do not want to go more deeply into this aspect of the matter. It will be sufficient to state that the students have good reasons to revolt; and if the reasons they actually advance are bad, one should remember that the educational institutions have cut them off from the life of reason so effectively that they cannot even articulate the causes of their legitimate unrest.

By the irrational violence of the attack, the revolt could expose the flabbiness and emptiness of the institutionalized climate and its personnel, but one should not expect the life of reason to emerge from the confrontation of two vacua. More important than the spectacular events is the quiet erosion of the climate through the historical sciences. The nature of man can be deformed by the dominant opinions—the other day I heard a well-intentioned but helpless colleague cry out in anguish: Our world is fragmented!—but it is indestructible and finds ways to reassert itself. The metaleptic reality that is brushed aside as stuff and nonsense, if it claims in public to be the primary concern of man, has deviously crept in again under the respectable cover of comparative religion, comparative literature, the history of art, the science of the myth, the history of philosophy, intellectual history, the exploration of primitive symbolisms in ethnography and anthropology, the study of ancient civilizations, archeology, and prehistory, of Hinduism, Islam, and the Far East, of Hellenistic mystery religions, the Qumran texts, and Gnosticism, of early Christianity and the Christian Middle-Ages, and last not least by classical studies. In the cultural history of Western society, the splendid advance of the historical sciences has become the underground of the great *resistance* to the climate of opinion. In everyone of the fields enumerated, we find the men who devote their life to it, because here they find the spiritual integrity and wholeness of existence which on the dominant level of the universities has been destroyed. No critical attack on the insanity of the "Age" can be more devastating than the plain fact that men who respect their own humanity, and want to cultivate it as they should, must become refugees to the Megalithicum, or Siberian shamanism, or Coptic Papyri, to the petroglyphs in the caves of the Ile-de-France, or to the symbolisms of African tribes, in order to find a spiritual home and the life of reason. Moreover, this underground has become the refuge not only for scholars but also for the more sensitive students, as one can ascertain by browsing for an hour in a college bookstore; the nature of man asserts itself, even if these poor fellows, deprived of proper guidance, grope for support in such exotica as the I-Ching.

Under the historical cover, thus, the substantive knowledge concerning the nature of man is present in our universities. Thanks to the fantastic enlargement of the historical horizon in time and space that has occurred in the present century, this knowledge has even become more comprehensive and penetrating than at any other time in the history of our universities. At the same time it has become more easily accessible to everybody—I have only to compare the difficulties of access in the 20s, when I was a student, with the present plethora of paperbacks. This formidable presence, however, is slow to develop into a formative force in our institutions of higher learning. One of the reasons for this odd state of things will become apparent from an incident, a few years ago, at a conference on comparative religion: One of the participants broke the great taboo and flatly put it to his *confrères* that the subject-matter they were treating was irrelevant by the standards of opinion to which most of them seemed to adhere; sooner or later they would have to make up their mind whether the science of comparative religion was an occupational therapy for persons otherwise unemployable, or whether it was a pursuit of the truth of existence which its subject-matter substantively contained; one could not forever explore "religious phenomena," and pretend to their importance, without unreservedly professing that man's search for the divine ground of his existence, as well as the revelatory presence of God in the motivation of the search, constituted his humanity; in brief, he confronted them with the question of truth implied in their admirable achievements as historians. Not everybody present was pleased by such tactlessness. The historical cover, thus, is a sensible device as long as it secures a degree of freedom for the life of reason in institutions which are dominated by an essentially totalitarian climate, but it is in danger of becoming itself a part of the climate, as this incident shows, if the cover is used to sterilize the content and prevent it from becoming effective in our society. The cover will then degenerate into the ideology of historical positivism.

The advance of the historical sciences concerning the nature of man in its various manifestations has arrived at a critical juncture: In retrospect from a future historical position, will it be the massive basis for a restoration of the life of reason? or will it be an interesting last gasp of reason, exhaled by little men who did not have the courage of their convictions, before the totalitarian climate strangled it off for a long time to come?

Assuming the first alternative to be realized, classical studies will have an important function in the process, for in its Greek manifestation man's nature has achieved the luminosity of noetic consciousness and developed the symbols for its self-interpretation. The Greek differentiation of reason in existence has set critical standards for the exploration of consciousness behind which nobody is permitted to fall back. This achievement, however, is not a possession forever, something like a precious heirloom to be handed on to later generations, but a paradigmatic action to be explored in order to be continued under the conditions of our time. But at this point I must stop, for the great question how that is to be done cannot be answered by jotting down a program; concrete action itself would be necessary; and as the Greek manifestation of man's nature covered the range of a civilization, that feat cannot be performed here and now. Hence, I shall conclude these reflections with the designation of two general areas in which no major advance of science beyond its present state seems possible without recourse to, and continuation of, the Greek noetic effort.

1. If anything is characteristic of the present state of the historical sciences, it is the discrepancy between the mountains of material information and the poverty of their theoretical penetration. Whenever I have to touch on problems of the primitive myth or the imperial symbolism of Egypt, of Israelite prophetism, Jewish apocalypse, or Christian gospels, of Plato's historical consciousness compared with that of Deutero-Isaiah, of the Polybian ecumenic consciousness compared with that of Mani, of magic or hermetism, and so forth, I am impressed by the philosophical and text-critical work done on the sources but feel frustrated because so little work is done to relate the phenomena of this class to the structure of consciousness in the sense of noetic analysis.

2. One of the great achievements of the Greek struggle, both against the older myth and the Sophistic climate of opinion, for insight into the order of man's existence is the exploration of existential deformation and its varieties. Again, very little is done to explore this achievement, to develop it further, and to apply it to the modern phenomena of existential deformation. We do not even have a good study on "alienation," though this very topical subject ought to stir up any classical scholar to voice what he has to say about it on the basis of the sources he knows best.

Accepting the [illegible] [illegible] most [illegible] looks [illegible] for the exploration of [illegible]. This [illegible]ment, however, is not a [illegible] something [illegible] to be [illegible] after the entrance of [illegible]. But at this point [illegible] the great question [illegible] is to be [illegible] cannot be [illegible] definition of [illegible] the range of [illegible] cannot be performed here and now [illegible] as well as [illegible] science [illegible] communication [illegible].

[illegible] the [illegible], if [illegible] discussion [illegible] information and the [illegible] of their theoretical conception. Whereas [illegible] of the [illegible] symbolism of Egypt, of [illegible] Chinese [illegible] compared with that of [illegible] of the [illegible] by [illegible] work [illegible] on the [illegible] so little [illegible] phenomenon [illegible] the structure of [illegible] in the [illegible].

[illegible] great [illegible] Greek [illegible] against the older myth and the Sophistic [illegible] of [illegible] into the [illegible] existential [illegible] and [illegible] to [illegible] phenomenon of existential determination we do not even have a good study on [illegible] very [illegible] subject ought to [illegible] classical scholars to voice what he has to say about it on the basis of the sources he knows best.

14/Politics

What Is the Purpose of Politics?*

Stephen Tonsor

I SUPPOSE THAT IF ONE were to ask the question, "What is the purpose of politics?" of Mayor Richard Daley (in one of his candid and relaxed moments), he would say, "The purpose of politics is to get elected," and if one were to ask that same question of Mr. John Dean, lately of the White House Staff, he would reply, "The purpose of politics is to get appointed." Now, however crass these answers may seem, they are not bad answers, for getting elected and getting appointed are political actions of great importance. They are not, however, the end or purpose of politics even though they have come to seem the very essence of political life. Politics for the general public increasingly means "something," or better said, a set of activities engaged in by politicians to their own great advantage and to the general disadvantage of the public. Politics for many is no longer viewed as the source of community and order in society and has come to be regarded as the preserve of professionals who have learned to make the system function to their benefit.

The state of mind which is frequently described as "political alienation" or more succinctly as "dropping out" derives at least in part from the feeling that politics is for politicians and that ordinary men and women can have little or no effect on their political destinies. It is better, so many believe, to take refuge in a thoroughgoing cynicism and withdrawal from public life than

* From *Modern Age*, vol. 18, no. 2 (Spring 1974). Copyright © 1974 by the Foundation for Foreign Affairs, Inc. Reprinted by permission.

to court the disillusionment which follows on the discovery of the political ineffectuality of the individual.

The characteristic mark of the age in which we live is an overwhelming skepticism with respect to the organized and institutionalized structures of our common life. The retreat into the private sphere is a reflection of this general distrust of politics, for politics reach beyond the governmental into every community activity. Survey research and public opinion polls reveal the steep decline of public confidence with respect not only to government but religion, education, medicine, labor, science, business, the press, and, significantly, even the family. All of these institutions have well developed political structures, are in fact a part of politics and so what we see so evidently manifested is the decline of politics, the massive desertion of the political and communal for the private and individual.

This underestimation of the effectiveness of politics is the mirror image of the overestimation of the possibilities of political action. In fact, the retreat to the private sphere has recently often been a consequence of the disappointed expectations men held with respect to their most honored and powerful institutions. As Henry Fairlie has pointed out in his book, *The Kennedy Years,* the current mood of depression and dismay in American society stems in part, at least, from the grandiose dreams engendered on the New Frontier and by the Great Society. In those years American political leaders held out hopes and aspirations to men which simply could not be fulfilled through political action. Something of the same mood dominated the Roman Catholic Church during the pontificate of Pope John and in the brief period following the first session of Vatican II. When the inflated rhetoric had exhausted itself, when the great gestures had been made, when the eulogies had been organized and the money spent, when the manifestos had been issued and the council documents promulgated, the milennium had, alas, still not been achieved and we discovered that we were still stuck with our recalcitrant and unregenerate human natures. It was a dismaying experience. We ought to have learned from it not that politics can do nothing but that it cannot do everything. Many, however, came to believe not that politics could not do everything but that the wrong sort of politics could not do everything. The belief is now widespread that if only John Kennedy had been more pure in his intentions, had not been at heart a cold warrior, had been more deeply convinced on the issue of civil rights, had been more revolutionary in domestic commitments then today we would indeed be living in a sort of Camelot.

Both these positions are the consequence of a defective knowledge of the nature of politics. Both those who cop out and refuse political action and those who hope for fulfillments which political action can never bring to pass, fail to understand the nature of politics. Let us ask again then, "What is the Purpose of Politics?"

Politics is the institutional organization of society whether the form is that of the family, the community, the factory, the voluntary association, or even that of business. Of course, much of the politics of these groups is informal and only in the most highly developed communities does politics become organizational. Nonetheless, wherever the individual touches on or is connected with society political life and political activity result.

Being fully human involves acting politically and this is the root of Aristotle's famous dictum. Nor can we as individuals avoid social or political involvement. Even Robinson Crusoe discovered that although he was autonomous he was not self-sufficient. It is an interesting fact that the more highly intellectualized and spiritualized, the more elaborately cultural human societies become, the more political they are. Diversity and complexity, both of which make autonomy not only possible but meaningful, can exist and be optimized where society and politics are highly developed. It has often been remarked that Thoreau was able to conduct his experiment at Walden pond only because Cambridge lay nearby and his family and friends provided that infrastructure of community which permitted the full flowering of anarchistic individualism.

Much has been written during the past decade concerning "libertarianism" and "anarchism." Many poses have been struck. The roads and the parks, at least in theory, have been sold over and over again and the defense establishment has been let out to contract, theoretically, to a hippy commune in central Colorado who promise to bite to death the enemies of people of the United States. For the most part, libertarians and anarchists have not dealt realistically with either the problem of community or the problem of politics. Their recently invented social and political systems resemble nothing so much as the fanciful perpetual motion machines of the 17th and 18th centuries. Liberty is a reflection of social complexity and political sophistication. It does not result in anarchism. Rather, it always creates and it requires obligation. Consequently, the question is not whether or not one has the right to withdraw from society, to make the great refusal, to break the bonds which bind men together for purposes of mutual fulfillment; the question is not whether we shall be political or not, but rather, how we shall be political and what the ends of our politics shall be. To be fully human is to live politically. The condition of alienation is a reflection of the impossible dream of total self-sufficiency. The madman who invents and peoples a world in his imagination is the only unpolitical man.

Liberty and obligation are indissolubly linked. To be free to do anything means to be obligated to do something. We are free to choose; that is, we are autonomous but the very possibilities of choice open to us are the products of the social matrix in which we have our being and in which we find our fulfillment. All politics and all community have their roots in the inadequacy of the individual, acting alone, to achieve the objectives he finds desirable. These objectives go to the heart of human existence, for human survival depends on man's ability to organize societies to meet the challenge of the environment. Beyond survival all those things which make life worth living and which offer us a foretaste of eternity are communal in nature. In this respect the Christian conception of the Trinity has always seemed to me, purely from a symbolic standpoint, a much more satisfactory representation of the Godhead than Aristotle's self-sufficient, self-contemplating unmoved mover. The image of the beautific vision in the Christian tradition is the image of community, the "communion of saints." But aside from these startling and profound images it is apparent that we ought to view our individual insufficiency not as limitation and as frustration but as the key to fulfillment. As the French are reported to say, "*Vive la difference*!"

It follows from this that the bonds of obligation in society are not exclusively or even predominately contractual; that is, social structures and political forms are not simply arrangements in which the costs and benefits are calculated and nicely weighed and when cost exceeds benefit the contract is nullified. Attempt running a family on that basis some time, or better still rearing a family of teen-age children.

Having said this I must add that I reject the communitarian position which argues that unless there is a common religion, unless there are commonly shared political myths and unless there are pervasive and commonly accepted cultural values about which there is no debate there cannot be an orderly and coherent society. This is neither logically necessary nor is it the experience of mankind.

Common action follows on the acceptance of a common task, the confrontation with a common challenge. Politics does not begin with contract or consensus. The origins of society do not lie in so ethereal a thing as community or so rational and calculated a thing as contract. Life is not quite so simple a matter. As soon as individual men, no matter how diverse they are in origins, heterodox in religion, pluralistic in custom, and different in culture, perceive a common need or confront a common challenge, politics is born. Community and contract are not antecedent to political action but derive from it.

Politics then takes its rise from individual insufficiency. Does it follow that men acting together can do all things? Does it follow that there are no limits to political action? We have been speaking, up to this point, of politics in very broad terms, the politics of the family, the politics of the office, the politics of the playing field. Let us now speak quite specifically of the politics associated with government. Whatever the objectives of political activity in the family, the church, the military, these politics are in a striking way different from the politics of government or what we most frequently call simply "politics." Are there any limitations to the actions of government? What is the purpose of the politics of the "state"?

To ask that question is to raise a series of issue of the utmost consequence for contemporary society. The historical record in the Western World for the past one thousand years reveals the steady growth and concentration of the powers of the state, an enormous increase in its activities and absorption into itself of all other political forms and structures.

The state has clothed itself with the mystique and the liturgical forms of religion; it has become the moral arbiter of society; it has steadily drawn all the activities of the culture-creating elites into its ambit; it has assumed the dominant position in education; it has usurped many of the functions and the roles of the family; it has continuously enlarged its activities in the economic sphere and threatens now to engulf all enterprise, production and distribution of goods and income; it licenses and restricts and eventually will destroy as Rousseau hoped and Tocqueville predicted all intermediary groups and voluntary associations.

The growth of the powers of the state has been the single greatest fact in modern European history. The French and Russian revolutions and the development of nationalism are only incidents in the history of the evolution of statism.

This growth in the power and the authority of the state gives the politics of the state a wholly new meaning and imposes on it forms which in other eras would have been thought totally inappropriate. We have come to view these new political forms as authoritarian and totalitarian. They are political nonetheless though the form of political participation may be very different from the forms characteristic of other eras and other political structures. For example, totalitarian politics casts itself increasingly in the religious and liturgical mold. Participation in the community is sacramental rather than conventionally political. The rites of solidarity on May Day or the anniversary of the revolution are a much more important form of political participation than casting a ballot or seeking electoral office.

Are genuine politics possible under such conditions? Has the evolution of Western governments been such that these are, in fact, the only type of politics possible? Is there a limit to what the state can and ought to do imposed by the nature of man and society? Or is the purpose of politics the augmentation of the authority and the power of the state until it becomes the gigantic though rusty mechanism of which Ortega spoke so eloquently in *The Revolt of the Masses*?

I assert that the politics of the state has one purpose and one purpose only and that is to enable men to live together in civil society. The purpose of politics is not to make men good or holy though that may be an indirect benefit which results from a properly ordered state. Politicians are not and can never become philosopher kings. When politicians speak of philosophy their accents are not those of Plato and St. Thomas but Marx, Rosenberg, Sorel, and Marcuse. And this is the case because the very act of attempting to establish absolute rather than relative justice, the very act of making all men virtuous or all men holy, the very act of allocating goods on the basis of the concept of equality poses a range of problems which lie beyond the powers of governmental action.

While governments cannot make men good they can create the conditions of peace and security which will enable men, singly and in groups to seek the multiform goods which have always been characteristic of any sophisticated society. While governments cannot make men virtuous they can maintain those conditions which make the pursuit of virtue possible. Above all, government will refuse the temptation to commit evil in the name of some higher and remoter good. Evil will not appear as a historical necessity pressed on mankind by the cycle of constitutions, by the invisible hands, the cunning of reason, or the next sequent step in the womb of time. "Historical necessity" is always another name for the abdication of moral responsibility. When politics attempts to achieve that which is beyond political action, it often resorts to evil, always believing it is temporary, always assuming that when the new dispensation has been ushered in, evil will have been forever banished.

The purpose of politics does not go beyond securing the conditions in which the creative potentialities of the individual and the groups and communities he and others create are liberated and facilitated. Note that such political action will always be concrete and related to the solution to specific and particular problems. It will not be general, vague, ideological, nor will it be premised on the belief that either man's nature or his environment can be perfected. The world is a marvelous and complicated place and our natures even more complex. To believe that absolute justice, innocence, or the perfection of person, time, or place this side of the grave is possible, is to indulge one of those groundless hopes which only idiots and revolutionaries entertain. Such notions are commonplaces with the monsters and deformities who serve as heroes in the novels of Dostoevsky. They are inexcusable in a world where every man's work is colored by ambiguity and tried by fire.

The great politicians of any age are not the dreamers and the idealists. They are practical men who have a vision of what is both desirable and possible for their societies. They are not the inventors of slogans such as the "classless society" or the "new frontier" or the "great society." They speak in terms of specific and concrete goals and they have some estimate of what the costs, material and social, will be. They realize that in a world of scarcity and conflicting demands to do anything means not to do something else. They are aware, moreover, that those actions which benefit one member of a society may not, probably will not, benefit another. They believe, therefore, that only those actions which benefit the whole of society more than they benefit any particular individual or group in society ought to be undertaken by government.

Even so, it is extremely difficult to calculate benefits with any degree of accuracy. For example, does public education benefit the individual more than it does the society or is the opposite the case? Does public housing benefit the society more than it does the recipient of the housing or is the opposite the case? How exactly is one to calculate and weigh benefits? These are extremely difficult problems but we might begin by making it a rule that individual welfare ought never to be the object of political action, just as private actions ought never to be the object of scrutiny by the police power or the society as a whole. Individual welfare may be and ought to be the object of politics or institutions other than the state. That, in fact, is the role of the family, the church, the voluntary association. That the happiness quotient in my family should remain high should not become the object of state action for the state. Aside from its ability to spend money (an action which in terms of happiness is very ambivalent) the state has little to offer which can increase our happiness. It can do a great deal, however, to make life for myself and my family a living hell. The language of political discussion ought to eschew discussions of private benefit.

One way in which the state can limit its actions to those which benefit the society as a whole is to refuse any actions which can be performed by other institutions or groups within the society. The state, following this rule, does not attempt to perform the functions of the family, does not attempt to provide education, does not organize charity, does not regulate the economy, and forgoes intrusions into the processes of production and consumption.

We have seen that the whole tendency of state action in the past five hundred years has been just the opposite of this. The state has constantly enlarged the sphere of its activity and increased the degree of centralization within society. I am not arguing that we need fewer social services, that individual need, dependency, helplessness is today less than it was a century ago though that may very well be the case. I am arguing that direct state action in these areas is inappropriate. I am arguing that these are not areas suitable for governmental politics. I am saying that governmental action is less apt to maximize welfare and liberty than alternative social solutions. Only in those cases in which a desired social objective cannot be achieved except by the intervention of the state and in the absence of alternative social institutions and structures ought the state to undertake public action. The community has every possible interest in the world in the collection and safe disposal of garbage. It does not follow from this that garbage ought to be collected by city employees who are paid out of tax money. The same argument can and ought more often to be made with respect to the postal service.

However, we would delude ourselves were we to assume that all those needs essential to the orderly and satisfactory functioning of society are now or have ever been all met by voluntary associations and corporations and institutions other than the state. Libertarians have reason but not history on their side when they argue for the "night-watchman" concept of the state. Most men, even contemporary liberals, wish that a state of such limited powers were capable of meeting the needs of our society. But even in America where the voluntary association has obtained a development unequaled anywhere else in the world men are forced, repeatedly, to turn to the state simply because private agencies and institutions are unavailable.

Moreover, we have seen in the past half century, and that at an increasing rate of acceleration, the decay and dispersal of communities. Rapid and unorganic suburban growth, the movement of large populations from the farm to the city, the industrialization and economic development of the southwest, northwest, west, and south, rapid social mobility and the erosion of the mores and the instituions which supported them in an older America; all of these factors have created an anomic and dislocated society in which the organs of community seem no longer capable of affording individuals and groups the services and protections they find necessary for survival. In consequence, when problems arise they devolve almost immediately upon the state. It alone seems to possess the organizational capacities, the experience, the skills and the resources necessary to deal with the problem. Finally, it seeks to provide an ideology to replace the lost faiths and the shattered myths which had at one time provided support for community.

The solution to this problem lies with the individual. He must deliberately choose to devote his time and talent to the location of community and the solution of the problems which his society confronts through common action. The individual must become a participant in the common tasks of the community. He must, increasingly, devote himself to the common good and to activities which have as their objective the securing of the common welfare. Indeed, the individual will discover his humanity most completely in these activities in which he brings to bear on the problems of his culture and time his gifts and insights. The alternative to participation freely and enthusiastically given is participation through the coercion of the state, participation often in solutions to pressing social problems which fly in the face of the moral, economic, cultural, and political views of the citizen. We do not have a choice as to whether we shall participate or not. In the early 1950s when West Germany began the grim business of rearming, slogans suddenly appeared stenciled on the walls and pavements, *ohne mich,* "without me!" That, however, is in any society never really an option. We cannot choose whether or not we will participate; we can, if we are fortunate, choose the method of our participation.

Beyond the cooperative action of individuals in the creation of community the state has a powerful and important role. It is in the interest of the state to encourage and foster voluntary association and nongovernmental institutional forms. These powerful corporate groups and institutions serve in all good societies to stand between the great power of the state and the helplessness of the individual. They act to check the power of single individuals and the power of other corporate groups in the society but above all they alone are capable of challenging state power and authority. The state will be able to fulfill its mission best when its tasks are clearly delineated and when the boundaries of its powers and activities are constantly patrolled by strong and capable competing communities.

For its own health, therefore, the state ought not to undertake activities which go beyond the preservation of the civic order unless it can anticipate a time in the fairly immediate future when its intervention will no longer be necessary. It ought always to be the object of politics to make men and their communities autonomous and independent rather than to coerce them into dependency and servitude. There will always be moments when the resources of individuals and communities are insufficient to meet the staggering problems of the community. The state must then exercise special care that temporary assistance does not become permanent servitude.

Authority and its reflection in the exercise of power is ultimately based upon the moral dispositions of its citizens and upon consent freely given. The moral character of the state, as Harold Laski pointed out long ago (1925) in his book *A Grammar of Politics,* is no different from that of any other association.

> It exacts loyalty upon the same grim condition that a man exacts loyalty from his friends. It is judged by what it offers to its members in terms of the things they deem to be good. Its roots are laid in their minds and hearts. In the long run, it will win support, not by the theoretic program it announces, but by the perception of ordinary citizens that allegiance to its will is a necessary condition of their well-being.

There have surely been few better definitions of the state or the purpose of politics.

15/Sports

Rooting, Agon*

Michael Novak

Rooting

The fan "roots." Yet in the tradition of rationalism and the Enlightenment, the highest stage of human development is to attain universality. Particularism is a scandal. Loyalties to a particular tradition, religion, region, group, or place are considered inferior and also immoral, as if they were the root of prejudice and conflict. Can an "enlightened person" be a fan? In this respect, the traditions of rationalism and of the Enlightenment seem at least partly antihuman. The metaphor of enlightenment itself seems pretentious. Human beings are not filled with pure light, are not angels. Their heads are firmly attached to solid, all-too-solid bodies. Enlightenment seems a trifle Manichean: dividing the world into light and darkness, making many pretend to a reasonableness they do not possess.

A human goal more accurate than enlightenment is "enhumanment." Sports like baseball, basketball, and football are already practiced as express liturgies of such a goal. One religion's sins are another's glories. Some "enlightened" persons feel slightly guilty about their love for sports; it seems less rational, less universal, than their ideals; they feel a twinge of weakness. The "enhumaned" believe that man is a rooted beast, feet planted on one patch of soil, and that it is perfectly expressive of his nature to "root." To be a fan is totally in keeping

* From *The Joy of Sports: End Zones, Bases, Baskets, Balls, and the Consecration of the American Spirit,* by Michael Novak, © 1976 by Michael Novak, Basic Books, Inc., Publishers, New York. Reprinted by permission.

with being a man. To have particular loyalties is not to be deficient in universality, but to be faithful to the laws of human finitude.

A team is not only *assembled* in one place; it also *represents* a place. Location is not merely a bodily necessity; it gives rise to a new psychological reality. Miami, Florida, is a different sort of city now that it has the Dolphins; Denver carries a new identity as the home of the Broncos. New teams in such cities needed a place to play, a stadium, colors, a name. But the cities gained a new persona. Thousands of their citizens gained a focal point for their affections and despairs.

In sports cities around the nation, millions of lives are affected by whether in the days of their youth they were privileged to cheer for winners or, good-naturedly, groaningly, grew up with perennial losers. Around Pittsburgh we went for decades without a winner in anything; inferiority matched the mood of the region. When the Pirates burst through as world champions, followed later by the Steelers, their success released pleasant feelings of vindication, and grounded a rectification of reality: it *was* a good region in which to grow up; national recognition was long overdue. In Detroit, in a year of predicted riots, the Tigers raced toward the championship and brought the city a unity of spirit, a cooling off of hostilities, and even a diminishment of crime no federal programs had been able to accomplish.

It is true that America is steadily being nationalized; the great television networks and the commercial giants require, and help to effect, a unification of consciousness. National sportscasts alternate the teams they telecast; the viewers sometimes cannot see their own teams but must accept the "game of the week." In fact, of course, since a third of the population is highly mobile, the game of the week gives fans who have moved away a chance to see their old hometown squad. That is how I get to see the Dodgers, for example, now that they have moved way out to California. To watch teams I hardly know sometimes satisfies a certain tepid curiosity; I'm glad to catch a glimpse of Yastrzemski, Vida Blue, and others I have heard of. But unless I have a personal stake in a team, a game between two teams unknown to me rarely grabs my attention. Sometimes the sheer drama and perfection of the game holds me at the set; sometimes there is nothing better to do; but for the most part, I depend for excitement on team loyalties.

One effect of contemporary mobility, however, is to have

given me multiple loyalties, at various levels of identification. At different times, I have lived near, or learned to love, five or six professional teams: Green Bay, Oakland, Pittsburgh, New York (the Jets), Washington, Minnesota. I like Don Shula, followed the Giants because I once met Fran Tarkenton, liked Baltimore because of John Unitas, kept an eye on the Bears because so many Notre Damers went there. When one or the other of these teams is playing, I have one or another peg on which to fix my affections. But that is the essential point. To watch a sports event is not like watching a set of abstract patterns. It is to take a risk, to root and to be rooted. Some people, it is true, remain detached; they seem like mere voyeurs. The mode of observation proper to a sports event is *to participate*—that is, to extend one's own identification to one side, and to absorb with it the blows of fortune, to join with that team in testing the favors of the Fates. The root of the word "fan" is not only "fanatic" but also "fantastic"; we have already noted its relation to the word for temple, *fanum,* the temple of the god of the place: by an exercise of imagination one places oneself under the fate of a particular group, becomes other than oneself, and risks thereby one's security. When Notre Dame loses, there is no reason for me to have allowed my security to be vulnerable; in rooting for Notre Dame, I open myself to their bad fortune as well as to their good. (Since, as David Hume says, there is a higher proportion of unhappiness than of happiness in every life, identification with another increases one's risks more than one's rewards. This was his argument against marriage; it also holds for sports fans.) A fan dies a thousand deaths. No team is, or can be, always perfect.

To the unbeliever, it is foolish to invest one's fortunes in a team, in a mere *game.* "How," they say, "can you care what happens to a group of silly men doing silly things?" Like attending cabinet meetings? I reply. Like attending press conferences? When I hear serious people talk about really Serious Things (a passion which I also indulge), my heart sometimes wanders in the middle of the conversation, particularly if at that very hour the Dodgers are playing. It is, I know, proper, well-behaved, mature, and adult to take seriously Summits, Diplomatic Shuttles, Crises of the Dollar, Get Out the Vote Campaigns, Riots in the Cities, Peace, War, Justice, Hunger, Dirty Air. It is not true, however, that these adult things are complex, and sports simple. On the contrary, the only difficult point on

Serious Issues is to discern which is the More Moral Side. As they say in Congress, look to see how Bella Abzug votes, since at least 30 others will use her as a flag to vote against. The older one gets, the more the Serious Issues seem to be the highest comedy of all. And the more basic and fundamental seem to be the realities of sport: community, courage, harmony of mind and body, beauty, excellence. Let the world burn, these realities endure. Let New Moralities come, and Old Moralities be despised; still, three strikes and you're out, and a base hit when your buddies need it is a deed of beauty.

In sports is reality; not all of it, but a great deal of everything important. In politics and social action is illusion; not all of it, but a great deal of what Serious People today think important. Last year's Big Reform is this year's simpleminded gaffe.

I do not want to overstate the case. Business must go on. For the sake of the Ship of State, someone has to get dirty hands down in the boiler room. I only want to assert that rooting for politicians, movements, and causes is not a simple moral matter; it is full of irony, disappointment, bitterness, and, most of all, illusion. (Read Henry Adams. It doesn't change.) The rabid partisans of right, left, and center seem to me no freer from illusions than the partisans of Gehrig, DiMaggio, and Mays. Political and social commentary seem amazingly simplistic, the more so as one learns of the difficulties inherent in politics and statecraft. Moreover, in politics and social thought, partisans seem to me too little enamored of excellence, too quick in praise solely of their own companions, too rabid in their denunciation of their opposition. In sports fans, I detect a richer and more sophisticated appreciation of excellence. I have watched ovations for a player on the other side. Even at the height of their rivalries, antagonists in sports commonly reflect more respect for each other than do Republicans for Democrats, or radicals for liberals. In terms of civility and an ability to see the virtues on the other side, I prefer the company of sports fans to the company of Activities in the Constituency of Conscience.

The most universal experience in America, historians say, is to have been uprooted. Rooting is a pressing national need. The human being needs roots, because the pretense of infinity, the search for total universality, may be proper to the spirit but not to the body; and whoever commits himself to such a search dooms himself to the disintegration of the embodied self, which is death.

In *Easy Rider,* the moment Captain America commits himself to absolute freedom (just as in *Anna Karenina,* when Anna commits herself to total love), one's dreading heart knows that the ending must be death; suspense is released only when, bloodily, death comes. The human body cannot bear infinity. It is not made to be universal. The human body is of a specific color, sex, bone and neural structure, weight, shape, height, genetic heritage, cultural location, point in time and space. Although we walk on legs, we are as rooted in the long spinning structure of history as an ivy plant in earth.

The mobility of the superculture of the United States (i.e., those who identify with no subculture) is our national version of the pursuit of romantic love. We try to be free in total liberty, for total love. If observers watch with dread, it is because they know the narrative laws of such a story. Our national ideal is antihuman. Resisting the rooting ties, we cut our spirits free from discipline; they grow too large, misshapen, distended, anomic, puffs of gas, figures by Goya and Bosch. Divorce, abortion, abandoned children, greed, power, mobility, affluence—we live in a kind of middle-aged pursuit of the unfettered life, fettered by the realities of the jagged walls up which we climb.

The liturgies of sports counter, though poorly, the national pursuit of rootlessness. Even though the national madness uproots teams from city to city, leading them to hopscotch across the continent like drunks pursuing dollars; even though trades and deals result in tearing heroes out of one field and replanting them in others; still, through it all, the Dodgers, even in Los Angeles, break one's heart in as many ways today as thirty years ago, and Notre Dame is still visited by miracles and plunged into that "vale of tears" the *Salve Regina* of the grotto warns us of. God knows, our families and marriages are even more discontinuous than our national sports. Brothers and sisters, spread out across the globe, learn of nieces and nephews by dittograph at Christmas time. Second and third spouses, and children of various parentage, may seem more distant, even, than the teams of memory and youth. Compared to most American affections, the teams of sports have roots of oak.

To root, to be a fan, is to identify oneself with an organism that in every contest faces death. That is why steady winners become so arrogant, so out of tune with reality, and why losing teams see a decline in patronage. Yet when Ralph Kiner played for Pittsburgh and led the National League in homers every year for seven years, the fans came out, over a million every year, even though the Pirates lost more games than they could win. The spirit and the excellence of Kiner drew them, even in defeat. The bumbling, stumbling Mets of the early years became the darling princes of defeat. In general, however, defeat is death; losing is too painful for the fans. The beauty of the game may still attract them, and the possibility that odds-on losers may pull a grand surprise. But most in adversity dim their identification with a team. Being a steady loser hurts too much. Christianity may teach that a fruitful grain of wheat must die; the religions of sport, less paradoxical and less transcendent, fear death considerably more.

To root is not necessarily to be incapable of larger visions. Sports belong to the Kingdom of Ends, but are not the End. They are foretastes of the End, little ends before the End.

Of course, there are fanatic fans, fans who eat and sleep and drink (above all, drink) their sports. Their lives become defined by sports. So some politicians are devoured by politics, pedants by pedantry, pederasts by pederasty, drunks by drink, compulsive worshipers by worship, nymphomaniacs by phalluses, and so forth. All good things have their perversions, good swollen into Good, idols into God. Every religion has its excess. Sports, as well.

The good is always helpless before corruption, and yet outlasts it. Richard Nixon, a great perverter of sports metaphors, tried to stretch a double, missed a base, bluffed, was caught in the most exciting rundown the nation has ever seen, was lightly tagged on a flapping bit of tape, and then thrown out in a call perfectly clear to everyone in the stadium, just before he slid home lamely. The national liturgy was vindicated. The decision of the judge was final. He was out. The game went on. The people, having seen it all before in metaphor, calmly turned to watch the hitter after him.

Agon

According to rationalists, the form of life is reason. In sports, the form of life is conflict. What grabs us in sports—grabs those, at least, who have the faith—is conflict. An athletic event is an agon. In the ideal event, the antagonists are closely matched and the stakes are as nearly final as possible. Even in an early season meeting, a contest between two top contenders has more significance than other contests because it sets the stage for later meetings; a kind of intimidation, a kind of momentum, is a factor. The winner will gain a later edge, if he can sow in the loser a sneaky fear that, do what he will, victory is impossible. The loser, on the other hand, hopes the winner will underestimate him next time, when he has the incentive of desperation and revenge.

When the teams are not evenly matched, when the outcome is not in doubt, the symbolic power of the metaphor of life and death is lost; the risk has evaporated. One contents oneself with the formal aspects of the play: the brilliant execution, the perfect design, the masterful movements. A championship team that allows itself to look ragged earns displeasure. The connoisseurs of the art want perfection every time. Champions should look like champions. Sloppiness is an aesthetic affront.

Yet the heart of sports is contestation. A test. A trial. A match. On the surface, significance resides in competing excellences: who is better? But deep down, the contest means more than that. A game is not a kind of measurement. If that were the only thing at stake, a computer could point out every relevant statistic and assign superiority in cold printed fact. An athletic contest introduces elements that go beyond measurement: on the one hand, Fate; on the other hand, spirit. About the first, we have perhaps said enough already. Two teams compete, not only by matching talent for talent but also by competing for the favor of the Fates. They compete as good or evil, death or life; they are beloved of the gods or damned. No matter how well the teams or individuals perform, a bad bounce, a fumble, an errant pass can turn the tide of play. Even the team that is statistically playing better—getting more hits, enjoying superior pitching, gaining more yards, containing the other side, shooting better, working a tighter defense—can lose a game. Even a team that nine times out of ten can beat its antagonist may lose the most important game. To win, one must defeat both the other team and Fate. Coaches war against mistakes, complacence, inattention, lapses in concentration—the ghostly extra players employed by Fate.

But the most satisfying element in sports is spirit. Other elements being equal, the more spirited team will win: the one that hits the hardest, drives itself the most, runs the swiftest, plays with the most intelligence. Even a team seriously outmanned can play with greater concentration or devise more wily tactics. Half the pleasure of football is the contest between wit and brawn. Jim Thorpe of the Carlisle Indians, perhaps the greatest runner the game has ever seen, said his secret was to "show the man a leg, and take it away"; his reflexes and shifts of direction were wilier than any of his opponents, however big or swift, could master.

There is nothing more satisfying in sports, especially for a player, than to face a team more highly rated, catch them when they are playing at their best, yet still refuse to yield to them. Nothing is ever so sweet as victory under such circumstances. It is, one knows, a triumph of spirit. One will concede that the other team is better, *should* have been favored, under most circumstances *could* have beat one's own team. But not today. "We knew what we had to do. We did it." It is for this sort of victory that sports were invented.

Sports are creations of the human spirit, arenas of the human spirit, witnesses to the human spirit, instructors of the human spirit, arts of the human spirit. Spirit is not always visible in sports; is not always actualized; is often dormant. But at any moment it may flash through. Athletes often store their energies, wait, coil, spring. They love to dare the impossible. They love to be given challenges no one has a right to expect them to beat, and to prove by deed that the impossible is possible. They have to prove to themselves that their capacities exceed their past accomplishments. Sometimes, deliberately, they will set themselves at a disadvantage, tempt their opponents to test them, move in a step or two and dare them to try to hit behind them—and then go racing back to pull in a line drive with a running over-the-head arms-outstretched catch. In any one game, a man cannot count on being given opportunities for greatness; over a season, or over a lifetime, the opportunities are finite, can be numbered, come at their own pace. Thus, one must be ever alert to grab greatness as it passes by—to seize every risk, accept every dare. The great ones attempt what the good ones let go by. This, too, is a window to the spirit.

If I had to give one single reason for my love of sports it would be this: I love the tests of the human spirit. I love to see defeated teams refuse to die. I love to see impossible odds confronted. I love to see impossible dares accepted. I love to see the incredible grace lavished on simple plays—the simple flashing beauty of perfect form—but, even more, I love to see the heart that refuses to give in, refuses to panic, seizes opportunity, slips through defenses, exerts itself far beyond capacity, forges momentarily of its bodily habitat an instrument of almost perfect will. Perhaps it is a form of Slavic masochism (we should never discount it), but all my life I have never known such thoroughly penetrating joys as playing with an inspired team against a team we recognized from the beginning had every reason to beat us. I love it when the other side is winning and there are only moments left; I love it when it would be reasonable to be reconciled to defeat, but one will not, cannot; I love it when a last set of calculated reckless, free, and impassioned efforts is crowned with success. When I see others play that way, I am full of admiration, of gratitude. That is the way I believe the human race should live. When human beings actually accomplish it, it is for me as if the intentions of the Creator were suddenly limpid before our eyes: as though into the fiery heart of the Creator we had momentary insight.

16/Revolution and the American Political Tradition

The American Revolution as a Successful Revolution*

Irving Kristol

I

As WE APPROACH THE bicentennial of the American Revolution, we find ourselves in a paradoxical and embarrassing situation. A celebration of some kind certainly seems to be in order, but the urge to celebrate is not exactly overwhelming. Though many will doubtless ascribe this mood to various dispiriting events of the recent past or to an acute public consciousness of present problems, I think this would be a superficial judgment. The truth is that, for several decades now, there has been a noticeable loss of popular interest in the Revolution, both as a historical event and as a political symbol. The idea and very word, "revolution," are in good repute today; the American Revolution is not. We are willing enough, on occasion, to pick up

* From *America's Continuing Revolution: An Act of Conservation* (Washington: American Enterprise Institute for Public Policy Research). Copyright © 1975 by American Enterprise Institute. The essay, "The American Revolution as a Successful Revolution," by Irving Kristol, was one of three selected from the above series of essays. In book form it was published by American Brands, Inc. as a means of marking the Nation's birthday. Copyright © 1975 by American Brands, Inc. Reprinted by permission of the American Enterprise Institute and American Brands, Inc.

an isolated phrase from the Declaration of Independence, or a fine declamation from a Founding Father—Jefferson, usually—and use these to point up the shortcomings of American society as it now exists. Which is to say, we seem to be prompt to declare that the Revolution was a success only when it permits us to assert glibly that we have subsequently failed it. But this easy exercise in self-indictment, though useful in some respects, is on the whole a callow affair.

It does not tell us, for instance, whether there is an important connection between that successful Revolution and our subsequent delinquencies. It merely uses the Revolution for rhetorical-political purposes, making no serious effort at either understanding it or understanding ourselves. One even gets the impression that many of us regard ourselves as too sophisticated to take the Revolution seriously—that we see it as one of those naive events of our distant childhood which we have since long outgrown but which we are dutifully reminded of, at certain moments of commemoration, by insistent relatives who are less liberated from the past than we are.

I think I can make this point most emphatically by asking the simple question: what ever happened to George Washington? He used to be a Very Important Person—indeed, *the* most important person in our history. Our history books used to describe him, quite simply, as the "Father of his Country" and in the popular mind he was a larger-than-life figure to whom piety and reverence were naturally due. In the past fifty years, however, this figure has been radically diminished in size and virtually emptied of substance. In part, one supposes, this is because piety is a sentiment we seem less and less capable of, most especially piety toward fathers. We are arrogant and condescending toward all ancestors because we are so convinced we understand them better than they understood themselves—whereas piety assumes that they still understand us better than we understand ourselves. Reverence, too, is a sentiment which we, in our presumption, find somewhat unnatural.

Woodrow Wilson, like most Progressives of his time, complained about the "blind worship" of the Constitution by the American people. No such complaint is likely to be heard today. We debate whether or not we should obey the laws of the land, whereas for George Washington—and Lincoln too, who in his lifetime reasserted this point most eloquently—obedience to law was not enough: they thought that Americans, as citizens of a self-governing polity, ought to have *reverence* for their laws. Behind this belief, of course, was the premise that the collective wisdom incarnated in our laws, and especially in the fundamental law of the Constitution, understood us better than any one of us could ever hope to understand it. Having separated ourselves from our historic traditions and no longer recognizing the power inherent in tradition itself, we find this traditional point of view close to incomprehensible.

Equally incomprehensible to us is the idea that George Washington was the central figure in a real, honest-to-God revolution—the first significant revolution of the modern era and one which can lay claim to being the only truly successful revolution, on a large scale, in the past two centuries. In his own lifetime, no one doubted that he was the central figure of that revolution. Subsequent generations did not dispute the fact and our textbooks, until about a quarter of a century ago, took it for granted, albeit in an ever-more routine and unconvincing way. We today, in contrast, find it hard to take George Washington seriously as a successful revolutionary. He just does not fit our conception of what a revolutionary leader is supposed to be like. It is a conception that easily encompasses Robespierre, Lenin, Mao Tse-tung, or Fidel Castro—but can one stretch it to include a gentleman (and a gentleman he most certainly was) like George Washington? And so we tend to escape from that dilemma by deciding that what we call the American Revolution was not an authetic revolution at all, but rather some kind of pseudo-revolution, which is why it could be led by so un-revolutionary a character as George Washington.

Hannah Arendt, in her very profound book *On Revolution,* to which I am much indebted, has written:

> Revolutionary political thought in the nineteenth and twentieth centuries has proceeded as though there never had occurred a revolution in the New World and as though there never had been any American notions and experiences in the realm of politics and government worth thinking about.

It is certainly indisputable that the world, when it contemplates the events of 1776 and after, is inclined to see the American Revolution as a French Revolution that never quite came off, whereas the Founding Fathers thought they had cause to regard the French Revolution as an American Revolution that had failed. Indeed, the differing estimates of these two revolutions are definitive of one's political philosophy in the modern world: there are two conflicting conceptions of politics, in relation to the human condition, which are symbolized by these two revolutions. There is no question that the French Revolution is, in some crucial sense, the more "modern" of the two. There is a question, however, as to whether this is a good or bad thing.

It is noteworthy that, until about 15 years ago, most American historians of this century tended to look at the American Revolution through non-American eyes. They saw it as essentially an abortive and incomplete revolution, in comparison with the French model. But more recently, historians have become much more respectful toward the American Revolution, and the work of Bernard Bailyn, Edmund S. Morgan, Caroline Robbins, Gordon S. Wood, and others is revealing to us once again what the Founding Fathers had, in their day, insisted was the case: that the American Revolution was an extremely *interesting* event, rich in implication for any serious student of politics. These historians have rediscovered for us the intellectual dimensions of the American Revolution, and it is fair to say that we are now in a position to appreciate just how extraordinarily self-conscious and reflective a revolution it was.

All revolutions unleash tides of passion, and the American Revolution was no exception. But it *was* exceptional in the degree to which it was able to subordinate these passions to serious and nuanced thinking about fundamental problems of political philosophy. The pamphlets, sermons, and newspaper essays of the revolutionary period—only now being reprinted and carefully studied—were extraordinarily "academic," in the best sense of that term. Which is to say, they were learned and thoughtful and generally sober in tone. This was a revolution infused by *mind* to a degree never approximated since, and perhaps never approximated before. By mind, not by dogma. The most fascinating aspect of the American Revolution is the severe way it kept questioning itself about the meaning of what it was doing. Enthusiasm there certainly was—a revolution is impossible without enthusiasm—but this enthusiasm was tempered by doubt, introspection, anxiety, skepticism. This may strike us as a very strange state of mind in which to make a revolution; and yet it is evidently the right state of mind for making a successful revolution. That we should have any difficulty in seeing this tells us something about the immaturity of our own political imagination, an immaturity not at all incompatible with what we take to be sophistication.

Just a few weeks ago, one of our most prominent statesmen remarked to an informal group of political scientists that he had been reading *The Federalist* papers and he was astonished to see how candidly our Founding Fathers could talk about the frailties of human nature and the necessity for a political system to take such frailties into account. It was not possible, he went on to observe, for anyone active in American politics today to speak publicly in this way: he would be accused of an imperfect democratic faith in the common man. Well, the Founding Fathers for the most part, and most of the time, subscribed to such an "imperfect" faith. They understood that republican self-government could not exist if humanity did not possess—at some moments, and to a fair degree—the traditional "republican virtues" of self-control, self-reliance, and a disinterested concern for the public good. They also understood that these virtues did not exist everywhere, at all times, and that there was no guarantee of their "natural" preponderance. James Madison put it this way:

> As there is a degree of depravity in mankind which requires a certain degree of circumspection and distrust; so there are other qualities in human nature which justify a certain portion of esteem and confidence. Republican government presupposes the existence of these qualities in a higher degree than any other form.

Despite the fact that Christian traditions are still strong in this country, it is hard to imagine any public figure casually admitting, as Madison did in his matter-of-fact way, that "there is a degree of depravity in mankind" which statesmen must take into account. We have become unaccustomed to such candid and unflattering talk about ourselves—which is, I suppose, only another way of saying that we now think democratic demagoguery to be the only proper rhetorical mode of address as between government and people in a republic. The idea, so familiar to the Puritans and still very much alive during our revolutionary era, that a community of individual sinners could, under certain special conditions, constitute a good community—

just as a congregation of individual sinners could constitute a good church—is no longer entirely comprehensible to us. We are therefore negligent about the complicated ways in which this transformation takes place and uncomprehending as to the constant, rigorous attentiveness necessary for it to take place at all.

The Founders thought that self-government was a chancy and demanding enterprise and that successful government in a republic was a most difficult business. We, in contrast, believe that republican self-government is an easy affair, that it need only be instituted for it to work on its own, and that when such government falters it must be as a consequence of personal incompetence or malfeasance by elected officials. Perhaps nothing reveals better than these different perspectives the intellectual distance we have traveled from the era of the Revolution. We like to think we have "progressed" along this distance. The approaching bicentennial is an appropriate occasion for us to contemplate the possibility that such "progress," should it continue, might yet be fatal to the American polity.

II

In what sense can the American Revolution be called a successful revolution? And if we agree that it was successful, why was it successful? These questions cannot be disentangled, the "that" and the "why" comprising together one's basic (if implicit) explanation of the term, "successful revolution." These questions are also anything but academic. Indeed I believe that, as one explores them, one finds oneself constrained to challenge a great many preconceptions, not only about the nature of revolution but about the nature of politics itself, which most of us today take for granted.

To begin at the beginning: the American Revolution was successful in that those who led it were able, in later years, to look back in tranquillity at what they had wrought and to say that it was good. This was a revolution which, unlike all subsequent revolutions, did not devour its children: the men who made the revolution were the men who went on to create the new political order, who then held the highest elected positions in this order, and who all died in bed.

Not very romantic, perhaps. Indeed, positively prosaic. But it is this very prosaic quality of the American Revolution that testifies to its success. It is the pathos and poignancy of unsuccessful revolutions which excite the poetic temperament; statesmanship which successfully accomplishes its business is a subject more fit for prose. Alone among the revolutions of modernity, the American Revolution did not give rise to the pathetic and poignant myth of "the revolution betrayed." It spawned no literature of disillusionment; it left behind no grand hopes frustrated, no grand expectations unsatisfied, no grand illusions shattered. Indeed, in one important respect the American Revolution was so successful as to be almost self-defeating: it turned the attention of thinking men away from politics, which now seemed utterly unproblematic, so that political theory lost its vigor, and even the political thought of the Founding Fathers was not seriously studied. This intellectual sloth, engendered by success, rendered us incompetent to explain this successful revolution to the world, and even to ourselves. The American political tradition became an inarticulate tradition: it worked so well we did not bother to inquire why it worked, and we are therefore intellectually disarmed before those moments when it suddenly seems not to be working so well after all.

The American Revolution was also successful in another important respect: it was a mild and relatively bloodless revolution. A war was fought, to be sure, and soldiers died in that war. But the rules of civilized warfare, as then established, were for the most part quite scrupulously observed by both sides: there was none of the butchery which we have come to accept as a natural concomitant of revolutionary warfare. More important, there was practically none of the off-battlefield savagery which we now assume to be inevitable in revolutions. There were no revolutionary tribunals dispensing "revolutionary justice"; there was no reign of terror; there were no bloodthirsty proclamations by the Continental Congress. Tories were dispossessed of their property, to be sure, and many were rudely hustled off into exile; but so far as I have been able to determine, not a single Tory was executed for harboring counterrevolutionary opinions. Nor, in the years after the Revolution, were Tories persecuted to any significant degree (at least by today's standards) or their children discriminated against at all. As Tocqueville later remarked, with only a little exaggeration, the Revolution "contracted no alliance with the turbulent passions of anarchy, but its course was marked, on the contrary, by a love of order and law."

A law-and-order revolution? What kind of revolution is that, we ask ourselves? To which many will reply that it could not have been much of a revolution after all—at best a shadow of the real thing, which is always turbulent and bloody and shattering of body and soul. Well, the American Revolution was not that kind of revolution at all, and the possibility we have to consider is that it was successful precisely because it was not that kind of revolution—that it is we rather than the American revolutionaries who have an erroneous conception of what a revolution is.

Dr. Arendt makes an important distinction between "rebellion" and "revolution." By her criteria the French and Russian revolutions should more properly be called "rebellions," whereas only the American Revolution is worthy of the name. A rebellion, in her terms, is a meta-political event, emerging out of a radical dissatisfaction with the human condition as experienced by the mass of the people, demanding instant "liberation" from this condition, an immediate transformation of all social and economic circumstance, a prompt achievement of an altogether "better life" in an altogether "better world." The spirit of rebellion is a spirit of desperation—a desperate rejection of whatever exists, a desperate aspiration toward some kind of utopia. A rebellion is more a sociological event than a political action. It is governed by a blind momentum which sweeps everything before it, and its so-called leaders are in fact its captives, and ultimately its victims. The modern world knows many such rebellions, and all end up as one version or another of "a revolution betrayed." The so-called "betrayal" is, in fact, nothing but the necessary conclusion of a rebellion. Since its impossible intentions are unrealizable and since its intense desperation will not be satisfied with anything less than impossible intentions, the end result is always a regime which pretends to embody these intentions and which enforces such false pretentions by terror.

A revolution, in contrast, is a political phenomenon. It aims to revise and reorder the political arrangements of a society, and is therefore the work of the political ego rather than of the political id. A revolution is a practical exercise in political philosophy, not an existential spasm of the social organism. It requires an attentive prudence, a careful calculation of means and ends, a spirit of sobriety—the kind of spirit exemplified by that calm, legalistic document, the Declaration of Independence. All this is but another way of saying that a successful revolution cannot be governed by the spirit of the mob. Mobs and mob actions there will always be in a revolution, but if this revolution is not to degenerate into a rebellion, mob actions must be marginal to the central political drama. It may sound paradoxical but it nevertheless seems to be the case that only a self-disciplined people can dare undertake so radical a political enterprise as a revolution. This is almost like saying that a successful revolution must be accomplished by a people who want it but do not desperately need it—which was, indeed, the American condition in 1776. One may even put the case more strongly: a successful revolution is best accomplished by a people who do not really want it at all, but find themselves reluctantly making it. The American Revolution was exactly such a reluctant revolution.

The present-day student of revolutions will look in vain for any familiar kind of "revolutionary situation" in the American colonies prior to '76. The American people at that moment were the most prosperous in the world and lived under the freest institutions to be found anywhere in the world. They knew this well enough and boasted of it often enough. Their quarrel with the British crown was, in its origins, merely over the scope of colonial self-government, and hardly anyone saw any good reason why this quarrel should erupt into a war of independence. It was only after the war got under way that the American people decided that this was a good opportunity to make a revolution as well—that is, to establish a republican form of government.

Republican and quasi-republican traditions had always been powerful in the colonies, which were populated to such a large degree by religious dissenters who were sympathetic to the ideas incorporated in Cromwell's Commonwealth. Moreover, American political institutions from the very beginning were close to republican in fact, especially those of the Puritan communities of New England. Still, it is instructive to note that the word "republic" does not appear in the Declaration of Independence. Not that there was any real thought of reinstituting a monarchy in the New World: no one took such a prospect seriously. It was simply that, reluctant and cautious revolutionaries as they were, the Founding Fathers saw no need to press matters further than they had to, at that particular moment. To put it bluntly: they did not want events to get out of hand and saw no good reason to provoke more popular turbulence than was absolutely necessary.

One does not want to make the American Revolution an even

more prosaic affair than it was. This was a revolution—a real one—and it was infused with a spirit of excitement and innovation. After all, what the American Revolution, once it got under way, was trying to do was no small thing. It was nothing less than the establishment, for the first time since ancient Rome, of a large republican nation, and the idea of reestablishing under modern conditions the glory that had been Rome's could hardly fail to be intoxicating. This Revolution did indeed have grand, even millenial, expectations as to the future role of this new nation in both the political imagination and political history of the human race. But certain things have to be said about these large expectations, if we are to see them in proper perspective.

The main thing to be said is that the millenarian tradition in America long antedates the Revolution and is not intertwined with the idea of revolution itself. It was the Pilgrim Fathers, not the Founding Fathers, who first announced that it was God's country, that the American people had a divine mission to accomplish, that this people had been "chosen" to create some kind of model community for the rest of mankind. This belief was already so firmly established by the time of the Revolution that it was part and parcel of our political orthodoxy, serving to legitimate an existing "American way of life" and most of the institutions associated with that way of life. It was a radical belief, in the sense of being bold and challenging and because this new "way of life" was so strikingly different from the lives that common people were then living in Europe. It was *not* a revolutionary belief. Crèvecoeur's famous paean of praise to "this new man, the American," was written well before the Revolution; and Crèvecoeur, in fact, opposed the American Revolution as foolish and unnecessary.

To this traditional millenarianism, the Revolution added the hope that the establishment of republican institutions would inaugurate a new and happier political era for all mankind. This hope was frequently expressed enthusiastically, in a kind of messianic rhetoric, but the men of the Revolution—most of them, most of the time—did not permit themselves to become bewitched by that rhetoric. Thus, though they certainly saw republicans as "the wave of the future," both Jefferson and Adams in the 1780s agreed that the French people were still too "depraved," as they so elegantly put it, to undertake an experiment in self-government. Self-government, as they understood it, presupposed a certain "way of life," and this in turn presupposed certain qualities on the part of the citizenry—qualities then designated as "republican virtues"—that would make self-government possible.

Similarly, though one can find a great many publicists during the Revolution who insisted that, with the severance of ties from Britain, the colonies had reverted to a Lockean "state of nature" and were now free to make a new beginning for all mankind and to create a new political order that would mark a new stage in human history—though such assertions were popular enough, it would be a mistake to take them too seriously. The fact is that Americans had encountered their "state of nature" generations earlier and had made their "social compact" at that time. The primordial American "social contract" was signed and sealed on the *Mayflower*—literally signed and sealed. The subsequent presence of all those signatures appended to the Declaration of Independence, beginning with John Hancock's, are but an echo of the original covenant.

To perceive the true purposes of the American Revolution, it is wise to ignore some of the more grandiloquent declamations of the moment—Tom Paine, an English radical who never really understood America, is especially worth ignoring—and to look at the kinds of political activity the Revolution unleashed. This activity took the form of constitution-making, above all. In the months and years immediately following the Declaration of Independence, all of our states drew up constitutions. These constitutions are terribly interesting in three respects. First, they involved relatively few basic changes in existing political institutions and almost no change at all in legal, social, or economic institutions; they were, for the most part, merely revisions of the preexisting charters. Secondly, most of the changes that were instituted had the evident aim of weakening the power of government, especially of the executive; it was these changes—and especially the strict separation of powers—that dismayed Turgot, Condorcet, and the other French *philosophes,* who understood the revolution as an expression of the people's will-to-power rather than as an attempt to circumscribe political authority. Thirdly, in no case did any of these state constitutions tamper with the traditional system of local self-government. Indeed they could not, since it was this traditional system of local self-government which created and legitimized the constitutional conventions themselves. In short, the Revolution reshaped our political institutions in such a way as to make them more responsive to popular opinion and less capable of encroaching upon the personal liberties of the citizen—liberties which long antedated the new constitutions and which in no way could be regarded as the creation or consequence of revolution.

Which is to say that the purpose of this Revolution was to bring our political institutions into a more perfect correspondence with an actual "American way of life" which no one even dreamed of challenging. This "restructuring," as we would now call it—because it put the possibility of republican self-government once again on the political agenda of Western civilization—was terribly exciting to Europeans as well as Americans. But for the American involved in this historic task, it was also terribly frightening. It is fair to say that no other revolution in modern history made such relatively modest innovations with such an acute sense of anxiety. The Founding Fathers were well aware that if republicanism over the centuries had become such a rare form of government, there must be good reasons for it. Republican government, they realized, must be an exceedingly difficult regime to maintain—that is, it must have grave inherent problems. And so they were constantly scurrying to their libraries, ransacking classical and contemporary political authors, trying to discover why republics fail, and endeavoring to construct a "new political science" relevant to American conditions which would give this new republic a fair chance of succeeding. That "new political science" was eventually to be embodied in *The Federalist*—the only original work of political theory ever produced by a revolution and composed by successful revolutionaries. And the fact that very few of us have ever felt the need seriously to study *The Federalist* and that Europeans—or in our own day, Asians and Africans—have barely heard of it tells us how inadequately we understand the American Revolution, and how distant the real American Revolution has become from the idea of revolution by which we moderns are now possessed.

This idea of revolution as the world understands it today is what Dr. Arendt calls "rebellion." It involves a passionate rejection of the status quo—its institutions and the way of life associated with these institutions. It rejects everything that exists because it wishes to create everything anew—a new social order, a new set of economic arrangements, a new political entity, a new kind of human being. It aims to solve not merely the political problem of the particular political community, at that particular moment, but every other problem that vexes humanity. Its spirit is the spirit of undiluted, enthusiastic, free-floating messianism: it will be satisfied with nothing less than a radical transformation of the human condition. It is an idea and a movement which is both meta-political and sub-political—above and below politics—because it finds the political realm itself too confining for its ambitions. Meta-politically, it is essentially a religious phenomenon, seized with the perennial promise of redeption. Sub-politically, it is an expression of the modern technological mentality, confident of its power to control and direct the processes of nature. Inevitably, its swollen pride and fanatical temper lead to tragic failure. But precisely because of this pride and this fanaticism, failure leads only to partial and temporary disillusionment. When this kind of revolution gets "betrayed"—which is to say, when the consequences of revolution lose all congruence with its original purpose—the true revolutionary believer will still look forward to a second coming of the authentic and unbetrayable revolution.

The French Revolution was the kind of modern revolution I have been describing; the American Revolution was not. It is because of this, one supposes, that the French Revolution has captured the imagination of other peoples—has become indeed the model of "real" revolution—in a way that the American Revolution has not been able to do. The French Revolution promised not only a reformation of France's political institutions, but far more than that. It promised, for instance—as practically all revolutions have promised since—the abolition of poverty. The American Revolution promised no such thing, in part because poverty was not such a troublesome issue in this country, but also—one is certain—because the leaders of this revolution understood what their contemporary, Adam Smith, understood and what we today have some difficulty in understanding: namely, that poverty is abolished by economic growth, not by economic redistribution—there is never enough to distribute—and that rebellions, by creating instability and uncertainty, have mischievous consequences for economic growth. Similarly, the French Revolution promised a condition of "happiness" to its citizens under the new regime, whereas the American Revolution promised merely to permit the individual to engage in the "pursuit of happiness."

It should not be surprising, therefore, that in the war of ideologies which has engulfed the 20th century, the United States is at a disadvantage. This disadvantage does not flow from any weakness on our part. It is not, as some say, because we have forgotten our revolutionary heritage and therefore have nothing to say to a discontented and turbulent world. We have, indeed, much to say, only it is not what our contemporaries want to hear. It is not even what we ourselves want to hear, and in *that* sense it may be correct to claim we have forgotten our revolutionary heritage. Our revolutionary message—which is a message not of the Revolution itself but of the American political tradition from the *Mayflower* to the Declaration of Independence to the Constitution—is that a self-disciplined people *can* create a political community in which an ordered liberty will promote both economic prosperity and political participation. To the teeming masses of other nations, the American political tradition says: to enjoy the fruits of self-government, you must first cease being "masses" and become a "people," attached to a common way of life, sharing common values, and existing in a condition of mutual trust and sympathy as between individuals and even social classes. It is a distinctly odd kind of "revolutionary" message, by twentieth century criteria—so odd that it seems not revolutionary at all, and yet so revolutionary that it seems utterly utopian. What the twentieth century wants to hear is the grand things that a new government will do for the people who put their trust in it. What the American political tradition says is that the major function of government is, in Professor Oakeshott's phrase, to "tend to the arrangements of society," and that free people do not make a covenant or social contract with their government, or with the leaders of any "movement," but among themselves.

In the end, what informs the American political tradition is a proposition and a premise. The proposition is that the best national government is, to use a phrase the Founding Fathers were fond of, "mild government." The premise is that you can only achieve "mild government" if you have a solid bedrock of local self-government, so that the responsibilities of national government are limited in scope. And a corollary of this premise is that such a bedrock of local self-government can only be achieved by a people who—through the shaping influence of religion, education, and their own daily experience—are capable of governing themselves in those small and petty matters which are the stuff of local politics.

Does this conception of politics have any relevance to the conditions in which people live today in large areas of the world—the so-called underdeveloped areas, especially? We are inclined, I think, to answer instinctively in the negative, but that answer may itself be a modern ideological prejudice. We take it for granted that if a people live in comparative poverty, they are necessarily incapable of the kind of self-discipline and sobriety that makes for effective self-government in their particular communities. Mind you, I am not talking about starving people, who are in a prepolitical condition and whose problem is to get a strong and effective government of almost any kind. I am talking about *comparatively* poor people. And our current low estimate of the political capabilities of such people is an ideological assumption, not an objective fact. Many of our frontier communities, at the time of the Revolution and for decades afterwards, were poor by any standards. Yet this poverty was not, for the most part, inconsistent with active self-government. There have been communities in Europe, too, which were very poor—not actually starving, of course, but simply very poor—yet were authetic political communities. The popular musical, *Fiddler on the Roof,* gave us a picture of such a community. It is always better not to be so poor, but poverty need not be a pathological condition, and political pathology is not an inevitable consequence of poverty, just as political pathology is not inevitably abolished by prosperity. Poor people can cope with their poverty in many different ways. They are people, not sociological creatures and in the end they will cope as their moral and political convictions tell them to cope. These convictions, in turn, will be formed by the expectations that their community addresses to them—expectations which they freely convert into obligations.

In *The Brothers Karamazov*, Dostoevsky says that the spirit of the Antichrist, in its modern incarnation, will flaunt the banner, "First feed people, and *then* ask of them virtue." This has, in an amended form, indeed become the cardinal and utterly conventional thesis of modern politics. The amended form reads: "First make people prosperous, and then ask of them virtue." Whatever reservations one might have about Dostoevsky's original thesis, this revised version is, in the perspective of the Judaeo-Christian tradition, unquestionably a blasphemy. It is also, in the perspective of the American political tradition, a malicious and inherently self-defeating doctrine—self-defeating because those who proclaim it obviously have lost all sense of what virtue, religious or political, means. Nevertheless, practically all of us today find it an inherently plausible doctrine, a staple of our political discourse. This being the case, it is only natural that we ourselves should have such difficulty understanding the American political tradition, and that when we expend it to the world, we distort it in all sorts of ways which will make it more palatable to the prejudices of the modern political mentality.

III

It would not be fair to conclude that the American political tradition is flawless, and that it is only we, its heirs, who are to blame for the many problems our society is grappling with—and so ineptly. The American Revolution was a successful revolution, but there is no such thing, either in one's personal life or in a nation's history, as unambiguous success. The legacy of the American Revolution and of the entire political tradition associated with it is problematic in all sorts of ways. Strangely enough, we have such an imperfect understanding of this tradition that, even as we vulgarize it or question it or disregard it, we rarely address ourselves to its problematic quality.

The major problematic aspect of this tradition has to do with the relation of the "citizen" to the "common man." And the difficulties we have in defining this relation are best illustrated by the fact that, though we have been a representative democracy for two centuries now, we have never developed an adequate theory of representation.

More precisely we have developed *two* contradictory theories of representation, both of which can claim legitimacy within the American political tradition and both of which were enunciated, often by the same people, during the Revolution. The one sees the public official as a "common man" who has a mandate to reflect the opinions of the majority; the other sees the public official as a somewhat uncommon man—a more-than-common man, if you will—who, because of his talents and character, is able to take a larger view of the "public interest" than the voters who elected him or the voters who failed to defeat him. One might say that the first is a "democratic" view of the legislator, the second a "republican" view. The American political tradition has always had a kind of double vision on this whole problem, which in turn makes for a bewildering moral confusion. Half the time we regard our politicians as, in the nature of things, probably corrupt and certainly untrustworthy; the other half of the time, we denounce them for failing to be models of integrity and rectitude. Indeed, we have a profession—journalism—which seems committed to both of these contradictory propositions. But politicians are pretty much like the rest of us and tend to become the kinds of people they are expected to be. The absence of clear and distinct expectations has meant that public morality in this country has never been, and is not, anything we can be proud of.

In a way, the ambiguity in our theory of representation points to a much deeper ambiguity in that system of self-government which emerged from the Revolution and the Constitutional Convention. That system has been perceptively titled, by Professor Martin Diamond, "a democratic republic." Now, we tend to think of these terms as near-synonyms, but in fact they differ significantly in their political connotations. Just how significant the difference is becomes clear if we realize that the America which emerged from the Revolution and the Constitutional Convention was the first democratic republic in history. The political philosophers of that time could study the history of democracies, but there was no opportunity for them to study both together. When the Founding Fathers declared that they had devised a new kind of political entity based on "a new science of politics," they were not vainly boasting or deceiving themselves. It is we, their political descendants, who tend to be unaware of the novelty of the American political enterprise, and of the risks and ambiguities inherent in that novelty. We simplify and vulgarize and distort, because we have lost the sense of how bold and innovative the Founding Fathers were, and of how problematic—necessarily problematic—is the system of government, and the society, which they established. Witness the fact that, incredibly enough, at our major universities it is almost impossible to find a course, graduate or undergraduate, devoted to *The Federalist.*

What is the difference between a "democracy" and a "republic"? In a democracy, the will of the people is supreme. In a republic, it is not the will of the people but the rational consensus of the people—a rational consensus which is implicit in the term "consent"—which governs the people. That is to say, in a democracy, popular passion may rule—*may,* though it need not—but in a republic, popular passion is regarded as unfit to rule, and precautions are taken to see that it is subdued rather than sovereign. In a democracy all politicians are, to some degree, demagogues: they appeal to people's prejudices and passions, they incite their expectations by making reckless promises, they endeavor to ingratiate themselves with the electorate in every possible way. In a republic, there are not supposed to be such politicians, only statesmen—sober, unglamorous, thoughtful men who are engaged in a kind of perpetual conversation with the citizenry. In a republic, a fair degree of equality and prosperity are important goals, but it is liberty that is given priority as the proper end of government. In a democracy, these priorities are reversed: the status of men and women as consumers of economic goods is taken to be more significant than their status as participants in the creation of political goods. A republic is what we would call "moralistic" in its approach to both public and private affairs; a democracy is more easygoing, more "permissive" as we now say, even more cynical.

The Founding Fathers perceived that their new nation was too large, too heterogeneous, too dynamic, too mobile for it to govern itself successfully along strict republican principles. And they had no desire at all to see it governed along strict democratic principles, since they did not have that much faith in the kinds of "common men" likely to be produced by such a nation. So they created a new form of "popular government," to use one of their favorite terms, that incorporated both republican and democratic principles, in a complicated and ingenious way. This system has lasted for two centuries, which means it has worked very well indeed. But in the course of that time, we have progressively forgotten what kind of system it is and *why* it works as well as it does. Every now and then, for instance, we furiously debate the question of whether or not the Supreme Court is meeting its obligations as a democratic institution. The question reveals a startling ignorance of our political tradition. The Supreme Court is not—and was never supposed to be—a democratic institution; it is a republican institution which counterbalances the activities of our various democratic institutions. Yet I have discovered that when you say this to college students, they do not understand the distinction and even have difficulty thinking about it.

So it would seem that today, two hundred years after the American Revolution, we are in a sense victims of its success.

The political tradition out of which it issued and the political order it helped to create are imperfectly comprehended by us. What is worse, we are not fully aware of this imperfect comprehension and are frequently smug in our convenient misunderstandings. The American Revolution certainly merits celebration. But it would be reassuring if a part of that celebration were to consist, not merely of pious clichés, but of a serious and sustained effort to achieve a deeper and more widespread understanding of just what it is we are celebrating.

17/Egalitarianism and the American Political Tradition

The Heresy of Equality*

M. E. Bradford

I

Let us have no foolishness, indeed.* Equality as a moral or political imperative, pursued as an end in itself—Equality, with the capital "E"—is the antonym of every legitimate conservative principle. Contrary to most Liberals, new and old, it is nothing less than sophistry to distinguish between equality of opportunity (equal starts in the "race of life") and equality of condition (equal results). For only those who *are* equal can take equal advantage of a given circumstance. And there is no man equal to any other, except perhaps in the special, and politically untranslatable, understanding of the Deity. *Not intellectually or physically or economically or even morally. Not equal!* Such is, of course, the genuinely self-evident proposition.[1] Its truth finds a verifi-

* From *Modern Age,* vol. 20, no. 1 (Winter 1976). Copyright © 1976 by the Foundation for Foreign Affairs, Inc. Reprinted by permission.

** This essay is a direct response to Harry Jaffa's "Equality as a Conservative Principle," *Loyola of Los Angeles Law Review,* VIII (June, 1975), pp. 471–505, which is itself a critique of *The Basic Symbols of the American Political Tradition* by Willmoore Kendall and George W. Carey. Lincoln's reading of the Declaration of Independence is the central subject of this entire exchange. Jaffa's piece invites direct comparison with mine.

[1] When pressed in debate by the righteous minions of Equality, an antebellum Northern congressman once called sentence two of the Declaration a "self-evident lie." Consider also *The Federalist,* No. 10.

cation in our bones and is demonstrated in the unselfconscious acts of our everyday lives: vital proof, regardless of our private political persuasion. Incidental equality, engendered by the pursuit of other objectives, is, to be sure, another matter. Inside of the general history of the West (and especially within the American experience) it can be credited with a number of healthy consequences: strength in the bonds of community, assent to the authority of honorable regimes, faith in the justice of the gods.

But the equality of Professor Jaffa's essay, even in the ordinary sense of "equal rights," can be expected to work the other way around. For this equality belongs to the post-Renaissance world of ideology—of political magic and the alchemical "science" of politics. Envy is the basis of its broad appeal. And rampant envy, the besetting virus of modern society, is the most predictable result of insistence upon its realization.[2] Furthermore, hue and cry over equality of opportunity and equal rights leads, *a fortiori,* to a final demand for equality of condition. Under its pressure self-respect gives way in the large majority of men who have not reached the level of their expectation, who have no support from an inclusive identity, and who hunger for "revenge" on those who occupy a higher station and will (they expect) continue to enjoy that advantage. The end result is visible in the spiritual proletarians of the "lonely crowd." Bertrand de Jouvenel has described the process which produces such non-persons in his memorable study, *On Power.*[3] They are the natural pawns of an impersonal and omnicompetent Leviathan. And to insure their docility such a state is certain to recruit a large "new class" of men, persons superior in "ability" and authority, both to their ostensible "masters" among the people and to such anachronisms as stand in their progressive way.

Such is the evidence of the recent past—and particularly of American history. Arrant individualism, fracturing and then destroying the hope of amity and confederation, the communal bond and the ancient vision of the good society as an extrapolation from family, is one villain in this tale. Another is ration-

[2] See Helmut Schoeck, *Envy: A Theory of Social Behavior* (New York: Harcourt Brace Jovanovich, 1970).

[3] *On Power: Its Nature and the History of Its Growth* (Boston: Beacon Press, 1962).

alized cowardice, shame, and ingratitude hidden behind the disguise of self-sufficiency or the mask of injured merit. Interdependence, which secures dignity and makes of equality a mere irrelevance, is the principal victim. Where fraternity exists to support the official structure of a government, it can command assent with no fear of being called despotic or prejudiced in behalf of one component of the society it represents. But behind the cult of equality (the chief if not only tenet in Professor Jaffa's theology, and his link to the pseudo-religious politics of ideology) is an even more sinister power, the uniformitarian hatred of providential distinctions which will stop at nothing less than what Eric Voegelin calls "a reconstitution of being": a nihilistic impulse which is at bottom both frightened and vain in its rejection of a given contingency and in its arrogation of a godlike authority to annul that dependency.[4] As Robert Penn Warren has recently reminded us, distinctions drawn from an encounter with an external reality have been the basis for the intellectual life as we have known it: prudent and tentative distinctions, but seriously intended.[5] With the reign of equality all of that achievement is set at peril.

II

So much in prologue. Concerning equality Professor Jaffa and I disagree profoundly; disagree even though we both denominate ourselves conservative. Yet this distinction does not finally exhaust or explain our differences. For Jaffa's opening remarks indicate that his conservatism is of a relatively recent variety and is, in substance, the Old Liberalism hidden under a Union battle flag. To the contrary I maintain that if conservatism has any identity whatsoever beyond mere recalcitrance and rationalized self-interest, that identity must incorporate the "funded wisdom of the ages" as that deposition comes down through a particular national experience. Despite modifications within the prescription of a continuum of political life, only a

[4] See Eric Voegelin, *Science, Politics and Gnosticism* (Chicago: Henry Regnery Co., 1968), pp. 99–100.

[5] Robert Penn Warren, "Democracy and Poetry," *Southern Review*, Vol. II (January 1975), p. 28.

relativist or historicist could argue that American conservatism should be an utterly unique phenomenon, without antecedents which predate 1776 and unconnected with the mainstream of English and European thought and practice known to our forefathers in colonial times. Jaffa of course nods toward one face of Locke and, by implication, the chiliastic politics of Cromwell's New England heirs.[6] And I have no doubt that he can add to this hagiography a selective (and generally misleading) list of earlier patrons of his view. I cannot counter in this space the full spectrum of Straussian rationalism. To specify what I believe to be lacking in Jaffa's conservative model (and wrong with the intellectual history he uses in its validation), it will serve better for me to concentrate first on how I read the Declaration of Independence and then append, in abbreviated form, my estimation of Lincoln's lasting and terrible impact on the nation's destiny through his distortions upon that text. This of course involves me incidentally in Jaffa's quarrel with Kendall/Carey and *The Basic Symbols of the American Political Tradition.* But it must be understood that my object is not to defend these worthy gentlemen. To the contrary, my primary interest is in a more largely conservative view of the questions over which they and Professor Jaffa disagree. And therefore, incidentally with the operation and quality of my adversary's mind which lead him to conclusions so very different from mine. With those concerns I propose to organize and conclude my remarks.

III

Professor Jaffa begs a great many questions in his comment on the Declaration. But his greatest mistake is an open error, and supported by considerable precedent in both academic and political circles. In truth, his approach is an orthodox one, at least in our radical times. I refer to his treatment of the second sentence of that document in abstraction from its whole: indeed, of the first part of that sentence in abstraction from its remainder, to say nothing of the larger text. Jaffa filters the rest of the Declaration (and later expressions of the American political faith) back and forth through the measure of that sentence until

[6] See my "A Writ of Fire and Sword: The Politics of Oliver Cromwell," in no. 3 of *The Occasional Review* (Summer 1975), pp. 61–80.

he has (or so he imagines) achieved its baptism in the pure waters of the higher law. He quotes Lincoln approvingly that "the doctrine of human equality was 'the father of all moral principle [amongst us].' "[7] Jaffa sets up a false dilemma: we must be, as a people, "committed" to Equality or we are "open to the relativism and historicism that is the theoretical ground of modern totalitarian regimes." The Declaration is, of course, the origin of that commitment to "permanent standards." And particularly the second sentence. The trouble here comes from an imperfect grasp of the Burkean calculus. And from the habit of reading legal, poetic, and rhetorical documents as if they were bits of revealed truth or statements of systematic thought. My objections derive primarily from those antirationalist realms of discourse. For I assume, with Swift, that man is a creature capable of reason, *capax rationis,* but not a rational animal. Therefore the head and heart must be engaged together where instruction is attempted. The burden of poetry and rhetoric is inherent in the form through which that idea is embodied: its meaning *is* its way of meaning, not a discursive paraphrase. And it achieves that meaning as it unfolds. According to this procedure we are taught from of old that the soul may be composed, the sensibility reordered. Reason enters into this process with modesty and draws its sanction for whatever new truth it may advance from cooperation with sources and authorities that need produce no credentials nor prove up any title with the audience assumed. For in poetry as in law and rhetoric all matters are not in question. There is a prescription, or something equivalent to what Burke calls by that name. And usually a theology to channel and gloss the prescript. Tropes and figures, terms weighted more or less by usage, norms of value configured and dramatic sequences of associated actions discovered through an unbroken stream of place and blood and history

[7] Doctrine is a loaded word. It is here suggestive of theology, revealed truth, though Lincoln means by it the kind of demonstrable "abstract truth" of the sort Jefferson "embalmed" into a "merely revolutionary document." See Lincoln's letter to Messrs. Henry L. Pierce & Others, April 6, 1859, on pp. 374–76 of Vol. III of *The Collected Works of Abraham Lincoln* (New Brunswick, N.J.: Rutgers University Press, 1953). The usage is thus a device for "having it both ways," as does Jaffa when claiming that the commandments of Sinai are knowable by unassisted human reason. For the commandments are explained only in Christ—a scandal to the Greeks.

operate in this mode of communication as something logically prior to the matter under examination. And likewise the law, especially where the rule is *stare decisis*. Where myth or precedent or some other part of the "wise prejudice" of a people is presupposed and identity therefore converted into a facet of ontology, a providential thing ("inalienable" in that word's oldest sense, not to be voted, given, or reasoned away), there is nothing for mere philosophy to say. And that *philosophe* abstraction, political Man, who once theoretically existed outside a social bond, nowhere to be seen. As a wise man wrote, "Where the great interests of mankind are concerned through a long succession of generations, that succession ought to be admitted into some share in the councils which are so deeply to affect them."[8] For the "moral essences" that shape a commonwealth are "not often constructed after any theory: theories are rather drawn from them"—the natural law, made partially visible only in the prescription, but made visible nonetheless.[9]

IV

To anyone familiar with English letters and the English mind in the 17th and 18th centuries, the Declaration of Independence is clearly a document produced out of the *mores majorum*—legal, rhetorical, poetic—and not a piece of reasoning or systematic truth. No sentence of its whole means anything out of context. It unfolds *seriatim* and makes sense only when read through. Furthermore, what it does mean is intelligble only in a matrix of circumstances—political, literary, linguistic, and mundane. Nevertheless, no one trained to move in the rhetorical world of Augustan humanism would take it for a relativistic statement any more than they would describe Dryden's *Religio Laici,* Addison's *Cato,* Johnson's *Rasselas,* or Burke's *Reflections on the Rev-*

[8] Edmund Burke, *Reflections on the Revolution in France* (Chicago: Henry Regnery Co., 1955), p. 240.

[9] *ibid.*, p. 244. See also on this manner of thinking Louis I. Bredvold's *The Intellectual Milieu of John Dryden* (Ann Arbor: University of Michigan Press, 1934) and also *The Brave New World of the Enlightenment* (Ann Arbor: University of Michigan Press, 1961) by the same author. Swift is a major illustration of this intellectual *habitus*. I identify with it.

olution in France in that fashion.[10] Jaffa revives the error of his master, Leo Strauss, in speaking of the bugbear historicism and of "mere prescriptive rights."[11] For it is in our day the alternatives which carry with them a serious danger of the high-sounding despot. Radicals (to use his term, meaning the Liberals who see in politics a new "Queen of the Sciences" and employ a sequence of private revelations to exalt her condition) believe in a "higher law"—have done so at least since the politics of secularized Puritanism first appeared in European society.[12] Even Marxists finally worship the demiurge of history—and rest the remainder of their argument upon that authority. And the goddess Reason is still with us, available to sanction whatever her hand finds to do in erasing all that survives from what Peter Gay rightly labels the mythopoeic vision.[13] I agree with Professor Jaffa concerning the danger of relativism. A Christian must. And also about behavioristic political science. Such study is description only, or else mere manipulation. But, hunger for the normative aside, we must resist the tendency to thrust familiar contemporary pseudoreligious notions back into texts where they are unlikely to appear. Any Englishman of 1776 (colonial or not) should not be expected to construe natural rights so rigorously as Justice Black—except perhaps for hyperbole and in argument. In between our day and that first July 4 stand a number of revolutions, especially the French. And also two

[10] I borrow from the title of Paul Fussell's *The Rhetorical World of Augustan Humanism* (Oxford: The Clarendon Press, 1965). In the same connection see J. T. Bolton's *The Language of Politics in the Age of Wilkes and Burke* (Toronto: University of Toronto Press, 1963).

[11] See Jaffa's *Equality and Liberty: Theory and Practice in American Politics* (New York: Oxford University Press, 1965), p. 122; and Leo Strauss' *Natural Right and History* (Chicago: University of Chicago Press, 1953), pp. 1–9.

[12] Jaffa accepts the Puritan typology for the American venture. There are, we should remember, alternative formulations (*Equality and Liberty*, pp. 116–17)—formulations less infected with secularized eschatology. And if Jaffa pursues his analogue, he should remember that there was slavery in Israel and among the ancient Jews a racism so virulent that they considered some neighboring peoples too lowly even for enslavement and fit only for slaughter. Or too wicked (Indians, the Irish at Drogheda, etc.).

[13] Peter Gay, *The Enlightenment: An Interpretation* (New York: Alfred A. Knopf, 1966), pp. ix–xiv.

hundred years of liberal and radical thought. We are bemused by the spectre of Locke (an authority to some of the revolutionary generation, but read loosely and in the light of Sir Edward Coke and William Petyt, and the 1628 Petition of Right, and the 1689 Declaration of Rights).[14] The legacy of English common law is lost upon us. And in the process we have forgotten, among other things, that Edmund Burke is our best guide to the main line of Whig thought: *not Locke or Paine, or even Harrington, but Burke.* It is, of course, a truism that all colonial Americans did their political thinking inside the post-1688 Whig legal tradition.[15] Some years ago Professor Jaffa attempted to counter this line of objection to his Lincolnian construction of the Declaration by setting Paine and Locke (plus an irrelevant bit of Blackstone) upon Daniel J. Boorstin's excellent *The American: The Colonial Experience.* But in so doing he only evaded his antagonist and obfuscated the question of what is typically Whig and behind our "revolution."[16] For Locke is not so consistent a source of equal rights as Jaffa would lead us to believe. Indeed, that worthy theorist of liberty was an eager party to the creation of a slaveocracy in South Carolina.[17] And on occasion he justified the peculiar institution with nothing more sophisticated than an appeal to race or right of conquest.[18] Blackstone, for his part, was a high Tory and a poor sponsor for equality of any sort. And Paine relates to very little that became American in our Constitution of 1787. Recent scholarship on early American history has, by and large, exhibited an anachronistic tendency to ignore all patriot utterances that do not sound like Locke in his

[14] See Maurice Ashley, *The Glorious Revolution of 1688* (New York: Scribner's, 1966), pp. 97–106.

[15] And this of course includes certain established rights, plus a balance between the values of liberty and community. I do not mean to minimize the value of these achievements. Clearly I identify with them.

[16] *Equality and Liberty,* pp. 114–39. For correction (in some respects), see Leonard Woods Labaree's *Conservatism in Early America* (Ithaca: Cornell University Press, 1959), pp. 119–22; and Clinton Rossiter's *The Seedtime of the Republic* (New York: Harcourt, Brace & World, 1953), especially p. 345; also Ashley, *op. cit.,* pp. 193–98.

[17] David Duncan Wallace, *South Carolina: A Short History, 1520–1948* (Columbia: University of South Carolina Press, 1966), p. 25.

[18] *John Locke, Two Treatises of Government: A Critical Edition with Introduction and Apparatus Criticus,* by Peter Laslett (Cambridge, England: Cambridge University Press, 1960), p. 159.

highest flights of freedom or Paine before the Mountain: like the Whig "Left," in other words.[19] They have ignored the problems in logic set up by "all men are created equal" when understood as one of Lincoln's beloved Euclidian propositions and the larger problems for libertarians determined not to call for equality of condition when they start from such a postulate.[20] Along with the political philosophers they have approached the task of explication as if the Declaration existed *sui generis,* in a Platonic empyrean.[21] A gloss upon what transpired in a real (*i.e.,* intellectually "messy") convention in a real Philadelphia seems not to interest these sages: what with reason could be expected to occur.[22] With a non-Lockean Whig machinery (and as a practicing rhetorician) I will attempt to draw the inquiry down toward such probabilties.

[19] For examples consider Bernard Bailyn's *The Ideological Origins of the American Revolution* (Cambridge, Mass.: Harvard University Press, 1967); and Gordon S. Wood's *The Creation of the American Republic, 1776–1787* (Chapel Hill, N.C.: University of North Carolina Press, 1964). Somewhat better are H. Trevor Colbourn's *The Lamp of Experience: Whig History and the Intellectual Origins of the American Revolution* (Chapel Hill, N.C.: University of North Carolina Press, 1965); and Merrill Jensen's *The Founding of a Nation: A History of the American Revolution, 1763–1776* (New York: Oxford University Press, 1968). These last two books are especially good on the "reluctant rebels," who were Burkean, not Lockean Whigs, postulating law, not a state of nature (i.e., where a fullscale, new contract can be drawn). See also Wallace (*South Carolina,* p. 273) for an account of a prescriptive South Carolina patriot—William Henry Drayton.

[20] In strict logic there is a problem with quantification if the proposition is supposed to be universal: a universal proposition would read "every man is created equal to every other man." Jefferson's phrase is merely a loose generalization, when seen in this light. For the libertarian the trouble goes the other way around: if all men are by nature equal (morally, in will, intellect, etc.), then only circumstances can explain the inequalities which develop. And these circumstances are thus offences against nature and the Divine Will—offences demanding correction. What some libertarians try to get out of "created equal" is "created unequal, but given an equal start." Jefferson's phrase will not submit to this.

[21] An exception is Russell Kirk's *The Roots of American Order* (La Salle, Ill.: Open Court, 1974).

[22] One has the temptation to say, as Socrates did of the rhapsode in Plato's *Ion,* that they understand the subject not by art or knowledge but by "inspiration."

V

Contrary to Professor Jaffa, it is my view that the Declaration of Independence is not very revolutionary at all. Nor the Revolution itself. Nor the Constitution. Only Mr. Lincoln and those who gave him support, both in his day and in the following century. And the moralistic, verbally disguised instrument which Lincoln invented may indeed be the most revolutionary force in the modern world: a pure gnostic force.[23] The Declaration confirms an existing state of affairs, even in its announcement of a break with George III. For the colonies existed as distinctive commonwealths with (and out of) English law. Yet they were English with a difference. It required only a fracturing of spiritual bonds that it be made official. In the spring and summer of 1776 things came to a head. As Jefferson wrote, a British army was descending upon Long Island: an army bent on putting an end to petitions, inquiries, declarations, and all such irritants. The King had declared the members of the Continental Congress rebels, without the law. And likewise those who thought themselves represented by that body. No security from deportation for trial, summary execution and confiscation were the alternatives to unconditional submission and allegiance outside the law.

Rhetorical criticism begins with a careful description of circumstances antedating composition.[24] For without that information well established, the meaning of language is uncertain; and a piece of literature may be treated as if it had been prepared only for the gods. Connection of a document with a set of writings made and/or exchanged before or after its appearance is certainly such necessary information. There is no Declaration apart from it. Effacing himself, Thomas Jefferson wrote what completed a conversation concerning the law which had gone back and forth across the Atlantic for many years before exhausting its purpose. Everything in this sequence appeals to

[23] I began to develop this view in "Lincoln's New Frontier: A Rhetoric for Continuing Revolution," *Triumph,* May 1971, pp. 11–13 and 21; June 1971, pp. 15–17. I use the term from Eric Voegelin's *New Science of Politics* (Chicago: University of Chicago Press, 1952).

[24] For a chronicle of these events see Jensen, *Founding of a Nation,* and Lawrence H. Gipson's *The Coming of the Revolution, 1763–1775* (New York: Harper, 1954).

the *consensus gentium* of sensible men (common reasonableness, but not philosophy) and to English law. James II had set himself outside that rule, using the dispensary powers to invent a new equality of rights. This usurpation resulted in a royal "abdication" and a new king who promised to uphold the charters and ancient laws and thus to preserve to Englishmen and their posterity the rights they had inherited through a providentially blessed history. This was the common understanding of that period. It is implicit in the dialogue between Philadelphia and Whitehall and in the antecedent quarrel between the Crown and various colonial assemblies after the Stamp and Declaratory Acts and the Albany Congress. The American "parliament" first convened in September of 1774 and soon issued its "Declaration and Resolves of the First Continental Congress, October 14, 1774." Even there it is unmistakably clear that a composite identity is addressing a related composite identity, that the mode of address is forensic (determining praise or blame between respective parties in dispute over the meaning of a "given" phenomenon), and that the point of reference is not divine revelation or a body of doctrine maintained according to the precepts of philosophy, but rather a wisdom inherited as prescription, to be applied reasonably, but not in *Reason's* name. This particular declaration makes it plain that Englishmen are in dispute with Englishmen, groups with groups, and on English grounds. The colonial charters set up this situation. At law they connect the colonies to a paternal source, even while they set them apart. They create an ambiguity in relations with the English parliament and the independent reality of other governments. And they leave law and king and common enemies to hold the mix together.[25]

In their first declaration we learn that the remonstrants are entitled to "life, liberty and property"; that these basic rights come from their ancestors (God perhaps acting through them); that removal over the sea can involve no alienation of such inherited rights; that such alienation is now proposed by way of taxation *and by the machinery for enforcing that tax*; and, finally, that kindred offences against "immunities and privileges granted and confirmed" by royal charters and "secured by their several

[25] Charter and compact are usually synonyms in the language of the Whigs, and usually imply a relation of unequals.

codes of provincial law" are in prospect. Here and in the later (and similarly argued) "Declaration of the Causes and Necessities of Taking up Arms, July 6, 1775," we can recognize the lineaments of a position finally developed in July of 1776. And also a line of thought coming down directly from the Great Charter of 1689—or even more remotely from Bracton and Fortescue. The king is the king, the subject the subject, only within the law. The American colonies are by blood and law part of the English *res publica,* set apart from the old Island Kingdom by England's destruction of that organic relationship. To repeat, it is well to remember that the king declared them "rebels" (Prohibitory Acts, August 1775) well before they accepted that title for themselves. As they insist, it is for no "light or transient causes" that they make his appellation official. Their charters have become mere paper. By virtue of relocation across the seas they have been defined as alienated Englishmen, without security even in such fundamental matters as life, liberty, and the fruits of their labors. And all men recognize these rights as being the precondition of submission to any government. Their fathers had, of course, grown violent over much smaller affronts. But the "authors" of the Declaration are determined to keep within the law and to appear as unusually conservative men. Only when the king denies them all representation, asserts his right to bind them *collectively,* to seize their goods *collectively,* to quarter an angry army upon them, and to punish their entreaties that he restrain his servants to observe the Bill of Rights—only then will they close with a last "appeal from reason to arms."

VI

We are now prepared to ask what Mr. Jefferson and his sensible friends meant by "all men" and "created equal." Meant together—*as a group.* In rhetoric, it is a rule to ask how the beginning leads through the middle to the end. If end and beginning consort well with one another, if they point in one direction, that agreement defines what may be discovered in between.[26] The last three-fourths of the Declaration (minus the

[26] There is no room for "secret writing" in public declarations.

conclusion, its original draft) is a bill of particulars.[27] The king (their only acknowledged link with England) has decapitated the body politic and hence is no longer king on these shores. The law/prescription cannot otherwise be preserved. And these men intend such a preservation. Something in existence declares itself in possession of "honor" and "sensible of the regard of decent men," prepared to draw a new charter out of those it possesses, to act as an entity in forming a confederal government. But first these commonwealths must file an official bill of divorcement, designed to the pattern of a countersuit in an action already initiated on the other side. The generation of a new head for this body is not yet, but will, we can assume, present no problem when a necessity for its creation is made explicit.[28]

The exordium of the Declaration begins this appeal with an argument from history and with a definition of the voice addressing the "powers of the earth!" It is a "people," a "we" that are estranged from another "we." The peroration reads the same: "we," the "free and independent states," are united in our will to separation—and prepared to answer to high and low for that temerity. They act in the name (and with the sanction) of the good people whose several assemblies had authorized their congregation. This much formally. No contemporary liberal, new or old, can make use of that framework or take the customary liberties with what is contained by the construction. Nor coming to it by the path I have marked, may they, in honesty, see in "created equal" what they devoutly wish to find. "We," in that second sentence, signifies the colonials as the citizenry of the distinct colonies, not as individuals, but rather in their corporate capacity. Therefore, the following "all men"—created equal in their right to expect from any government to which

[27] I cite Volume I of Julian P. Boyd's edition of *The Papers of Thomas Jefferson* (Princeton: Princeton University Press, 1950), pp. 315–39 and 414–33. Carl Becker, in his valuable *The Declaration of Independence: A Study in the History of Politics and Ideas* (New York: Vintage Press, 1958), argues unreasonably that this bill of particulars is not really important to the meaning of the Declaration. He was, however, as we should remember, an admirer of the *philosophes*—and no rhetorician.

[28] The image here is drawn from one of the Fathers of English law, from chapter 13 of the *De Laudibus Legum Angliae* (1471) of Sir John Fortescue (Cambridge, England: Cambridge University Press, 1949), the edition and translation by S. B. Chrimes.

they might submit freedom from corporate bondage, genocide, and massive confiscation—are persons prudent together, respectful of the law which makes them one, even though forced to stand henceforth apart: equal as one free state is as free as another.

Nothing is maintained concerning the abilities or situations of individual persons living within the abandoned context of the British Empire or the societies to be formed by its disruption. No new contract is drawn. Rather, one that exists is *preserved by amputation.* All that is said is that no component of a society can be expected to agree, even though it is part of that society by inheritance, that it is to be bereft of those securities that make life tolerable simply by geographical remoteness. And, if even the Turk and infidel would not as a people submit to a government such as George III proposes to impose through Lord Howe's army, how can Englishmen be expected to agree to that arrangement? So much is "obvious" to everyone, in other words, "self-evident." Thus even if the law of nature and of nations is drawn into our construction of "endowed by their Creator," what is left to be called "inalienable" with respect to American colonials and demonstrative of a certain minimal equality of rights in their collectivities is not so much. What happens in the remainder of the Declaration, following sentence two, is even more depressing to the contemporary Jacobin who would see in the new beginning a departure from the previous political history of Western man. Note particularly the remarks concerning the part played by the king's servants in encouraging a "servile insurrection," the xenophobic objections to the use of foreign mercenaries, and the allusion of the employment of savages as instruments of royal policy. Note also Jefferson's ironic reference to "Christian Kings" and anger at offences to the "common blood." These passages draw upon a received identity and are not "reasonable" in character. Certainly they do not suggest the equality of individual men. But (and I am sure Professor Jaffa will agree with me on this), even though racist, xenophobic, and religious assumptions have no place in the expression of philosophic truth, they can readily operate in an appeal to prescriptive law. And therefore, I say, in our Declaration of Independence.

VII

Though I agree with Kendall/Carey that there is a distance between the Declaration and the Constitution of 1787, and that silence on equality in the latter reflects a conscious choice, I agree also with Professor Jaffa that the two are not in conflict. The Constitution, like the Articles of Confederation before it, built a structure of common government (to handle all difficulties made by being one and thirteen) upon a common legal inheritance, common origins, and an established unity of purpose. It *is* a limited contract, resting on an external and prior bond of free and independent states, perfecting or improving their union.[29] It *does not* abrogate what it rests upon. The Declaration was a necessary prologue to its adoption. But, in logic, the Declaration is not implicit in the Constitution except as it made possible free ratification by the independent states. In truth, many rights are secured under the Constitution that are not present in the Declaration, however it be construed. Yet not equal voting rights in state or federal elections. Or economic rights in taxation. Or rights for women. Or even equal footing for various religions—or species of irreligion. To say nothing of slaves. All of this is well known. But, if we reasoned as do some gifted scholars, it might be maintained that the Constitution takes us even further away from equality for slaves than does the Declaraction.[30] For in Article I, Section 9, provision is made

[29] Jaffa's argument that one national Union was decided upon in 1774–1776 or before is easily refuted by John R. Alden's *The First South* (Baton Rouge: Lousiana State University Press, 1961); in Alden's *The South in the Revolution, 1763–1789* (Baton Rouge: Louisiana State University Press, 1957); and in Donald L. Robinson's *Slavery in the Structure of American Politics, 1765–1820* (New York: Harcourt Brace Jovanovich, 1971), p. 146 *et seqq. passim.* More than one Union has always been a possibility to be entertained by deliberate men. See Staughton Lynd's "The Abolitionist Critique of the United States Constitution," in *The Antislavery Vanguard: New Essays on the Abolitionists,* ed. Martin Duberman (Princeton: Princeton University Press, 1965), pp. 210–39.

[30] For instance, Professor Jaffa in forcing the notion of a Union before the Constitution into the "We the People" of the Preamble. Few scholars deny that the people acted through the states to ratify—as they had to form a Constitutional Convention. To this day they act through the states to amend. They existed at law through the maintenance of their several freedoms in battle. They formed the Confederation. The

that no law shall be passed by Congress to restrict the slave trade prior to 1808. Slavery exists by acknowledgment of the same document. Yet it encourages that there be more slaves in the Republic than are present in 1787. More in a proportion that twenty-one years can be expected to provide. Hence this provision can be described in logic as presenting Negro slavery as a positive good. For reasons of history I do not insist upon this commentary. The evidence of what lies behind the text suggests another view.[31] And for the same reasons I cannot follow the practical advice of the late Everett McKinley Dirksen and "get right with Lincoln."[32]

VIII

It would be unreasonable for me to attempt to develop in this essay all that I wish to say in objection to the politics of Abraham Lincoln. For it is a great deal and will perhaps involve some years. Therefore I must, in returning the courtesy of this review, raise only my primary objections, most of them proceeding from Lincoln's misunderstanding of the Declaration as a "deferred promise" of equality. I am of course close to the late Professor Kendall in these matters and have learned much from him and

---

Declaration was only a negative precondition to a Union and to the firmer connection that followed. Underneath all of this may stand an unwritten Constitution, joining the partners of the Declaration in more ways than are specified in 1787. And perhaps also committing them to other ends: ends which Professor Jaffa would not care to consider. That compact was the prescription which sanctioned the Continental Congress—a creature of the chartered colonies. If the Declaraction commits to anything, it is to that prescription—a compact of "the living, dead, and yet unborn." The continued operation of a society united in such a compact constitutes assent, regardless of official legal relations. New members are the only ones who are "sworn in."

[31] For instance, the 32 acts passed by Virginia's colonial House of Burgesses which called for a restriction of the trade, all of them negated by the Crown at the behest of Northern traders. Reports of the Constitutional Convention of 1787 indicate the same sort of pressures, resolved there by reasonable men determined to close out a divisive subject.

[32] See "Getting Right with Lincoln," pp. 3–18 of David Donald's *Lincoln Reconsidered* (New York: Vintage Press, 1961).

from Professor Carey.[33] For one thing, I agree with those gentlemen that Lincoln's "second founding" is fraught with peril and carries with it the prospect of an endless series of turmoils and revolutions, all dedicated to freshly discovered meanings of equality as a "proposition." I do not, however, look so much as they do to New England. It is not my preference for a colonial precedent to the national identity.[34] The millenarian infection spread and almost institutionalized by Lincoln (and by the manner of his death) has its impetus from that "other Israel" surrounding Boston.[35] And its full potential for mischief is yet to be determined. What Alexander Stephens called Lincoln's "religious mysticism" of Union, when combined in "cold, calculating reason" to the goal of "equal rights" and an authoritarian (that is, irrational) biblical rhetoric, constitutes a juggernaut powerful enough to arm and enthrone any self-made Caesar we might imagine: even an unprepossessing country lawyer from Illinois. For by means of that mixture and solution a transfer of authority and energy is effected, from the Puritan dream of a New Jerusalem governed by an elect to the manifest destiny of American democracy led by keepers of the popular faith. Both are authorized from on High to reform the world into an imitation of themselves—and to lecture and dragoon all who might object. Both receive regular intimations of the Divine Will through prophets who arise from time to time to recall them to their holy mission. And both operate from that base to paint all prospective opposition in the darkest of colors, the rhetoric of polarity being a fundamental correlative of all genuinely Puritan activity, with no room for shadings in between and no mercy for the wicked.

This is, of course, not to minimize the role played in Lincoln's rise to power by the tireless "engine" of his ambition. Nor his

[33] And especially from Kendall's "Equality: Commitment or Ideal?" *Phalanx,* Vol. I (Fall 1967), pp. 95–103, which answers some of Jaffa's complaints about Kendall's silences. I find it curious that Jaffa does not mention this piece.

[34] Except for reasons of strategy (guilt by association), I cannot see why Jaffa identifies *Basic Symbols of the American Political Tradition* with the South. For Kendall and Carey begin with Massachusetts and Connecticut.

[35] See p. 226 of Jaffa's own *Crisis of the House Divided.*

political gifts—for which I have an ever-growing admiration. As is announced obliquely in the "Address Before the Springfield Young Men's Lyceum, 1838," Lincoln was, very early, touched by a Bonapartist sense of destiny. His papers (all ten volumes, plus a recent supplement) reflect a steady purpose, an inexorable will to rise, to put his stamp upon the world.[36] Yet there was always another side to his nature—glum, ironic, pessimistic, self-deprecatory: in a word, inscrutable. It has deceived and puzzled many. Yet, as is ordinary in a Puritan, this meandering reflected private doubt of the wisdom behind personal choices and (perhaps) the status of motives which directed him toward their enactment: self-doubt, but not doubt of ideals. And he knew how to cure the ailment—by "striving to finish the work." He had his ends in mind, his religion of Union *in* Equality, but he left it to the "providential" flow of history to carry them to realization. However, after 1854 he condescended to give that flow a little help. The Kansas-Nebraska Act *made* the political career of Abraham Lincoln, opened the door for the "Reign of Reason," made it possible to put behind the "living history" of the revolutionary generation ("oaks," an organic image), and provided for an opportunity to roll out the big guns of priestly language to give what he meant by "freedom" that "new birth" he came to speak of at Gettysburg. He played with consummate skill the circumstances of free-soil reaction in '54 and then the tumult surrounding the campaigns of '58 and '60. Nor are there many scholars who do not find some mystery or subtle craft in his first months as President, to say nothing of his subsequent

[36] See Edmund Wilson's magisterial *Patriotic Gore: Studies in the Literature of the American Civil War* (New York: Oxford University Press, 1962), pp. 99–130. Surely Wilson cannot be mistaken in arguing that Lincoln saw himself in his portrait of the "new founder." For Lincoln clearly knows the animal he describes on a more intimate basis than mere speculation or observation could provide. Wilson compares Lincoln (pp. xvi–xx) to Bismarck and Lenin—the other great founders of our age. Another useful analogue (a firm higher-law man, and no legalist or historicist) is Adolf Hitler. For he writes in *Mein Kampf* that "human rights break state rights," calls for illegal as well as legal instruments in "wars of rebellion against enslavement from within and without," observes that all governments by oppression plead the law, and concludes, "I believe today that I am acting in the sense of the Almighty Creater . . . fighting for the Lord's work." (I cite the edition of 1938, published in New York by Reynal and Hitchcock, pp. 122–23 and 84).

conduct. But that story, as I read it, is a large book—larger than Professor Jaffa's. Suffice it to say that Lincoln was indeed a man whose "policy was to have no policy."[37] He loved to quote from *Hamlet* that "there is a divinity that shapes our ends,/Rough-hew them how we will."[38] And from the total pattern of his conduct we can extract the following formula: Wait, set up or encourage pressure, then jump, and call it God. The original behind this procedure could be any one of a dozen historic tyrants, all of whom announced a noble purpose for their acts. But when the pattern is encapsulated by the high idiom of Holy Scripture (the authority of which no man can examine), the Anglo-Saxon prototype emerges as Oliver Cromwell, the Lord Protector. And in searching for what is significant in that analogy, the logical point of departure is the House Divided speech to the Illinois Republican convention of June 1858.

IX

Lincoln's political gnosticism does not come to a head in the House-Divided speech, and does not begin there. For even in the Springfield Lyceum address (made when he was twenty-nine), he concludes on a Puritan note: Let us refound the Union, and "the gates of hell shall not prevail against it." The new founder, having propped up the temple of Liberty/Equality on the solid pillars of "calculating reason," will therefore be, in relation to the powers of evil (*i.e.,* those who do not care for the arrangement) as was the faith of Peter to the Christian church after its foundation. And God is thus, by implication, the security for the quasi-religion of Equality. In a similar fashion Lincoln finds God as a verification for his rectitude as President in his address to Northern moderates, men who loved the old "divided" house, which we find in his Second Inaugural. Here is the heresy of a "political religion" at the beginning of Lincoln's political career, and also at its end. But one prudent shift is observable. Except for an occasional mention of "propositions" or their equivalent, the debt to European rationalism (the source

[37] Donald, *Lincoln Reconsidered,* p. 131.

[38] Roy P. Basler, *The Touchstone for Greatness: Essays, Addresses and Occasional Pieces about Abraham Lincoln* (Westport, Conn.: Greenwood Press, 1973), pp. 206–27.

of Lincoln's puzzling theological heterodoxy), fades into the background once Honest Abe appears on the center of the national stage in Peoria, Illinois (October 1854). And in the opposite direction the biblical element grows to be more and more dominant after 1858. But we should not infer from this that Lincoln's design changed after he got the Republican nomination against Douglas. Only his perception (drawing from the abolitionists) of the proper instrument for its execution.

The House-Divided speech was, beyond any question, a Puritan declaration of war. And therefore also Lincoln's election on the basis of its contents as transcribed in the Republican platform of 1860. A Lincoln admirer, Don E. Fehrenbacher, in his *Prelude to Greatness: Lincoln in the 1850's,* calls it "Garrisonian."[39] The South saw it that way, as did much of the North. And neither forgot those words:

> A House Divided against itself cannot stand. I believe this government cannot endure, perpetually half *slave* and half *free*. I do not expect the Union to be *dissolved*—I do not expect the house to *fall*—but I *do* expect it will cease to be divided. It will become *all* one thing, or *all* another.

Yet we should not abstract the speech from the intellectual milieu to which it belongs. By means of his political manipulation, Lincoln, in the words of his one-time friend, Alexander Stephens, "put the institution of nearly one-half the states under the ban of public opinion and national condemnation." And, continued Stephens, "this, upon general principle, is quite enough of itself to arouse a spirit not only of general indignation, but of revolt on the part of the proscribed."[40] Other people in these days made noises like Lincoln. After 1854 they got a good hearing. One of them, old John Brown, received beatification from the Northern newspapers which supported Mr. Lincoln in 1860. What this juxtaposition signified, despite certain cluckings of disapproval among Republican stalwarts, no one could mistake.

[39] Jaffa praises Fehrenbacher's work.

[40] *A Constitutional View of the Late War between the States* (Philadelphia: National Publishing Co., 1868), Vol. II, p. 266.

Of course the central motif of the House Divided speech, as quoted above, echoes the Bible (Mark 3:25): Christ speaking of the undivided hosts of Satan.[41] Lincoln's authority is thus, by association, elevated to the level of the hieratic. But he adds something to the mixture. The myth that slavery will be either set on its way to extinction by an official gesture on the part of the federal government or else all states will eventually become slave-states establishes a false dilemma, describes a set of conditions which, once fixed in the minds of his free-soil audience, was certain to create in them a sense of alarm. Thus he participates in what Richard Hofstadter calls the "paranoid style" in politics.[42] Fear of the slave power (Southern political and economic domination) and racist hostility to the idea of massive Negro influx, free *or* slave, into the North made predictable that one of these alternatives would be perceived as intolerable—and we can guess which one. Thus the size of the Republican Party might be augmented from the ranks of persons who despised Abolition and all its works.

For Lincoln to say after 1858 that the Constitution and the laws were sacred to him, that he would "preserve" the "old Union of the Fathers," is mere window dressing. For to argue that your enemy is evil incarnate (the burden of his rhetoric), in league with Satan, and then add that you respect him and his legal rights is to indulge in pietistic arrogance—as Alexander Stephens specified in the passage I quoted just above. Jaffa confuses matters no end in maintaining that Lincoln addressed a real danger in his imaginary "division." As the South perceived the question, the real issue in Kansas and Nebraska was whether or not there could be a federal policy on the "morality" of its conduct in any connection not covered by the original federal covenant: whether they could stay under the gun.

For houses are always divided, in some fashion or another. And, no doubt, should slavery be gone, some new infamy was bound to be discovered by the stern examiners whose power depends upon a regularity in such "crusades." A law prohibiting slavery in the territories, in that it affected the ability of a new state to

[41] Lincoln's use of this passage is curious. For, as the context makes clear, Christ's point in setting up the dichotomy is that the Devil would not help his servants to ruin his own plans.

[42] See David Brion Davis' *The Slave Power and the Paranoid Style* (Baton Rouge: Louisiana State University Press, 1969), especially pp. 10–11.

grow to maturity as a child of the total Union, would define the South as outside of that communion. Furthermore, it would set in motion a chain of circumstances that could be used against the region in any connection where antinomian morality could be read into law—could touch slavery or any other "peculiarity," unless a Constitutional amendment (requiring a three-fourths vote of the states) existed to protect it. A Union of this sort was not the old Union. Nor was its issue, a Union by force—in 1865 or *now.* Whatever the intent of armies in blue, it could not be the same—not the contract ratified by all the states who were party to it. Rather, it involved Lincoln's worship of the law as the Constitution *with the Declaration drafted into (and over) it*—Lincoln's Declaration: and therefore (*vide supra*), no worship of the law whatsoever, but instead devotion to perpetually exciting goals, always just beyond our reach. Thus, under the aegis of a plurality president, the principle of assent is put aside for the sake of an idea (read ideology) which only a small minority of Americans could be expected to approve, either in 1860 or to-day. And the entire project accomplished by rhetoric—Kendall's "magic." On the record of American history since 1858, Lincoln stands convicted as an enemy of the "foundings."[43] Which is to say, as our new Father—even though many of us still refuse to live in the cold uniformitarian temple he designed.

Of course, military resistance to radical Union (*i.e.,* statism covered by a patina of law) ended in 1865. Lincoln saluted these developments at the beginning of his second term. And I must conclude my remarks on Lincoln's politics with some observations on that address. His conduct in using the presidential powers has been treated to my satisfaction by Gottfried Dietze.[44] What that conduct amounts to is the creation of an Eastern priest/king—an epideictic personage such as we hear in the voice at Gettysburg. Speech and deeds together did change the country—and in respects more important than the abolition of Negro slavery: together opened the door to protentous changes that

[43] I use quotation marks because I deny that they were ever founded, in that term's strict sense.

[44] *America's Political Dilemma: From Limited to Unlimited Democracy* (Baltimore: Johns Hopkins Press, 1968), pp. 17–62. He is supported by papers published in *National Review* by the late Frank Meyer (August 24, 1965; January 25, 1966).

finally touch even liberty.[45] The argument of this essay is, in sum, that what Lincoln did to preserve the Union by expanding and enshrining equality left the prescription of the revolution of law in our national beginning and the "unwritten constitution" of our positive pluralism very much in doubt. Such was his purpose. But (and I again repeat) this plan is something which he concealed until he prepared the Second Inaugural—where in victory he became a scripture in himself.

X

There is of course a clear conflict between the Cooper Union speech, the First Inaugural, Lincoln's letters of the time, and the posture Lincoln assumed a few weeks before Lee's surrender. If we would discover in Father Abraham the "crafty Machiavel," the conflict between his assent to a constitutional amendment making slavery "perpetual" where established and the House Divided speech is our point of departure. But the Lincoln who kept Kentucky and Missouri from secession is hard to penetrate. It is wise to assume that he followed the times. For it cannot be demonstrated that he ever really attempted to pacify Southern anxieties without reconstituting the Republic. Certainly he wanted no peace on any grounds but unconditional surrender. And in 1865, he looked back on his five years as national leader, "scanned the providences," and "found himself approved."

When seen in the context of his career after 1858 and within the pattern of a lifetime of deliberate utterances, Lincoln's Second Inaugural turns out to be something very different from what most Americans have believed it to be: a completion of a pattern announced in the House Divided speech, unfolded in its fullness at Gettysburg, and glossed in a letter to Thurlow Weed written just before his death. Historically, the misconception of this performance may be attributed to a disproportionate emphasis upon the final paragraph of the Second Inaugural treated (once again) as if it had an independent existence out-

[45] Liberty is clearly the American value of greatest traditional authority—meaning "liberty to be ourselves," a nation which assumes an established, inherited identity. On the part played by the Gettysburg Address in this process, see my *Triumph* essay cited above.

side the total document. Furthermore, what Lincoln means by "malice toward none" and "bind up the nation's wounds" is, even within this single paragraph, modified beyond recognition by "as God gives us to see the right." For he means here revelation, not conscience. Americans are so accustomed, since Lincoln's time, to a quasireligious rhetoric in their public men that the combination has passed without notice for a century and more. But to discover its full meaning we must look up into the body of the speech. There it becomes clear what Lincoln is about behind his mild forensic tone.

Said another way, what I here contend is that the attribution of his own opinions to an antinomian revelation of divine will as regards America's political destiny is more completely and intensively visible in this particular Lincoln document than in any other. For what he does in the Second Inaugural is to expand the outreach of his rhetorical manicheanism beyond the limits made familiar to us in a thousand expressions of piety toward the Union (and most particularly at Gettysburg) to include not only his obviously beaten enemies in the South but also all those who accepted the Union as it had existed from the Founding until 1860. Indeed, the targets of his rhetoric on this occasion are all moderate Unionists who did not aforetimes recognize, as did their prophet for the day, the necessity for a greater perfection in their bonds. The war was long, says Father Abraham, not simply because the rebels were wicked but furthermore because many of their adversaries were reluctant. In the letter to Weed (March 15, 1865) Lincoln observes, in speaking of the unpopularity he expects to be the fate of the remarks in question, that "men are not flattered by being shown that there has been a difference of purpose between the Almighty and them. To deny it, however, in this case, is to deny that there is a God governing the world."[46] Since no Southerners were present to be offended by the Second Inaugural, and since Lincoln's teaching in that address refers chiefly to those who had been patient with the divided house, it is evident that his targets in interpreting long war and heavy judgment are those who did not see *before secession* the necessity of conflict. How this reading of the American teleology could be expected to bind up wounds in any conventional sense is difficult to determine. But the end

[46] Lincoln, *Collected Works,* Volume VIII, p. 356.

result is to give Lincoln a rhetorical upper hand he had not sought at any point in his presidency and to prepare him to do whatever he means by "finish the work." It is to leave him, finally, alone as the agent of his master, beyond the most ultra-Republicans as an instrument of providence and with an authority few mortal men have ever aspired to hold in their hands. Death confirmed him (or rather, his design) in that condition. Consider for an illustration Edward M. Stanton's words after reading the Gettysburg Address to an 1868 political audience in Pennsylvania: "That is the voice of God speaking through the lips of Abraham Lincoln. . . . You hear the voice of Father Abraham here tonight. Did he die in vain?"[47] Such politics are beyond reason, beyond law, though they may embody a rationalist objective. They are also Jaffa's model—from authority and passion. And with consequences I shall now consider.

XI

"Style," Sir Herbert Read once observed, "is the ultimate morality of mind." By style I would understand him to mean all the elements that go into the composition of a piece of rhetoric, its structural elements as well as its textural; and, in examining the "style" of this particular essay, I find an extraordinary laxity—which suggests that Professor Jaffa is not at his best. Indeed, I can hardly recognize here the consummate and ethical rhetorician of *Crisis of the House Divided,* a work which I obviously admire—though from a certain distance. The argument of this later essay is loose and meandering, like some ancient river that is constantly winding back on itself. Lincoln as a young legislative candidate once advocated (like a good, money-minded Whig) the straightening of such rivers by cutting off the neck of the loops. In closing, I shall attempt to do the same for Mr. Jaffa's argument, if only to indicate the tortuous nature of the "moral" impulse which lay behind its composition.

In the first place, as my metaphor suggests, this is an old river, an ancient argument which need not be developed again in detail since everyone is familiar enough with its tenets (i.e., the equation of the social-contract theory with some theory of equality). What is new in this lengthy diatribe is no more than the

[47] Donald, *Lincoln Reconsidered,* p. 8.

ostensible targets of Professor Jaffa's attack, Kendall and Carey. And indeed they could be a valid point of departure for an egalitarian like Professor Jaffa, since Kendall and Carey do define the true American political tradition as both conservative *and* hostile to Equality.

But unfortunately Kendall and Carey do not raise their standard on that spot of polemical ground where Professor Jaffa would like to do battle. They do not become overly preoccupied with slavery; and for obvious reasons Professor Jaffa would rather talk about slavery than the political documents which are the announced topic of *Basic Symbols.* And so he does, curving around obstacles to reach the sacred subject, turning his argument in that direction by charging that Kendall and Carey never mention the word in their study and that such an omission avoids the essential question of the American political experience. He repeats this charge several times during the windings of his thesis, despite the fact that it is unfounded (pp. 479, 486, and 491). For an instance, he ignores the following comment on page 92 of *Basic Symbols,* a passage that raises perhaps a most difficult question for him to consider:

> However, the assembly that approved the Declaration would not subscribe to the denunciation of slavery that Jefferson sought to include, so that we might be led to believe that the signers were talking of equality of men in a sense far short of that which modern egalitarians hold.

Small wonder that Professor Jaffa's rhetorical river veers sharply away from this high ground. Was it forgotten or ignored in order to avoid the issue it raises? Whatever the reasons, it flows off in that direction, attacking Kendall's review of *Crisis of the House Divided,* a Kendall essay in which the issues are relevant to slavery and furthermore a matter of historical interpretation. Soon we are curling and gliding through familiar territory, much of it mythic in nature and therefore simpler and purer than life. In Jaffa's imaginary history of the United States, Jefferson is the drafter of the Declaration, but *not* the slaveholder who wrote in *Notes on the State of Virginia* of his suspicion that blacks "are inferior to the whites in the endowments both of body and mind" and that this "unfortunate difference of colour, and perhaps of faculty, is a powerful obstacle to the emancipation of these people"; and *certainly not* the Virginian who called "Equality" a "mere abstraction" and its devotees a "Holy Alliance." There, Locke is the philosopher of *The Second Treatise*, but *not* the man responsible for *Fundamental Constitutions for Carolina*. Antebellum slavery is a kind of Buchenwald;[48] and the United States Constitution is drafted with a tacit understanding that "all men are [really] created equal," that this is a proposition with "constitutional status," *in spite of the fact* that the Constitution itself recognized the established legal institution of slavery and discouraged interpolation into its provisions of what is not clearly there. All of these oversimplifications ignore one overriding question, the question that Kendall and Carey raise and which Professor Jaffa is careful not to consider. Some "truths" are more important than the Truth. Even the Truth that we have a political tradition that is conservative and contrary to Lincoln. Thus, though the river of Professor Jaffa's argument seems erratic, its wanderings (like the wanderings of a real river) have a predictable pattern; they follow the course of least resistance. And it is in the pattern—tortuous and circuitous—that one can see the relationship between his "style" and his "ultimate morality of mind."

Yet we cannot entirely blame Professor Jaffa for these aberrations, this great falling away from scholarly rectitude and right reason. His errors are endemic among his kind—such Old Liberals as identify their politics with the Lincolnian precedent. As I have tried to indicate, such errors constitute what amounts to a "genetic flaw" within that intellectual tradition, a fracture impossible to heal. Trying to preserve property, secure tranquility, and promote equal rights, all at the same time, insures that none of these purposes will be accomplished. And insures also a terrible, unremitting tension, both among those in power and among those whose hopes are falsely raised. Especially with persistence in thinking of men outside of all history that is not

[48] This analogy smacks of Stanley Elkin's now discredited theory in *Slavery: A Problem in American Institutional Life* (Chicago: University of Chicago Press, 1959). For correction see Eugene D. Genovese's *Roll, Jordan, Roll: The World the Slaves Made* (New York: Pantheon Books, 1974). Also consider the fact that Jews were proscribed under Hitler—all Jews, in the same way—while antebellum Southern blacks could be slaves or freemen or even slaveholders.

Lincoln, and apart from the durable communions of craft and friendship, faith and blood. It has been, however, a distinctive trait of American political thought to do its worst as it touches upon the Negro: to break down when unable to make it through the aforementioned impasse of objectives. Class struggle has been the result, to say nothing of race conflict. And that failing attaches by definition to the Republican identity, flawing it perhaps forever as a viable conservative instrument. Said another way, the more a people derive their political identity from Lincoln's version of Equality, the more they are going to push against the given and providential frame of things to prove up the magic phrase. And, therefore, the more they will (to repeat one of my favorite images) kick the "tar baby."[49] And we all know how that story ends.

[49] "A Fire Bell in the Night: The Southern Conservative View," *Modern Age,* Vol. 17 (Winter 1973), pp. 9–15. In these pages I maintain that an expansive view of "natural rights" with respect to Negroes has undermined our inherited constitutional system.